A CONCISE HISTORY OF INDIA

Barbara Metcalf and Thomas Metcalf come together to write a concise history of modern India. While early histories were often composed as handmaids of British imperialism or as products of emerging nationalist identities, this book challenges the notion that a continuous meaning can be applied to social categories such as 'caste', 'Hindu', 'Muslim' or even 'India'. The narrative focuses on the fundamentally political theme of the imaginative and institutional structures that successively changed and sustained both colonial and independent India. It also documents the social changes and the rich cultural life that were constituted in interaction with that political structure and vision. Earlier chapters focus on the period of Muslim dynasties that preceded colonial conquest, and the book concludes with the dramatic recent events of the 1990s, including economic change, religious nationalism and India's emergence as a nuclear power. Illustrations and quotations from historical sources are integral to the narrative.

BARBARA D. METCALF is Professor in the Department of History, University of California, Davis. Her publications include *Islamic Revival in British India* (1982) and, more recently, *Making Muslim Space in North America and Europe* (1996). THOMAS R. METCALF is Professor of History and Sarah Kailath Professor of India Studies at the University of California, Berkeley. His publications include *Ideologies of the Raj* (1994, 1997) and *An Imperial Vision: Indian Architecture and Britain's Raj* (1989).

CAMBRIDGE CONCISE HISTORIES

This is a series of illustrated 'concise histories' of selected individual countries, intended both as university and college textbooks and as general historical introductions for general readers, travellers and members of the business community.

First titles in the series:

A Concise History of Germany
MARY FULBROOK

A Concise History of Greece
RICHARD CLOGG

A Concise History of France
ROGER PRICE

A Concise History of Britain, 1707–1795
W. A. SPECK

A Concise History of Portugal
DAVID BIRMINGHAM

A Concise History of Italy
CHRISTOPHER DUGGAN

A Concise History of Bulgaria
RICHARD CRAMPTON

A Concise History of South Africa
ROBERT ROSS

A Concise History of Brazil
BORIS FAUSTO

A Concise History of Mexico
BRIAN HAMNETT

A Concise History of Australia
STUART MACINTYRE

A Concise History of Hungary
MIKLÓS MOLNÁR

Other titles are in preparation

A Concise History of India

BARBARA D. METCALF
University of California, Davis

and

THOMAS R. METCALF
University of California, Berkeley

PUBLISHED BY THE PRESS SYNDICATE OF THE UNIVERSITY OF CAMBRIDGE
The Pitt Building, Trumpington Street, Cambridge, United Kingdom

CAMBRIDGE UNIVERSITY PRESS
The Edinburgh Building, Cambridge CB2 2RU, UK
40 West 20th Street, New York, NY 10011-4211, USA
10 Stamford Road, Oakleigh, VIC 3166, Australia
Ruiz de Alarcón 13, 28014 Madrid, Spain
Dock House, The Waterfront, Cape Town 8001, South Africa

http://www.cambridge.org

First published 2002

Printed in the United Kingdom at the University Press, Cambridge

Typeface Sabon 10/13 pt.   *System* LATEX 2$_\varepsilon$ [TB]

A catalogue record for this book is available from the British Library

Library of Congress Cataloguing in Publication Data

Metcalf, Barbara Daly, 1941–
A concise history of India / Barbara D. Metcalf and Thomas R. Metcalf.
p.   cm. – (Cambridge concise histories)
Includes bibliographical references and index.
ISBN 0 521 63027 4 (hardback) – ISBN 0 521 63974 3 (paperback)
1. India – History.   I. Metcalf, Thomas R., 1934–   II. Series.

DS461 .M47   2001
954 – dc21   2001035096

ISBN 0 521 63027 4 hardback
ISBN 0 521 63974 3 paperback

CONTENTS

ILLUSTRATIONS

MAPS

PREFACE

This is a concise history of India since the time of the Mughals. It comprises the history of what was known as British India from the late eighteenth century until 1947, when the subcontinent was split into the two independent countries of India and Pakistan, and of the Republic of India thereafter. (The history of Pakistan, and after 1971, of Bangladesh, is taken up in a separate volume in this series.)

In this work we hope to capture something of the excitement that has characterized the field of India studies in recent decades. Any history written today differs markedly from that of the late 1950s and early 1960s when we, as graduate students, first 'discovered' India. The history of India, like histories everywhere, is now at its best written as a more inclusive story, and one with fewer determining narratives. Not only do historians seek to include more of the population in their histories – women, minorities, the dispossessed – but they are also interested in alternative historical narratives, those shaped by distinctive cosmologies or by local experiences. Historians question, above all, the historical narratives that were forged – as they were everywhere in the modern world – by the compelling visions of nationalism. The first histories of India, written from the early decades of the nineteenth century, were the handmaid of British nationalism. They were subsequently challenged, and rewritten, by Indian nationalist historians. All of these histories, including those written from a Marxist perspective, were shaped by notions of 'progress' and what was seen as an inevitable progression toward presumably already known models of 'modernity' that included economic development and democracy. In recent years, Indian historians have taken the lead in breaking apart the old narratives, at the cost, some would argue, of a cherished cultural continuity and the stirring stories of heroism that foster patriotism. What they have given us in its place is what the leading 'subalternist' Partha Chatterjee calls 'fragments' of history. But such a history is no less critical for the formation of an informed citizenry of an individual nation, or of the world.

We focus in this concise history on the fundamentally political theme of the 'imagining' of India, and on the institutional structures that changed and sustained that 'India'. In so doing, we endeavour to show as well the social changes and the cultural values that were constituted in interaction with that political structure and that vision. We have chosen to place political history, and the doings of the social elite, at the centre of our narrative because they have been the driving force for historical change. A 'subalternist' might appropriately insist that such an emphasis does not do justice to the multiple mentalities and diverse lived experience of the bulk of India's population. An intriguing example of the gap between political history and individual memory has recently been analyzed by the historian Paul Greenough. Colonial and later census enumerators, he notes, required the recording of birth dates from populations who, for the most part, did not commemorate this event. Hence census personnel supplied respondents with lists of 'historic' events to help anchor memories. These included national events, such as the coronation of George V or the proclamation of the Republic of India, as well as local events such as natural disasters or corrupt elections. These latter events, in Greenough's view, proved most evocative in stirring recollections of the past, and so reveal a more 'subaltern' history than the official or textbook version. Yet, we would argue, in multiple ways the lives of those interviewed for the census were inevitably shaped, from the foods they ate and the lands they ploughed to the prospects for their children, by their existence as subjects of the colonial Raj, and later as citizens of the independent Indian state.

Like others who have come to recognize the implicit teleologies of 'national' history, we acknowledge that history is always written, and of necessity rewritten, to serve the needs of the present. One of those needs, in our view, is to show that commonsense notions of continuity, fostered by nationalism, must be replaced by an understanding of the newness of modern identities, and the new meanings infused into old terms ('caste', 'Hindu', 'Muslim', and even 'India' itself). This is what the political scientist Benedict Anderson has called the great paradox of nationalism: that nation-states, a product of recent centuries, must always claim to be very, very old. To show otherwise in the case of India is especially challenging; for the British colonialists had a powerful incentive to make of India a timeless and unchanging land in contrast to their own avowed 'progress', while Indian nationalists were driven by an equally insistent desire to claim the sanction of antiquity for their own cultural and political ideals. To understand how our cultures are constructed, however, is essential in giving us a critical distance on what otherwise seems part of nature. It is a distinctive contribution that history can make to civic life.

We call the reader's attention in particular to the extracted quotations and the illustrative figures threaded throughout the historical narrative. The extracts represent 'voices' of participants in the events being described. Where possible, we have chosen these extracts from works that are readily available to those who wish to explore these sources further. They exemplify the changing modalities of contemporaneous expression and behaviour. Similarly, the visual reproductions are not simple 'illustrations', but are intended to provide some sense of the visual world, including new media, of the times.

The maps provided in the volume are meant to help orient the reader to central elements of India's geography. The physical features of the Indian subcontinent have shaped its history in fundamental ways. Its size – some 2,000 miles from east to west, and another 2,000 miles from north to south – calls into question the label of 'subcontinent' given it by European map makers, whose own European 'continent' is hardly more extensive. The Indian subcontinent, like Europe itself, is a distinctive feature of the larger Eurasian land mass from which it projects. Unlike Europe, however, India was cut off by forbidding mountain ranges from Central Asia, so that it participated only marginally in the traffic in goods and people that over the centuries swept eastwards and westwards across the steppes.

Despite the persisting barrier to travel formed by the unbroken line of mountains reaching from the Pamirs and Karakoram in the north-west, across the central Himalaya to the dense jungle-clad hills of the Burmese border, India continually interacted with its neighbours. Such interaction commonly took place to the westward, where the Khyber and Bolan Passes provided easy access to the Afghan plateau. The earliest Indian civilization, that known as the Harappan or Indus (at its height 2000–1500 BC) possessed close trading ties with Mesopotamia. Central Asian peoples reached the subcontinent in the centuries around 1000 BC, bringing with them a language, the Indo-European, that also spread westwards into much of Europe. As a result the languages that grew up in northern and central India share fundamental linguistic patterns with those of many European countries. Greeks under Alexander the Great, followed by Central Asian Sakas, Scythians, and Huns, and finally Turks, Mongols, and Afghans, conquered, and frequently settled, in the north-west. Movements of peoples outwards from India into Central Asia also took place, most notably those of Buddhist pilgrims and teachers to Tibet and China, as well as traders in luxury goods.

The two arms of the Indian Ocean – the Bay of Bengal and the Arabian Sea – that define the remaining two sides of the Indian triangle mark out the region as a distinctive space and shape it as a distinctive climatic zone – that of the monsoon. Gathering force in the hot equatorial regions of the Indian Ocean, the monsoon rains sweep across India each summer. Indian agriculture is almost wholly dependent on these rains, which vary dramatically in their intensity, from 60 to 80 inches a year on the western and eastern coasts and the mountainous foothills, to a mere 15–20 inches in the Punjab. Sind and Rajasthan in the north-west lie outside the influence of the monsoon, and so are given over almost wholly to barren desert. The oceans also linked India to its neighbours. The seafaring Cholas of the far south were centrally important in the transmission of Buddhist and Brahmanic learning from India to South-East Asia. Indian merchants early learned to navigate with the monsoon winds as they sailed across the western Indian Ocean. From 1498, when Vasco da Gama, guided by a Gujarati pilot, brought his ship into an Indian port, India's European conquerors came from the west across the sea.

Its physical features, especially its mountains and rivers, divide India into regions no less distinctive than the various countries of Europe. These regions are characterized by differing ecological patterns, languages, and cultures. Paralleling the Himalaya are the rivers of the Gangetic plain, which unite to form the sacred 'Ganga', flowing from the north-west to the south-east into the Bay of Bengal. A rich agricultural zone, this region, known as 'Hindustan', was the heartland of northern empires and the goal of those invaders who entered from the north-west. The Indo-Gangetic plain, over 1,000 miles in extent, comprises the Punjab, whose 'five rivers' flow south-west into the Indus; the rich 'doab' area between Ganges and Jamuna; and farthest to the east, where the Brahmaputra joins it from Tibet, the fertile, heavily watered region of rice agriculture in Bengal.

Northern India is marked off from peninsular India, known as the Deccan, by ranges of low hills, scrub jungle, and westward-flowing rivers. Although not as forbidding a barrier as the towering Himalaya, nevertheless the central Indian hills permitted the settled peoples of south India, speaking languages derived from what is called the Dravidian family, to develop distinct cultural characteristics. Further, unlike the sweeping plains of the Gangetic valley, the land itself in the south, containing river valleys cut off from each other by hills, together with the coastal ranges known as the 'ghats', encouraged peoples to develop separate states and even languages. Despite all this diversity, however, by the Middle Ages unifying elements of what can be called an Indic civilization reached most areas of the subcontinent. Our volume begins with an examination of this medieval Indian civilization.

We wish to express our appreciation to a number of institutions which have made their facilities available to us during the writing of this book. These include the libraries of the University of California at Berkeley and at Davis, the Ames Library of the University of Minnesota, the British Library, and the Nehru Memorial Museum and Library, New Delhi. Several friends and colleagues, most notably Catherine Asher, Frederick Asher, Rebecca Brown, and Narayani Gupta have assisted us in procuring rare photographs used as illustrations. We are especially grateful to Rachel Sturman, who, in addition to giving the manuscript a careful reading, took upon herself the task of collecting illustrations and securing permissions for their use. More generally, we wish to thank our students, who, over the several decades since we began our teaching careers, by their questions and their enthusiasms have encouraged us always to think afresh about the history of India. We would especially like to acknowledge those who have shared ideas with us from research projects not yet published. These include Lisa Trivedi, Durba Ghosh, and Rachel Sturman, among others. We owe much as well to Marigold Acland, of the Cambridge University Press, who first encouraged us to take on this task and then prodded us to complete it in good time. Finally, we want to thank Kavita Datla and Ariana deRochefort Reynolds for preparing the index under intense time pressure.

GLOSSARY

bhakti   An approach to worship and spiritual practice in the Hindu tradition characterized by personal devotion to a Divinity, often mediated by a holy person or teacher

Brahman   The varna or status category identified in the classical Sanskrit tradition as most pure and entitled to perform priestly duties

Buddhist   A follower of Gautama Buddha (b. 560 BC). Like Mahavira Jain, he rejected the authority of Brahmanic ritual; he taught that suffering is inseparable from existence, and that one should strive to extinguish the self and the senses in order to achieve a state of illumination called nirvana. Supported by the great emperor Asoka (*c.* 269–32 BC), Buddhism essentially disappeared in the Indian subcontinent by the tenth century. It was revived in the mid-twentieth century by the 'untouchable' leader Ambedkar.

dalit   'Down-trodden', term used by former untouchables to describe their community. Has replaced Gandhi's term *harijan* 'children of God' in recent decades.

darbar   *see* durbar

durbar   Royal audience, hall of audience, court; executive government of a princely state

diwan   The chief civil administrator of an area under the Mughals; *diwani*, civil or revenue administration

factor   A commercial agent, here of the East India Company, resident in India; the term factory denoted a warehouse for storing trade goods

xix

farmer   A revenue term used for a person who bids to secure the right to collect the taxes of a given area in return for payment to the government of a fixed sum

hadith   Traditions of the Prophet Muhammad's sayings and actions

hartal   Closing of all shops in a market as a protest against oppression or ill-treatment

imam   A prayer leader; among Shi`a, venerated male descendants of the Prophet Muhammad, whose succession terminated after twelve incumbents for the majority of Shi`a followers, after seven for several smaller sects

jagir   The right to the assessed tax revenue of a piece of land, given for a limited term by the Mughals as a reward for service; the holder of a jagir is a *jagirdar*

Jain   A follower of Mahavira (b. 599 BC) who, like the Buddha, rejected the authority of Brahmanic ritual, and taught an ascetic, world-denying philosophical and ethical system. Particularly successful in business, Jains are a small community resident mostly in Gujarat and Bombay

Jat   A north Indian peasant and agriculturist community

Jesuit   A member of the Society of Jesus of the Roman Catholic Church, founded by St Ignatius Loyola in 1534; present in India from its earliest years with the establishment of Portuguese trading enclaves

jizya   A poll tax levied on non-Muslims that entitled them to protection and freed them from military service

jotedar   A revenue collecting intermediary in Bengal, between the peasant cultivator and the zamindar

Kayasth   North Indian caste group, many of whose members served from Mughal times in government bureaucracy and other institutions requiring literacy, accountancy, etc.

Khalifa (caliph)   A successor, particularly used for successors of the Prophet Muhammad

Khatri   North Indian caste group, many of whose members served from Mughal times in government bureaucracies and other institutions requiring literacy, accountancy, etc.

Khilafat (caliphate)   The office or dignity of the caliph; as 'Khilafat Movement', an organization that sought to secure the position of the Ottoman sultan as spiritual leader of all Muslims

Kshatriya The varna or status category identified in the classical Sanskrit tradition as those entitled to exercise military power and perform sacrifices

mansab A rank within the Mughal state system, carrying with it the obligation to supply horsemen in a number commensurate with the rank; the holder of a mansab is a *mansabdar*

nabob *see* nawab

naib A deputy, as of a governor of a province under the Mughals; title of respect

nawab Mughal governor; conventionally used in British India as a title for Muslim princes, chiefs, etc. The term *nabob*, a corruption of *nawab*, was used for Englishmen who gained sudden riches in India

Ottoman A vast empire in Asia Minor and the Balkans conquered in the fourteenth to sixteenth centuries by Osmanli Turks, who ruled until the empire's dissolution in 1918 following World War One

Pandit Title of respect for learned Brahman; passes into English as 'pandit', an expert or authority on some subject

panchayat Council, court for arbitration of disputes, for villages, castes or other groups; from traditional gathering of five (panch) elders

Parsi *see* Zoroastrian

Persian The literary and government language of the Delhi Sultanate, the Mughal Empire, and other pre-modern Indian states

peshwa Hereditary Maratha chief minister; from 1720 *de facto* ruler of the Maratha confederacy

pir 'elder', founder or head of a sufi order or shrine

presidency The residence of a 'president'; here used for the three East India Company centres of Madras, Bombay, and Calcutta established in the seventeenth century

Rajput A 'prince'. Rajput clans, based in northern and north-western India, emerged in the medieval and Mughal period as warrior princes and frequent allies of the Mughals

raja 'Ruler'. A title widely used in British India not only for princes but by chiefs, zamindars, etc.; customarily (but not always) confined to Hindus

sabha Association or society; assembly, council, court

Sanskrit   An Indo-European language which emerged in ancient times as the sacred language of legal and ritual tradition cultivated by Brahmans

satyagraha   'Truth force', a Gandhian neologism to describe his method of dispute settlement based on a shared pursuit of 'truth' with an opponent, together with mutual respect

Sayyid   Muslims who claim descent from the Prophet Muhammad

settlement   In British India a revenue term used in the context of agricultural taxation to specify an agreement with an individual or group for the responsibility to pay a fixed amount of tax on a given tract of land; often carried with it effective ownership of the land

Shaikh   (1) A title for a sufi (q.v.) master; (2) a Muslim claiming descent from the Companions of the Prophet

shari'at   The whole body of rules guiding the life of a Muslim in law, ethics, and etiquette

Shi'a   The minority of Muslims who reject the succession of the first four caliphs in favour of the rights of the Prophet Muhammad's son-in-law `Ali and his descendants, the imams

Shudra   The lowest varna or status category identified in the classical Sanskrit tradition; required to perform services for the three higher and pure varnas

Sikh   A 'Disciple', used in this case for the followers of the path (*panth*) of the teacher Guru Nanak. Also *see bhakti*

sufi   Those who cultivate the inner dimension of Islam through moral practices, disciplines, and association with sufi masters who act as guides, teachers, and mediators; a 'mystic'

Sunni   The majority of Muslims who accept the authority of the first four caliphs and the principle of consensus for choosing successors to the Prophet Muhammad (570–632 CE)

swadeshi   Of 'one's own land'; used by nationalists to encourage the production and use of products made within India

swaraj   Self-rule, self-government

'ulama (sg: *'alim*)   Authorities learned in Islamic legal and religious studies

Vaisya   The varna or status category identified in the classical Sanskrit tradition as businessmen and merchants and as men entitled to perform sacrifices

varna   The four ideal hierarchic categories comprising human society (Brahman, Kshatriya, Vaisya, and Shudra, q.v.) in the Brahmanic Sanskritic traditions, articulated above all the dharmasastra texts of Manu at the turn of the first millennium

yogi   A Hindu ascetic who practices disciplines intended to discipline the consciousness to achieve control and tranquility

zamindar   A 'landholder', the person who collects and transmits the revenue or tax claim to the government

zenana   The women's quarters of an Indian household

Zoroastrian   a follower of the Iranian teacher Zoroaster (b. 660 BC), roughly contemporary with the Buddha, Mahavira Jain, and the authors of the Upanishads, whose ethical monotheism, focused on the deity Ormazd, is predicated on a universal struggle between light and dark. Only small communities of Zoroastrians continued after the advent of Islam, including groups on the western coast of India known as 'Parsis' ('Persians').

PLACE NAMES: ALTERNATE SPELLINGS

British usage	Contemporary usage
Banaras	Varanasi
Bombay	Mumbai
Cawnpore	Kanpur
Ceylon	Sri Lanka
Dacca	Dhaka
Ganges	Ganga
Jumna	Yamuna
Madras	Chennai
Oudh	Awadh
Poona	Pune
Simla	Shimla

I

Sultans, Mughals, and pre-colonial Indian society

Imagine a time traveller standing in Mughal Delhi, amidst the splendor of the emperor Shah Jahan's (r. 1627–58) elegant, riverside city, in the year 1707 (plate 1.1). News had come of the death of Shah Jahan's long-ruling son, Aurangzeb (r. 1658–1707) in the distant Deccan, where he had been engaged in arduously extending his vast empire. The traveller, understandably wondering what the death of a mighty monarch would mean, might first have looked back in time a century, say to the death of Shah Jahan's grandfather, Akbar (r. 1556–1605). Had he done so, he would have seen the key institutions in place that had made the Mughals, in the intervening century, the most powerful empire the subcontinent had ever known. It was far greater in population, wealth, and power than the contemporaneous Turko–Mongol empires with which the Mughals shared so much: the Persian Safavids and the Ottoman Turks. The Mughal population in 1700 may have been 100 million, five times that of the Ottomans, almost twenty that of the Safavids. Given the trajectory of continuity and growth that had taken place in the seventeenth century, our time traveller at the turn of the eighteenth century might legitimately have imagined a Mughal future to match the glorious past.

But if, Janus-faced, the traveller then looked ahead a century, say to 1803, he would have found not continuity but extraordinary change. He would have seen an empire existing only in name amidst a landscape of competing regional powers. Among these regional states was one which, in 1707 only a minor European trading

Plate 1.1   Shah Jahan's Red Fort, Delhi.

body operating from coastal enclaves, was now transformed into a governing body based in the rich, eastern province of Bengal. The Mughal emperor, though still a symbolic overlord, was now confined to the area around Delhi, himself prey to Afghans, the western Deccan-based Marathas, and, in 1803, placed under the control of that very English Company which, as this new century turned, had lately come to a vision of creating an empire itself.

The most familiar ways of understanding the Mughal era in Indian history were forged in a framework created by the British as they themselves devised a national history for their own emerging nation. Central to their image of themselves, as well as to their image of what they came to see as a backward but incipient nation, was what the historian David Arnold has called the Orientalist 'triptych' of Indian history. In this vision, ancient 'Hindus' had once created a great civilization. With the advent of Islamic rulers in the early thirteenth century, Indian culture rigidified, political life gave way to despotism, and the gap between foreign 'Muslim' rulers and a native 'Hindu' populace of necessity made for a fragile structure. Moral arguments, particularly a focus on what became a caricature of Aurangzeb's 'intolerance', were central in explaining 'decline'. Stage three brought modern British colonial rule with its enlightened leadership, scientific progress, and – for some adherents to this vision more than others – tutelage to independence. This tripartite schema was explicit in much British writing, and it often underlay even anti-colonial Indian nationalist historiography. Even today it has been tenaciously persistent as unrecognized 'common sense' in historical writing; and, as we shall see in chapter 9, it is today treated as fact in Hindu nationalist ideologies.

Today historians of the centuries preceding the British period reject the earlier characterizations of the period of the Muslim dynasties. They also argue, perhaps surprisingly, in relation to the eighteenth century, that it was the culmination of long-term transitions in trade, finance, culture, and society that offered the English the very resources they needed to exercise their own remarkable innovations in finance, organization, and military and naval technology. This chapter introduces the middle frame of the 'triptych', covering roughly 1206 to 1707, when patterns were set that help explain our traveller's view both back in time and ahead.

THE DELHI SULTANATE

The common image of India's past has been profoundly influenced by two interrelated misperceptions: one that the classical texts of the Brahmans described an existing society; and, second, that, because India was 'timeless', the village and caste organization of colonial or even contemporary India was a guide to its historical past. In fact, the periods of the Sultanate and Mughal rule accelerated already existing patterns of change. These centuries saw the expansion of the agricultural frontier, extensive commercial networks, gradual technological change, and development of political and religious institutions. These changes, not some stagnant society, form the prelude to the colonial era. Nor, one might add, did Muslim rulers fit the caricature assigned them. It is, for instance, misleading to speak of them as 'foreign', for, in patterns set by the earliest Sultanates, Muslim and non-Muslim polities and cultures changed in interaction with each other. It is also misleading to speak of this era as the period of 'Muslim' rule. Such an expression exaggerates the differences between states ruled by Muslims and those ruled by non-Muslims. It also obscures the participation of non-Muslims in the Muslim-led polities. It may further suggest that there were religious practices, like mass conversion, that did not exist.

Successive Turko–Afghan regimes, collectively known as the Delhi Sultanate, dominated political life in the north, with periodic incursions into the south, during the late thirteenth and fourteenth centuries. These Turks and Afghans, like invaders before them stretching back two millennia, originally entered the subcontinent through the mountain passages of the north-west. One immediate corrective to much scholarship is to emphasize how much their kingdom had in common with other Indic polities of the day. Like these other states, including that of the celebrated Rajput Prithviraj Chauhan, the Turks and Afghans sought above all military successes in order to secure access to the agricultural surplus of the countryside. Like them, they possessed a fragmented political authority, with rights to a share of the land revenue of a specific area assigned to their subordinates as a form of compensation. Also like them, the Delhi Sultans offered scope to individual achievement, above all through military prowess. Any periodization predicated simply on the religion of the rulers would miss such fundamental similarities. The Turks and Afghans were invaders, but they behaved in ways that were familiar to their enemies. The 'Turks', as these rulers were conventionally called, were assimilated to such familiar categories as *yavana*, 'Ionian', the term used to describe the Greek invaders who followed Alexander the Great a millennium before, or *mlecca*, 'barbarians', a term for those outside the area of settled Indic civilization whether from distant areas or nearby jungles.

The core military and economic institutions of these dynasties were thus not specifically 'Islamic'. The sultans themselves were not religious leaders. Like non-Muslim rulers, they did not gain their authority through their own holiness or sacred learning but through their military and governing skill. They were expected, however, to patronize those who were holy and learned. The historian Peter Hardy has called the sultans 'pious policemen' collaborating with 'pious lawyers'. Muslim rulers patronized not only the learned legal scholars or *ulama*, who had mastered the sacred Arabic texts, but also the moral guides and spiritual intermediaries of the Muslim community, the *sufi shaikhs*. These two bodies of specialists had emerged as the foci of community life among Muslims from the eleventh century on. Non-Muslim rulers, whether warrior rajas or lesser lords, in similar fashion patronized Brahmans. The Brahmans both cultivated ritual and legal learning as recorded in the sacred Sanskrit texts, and played roles in the temple cults where devotional piety (*bhakti*) flourished in the centuries of Sultanate rule.

For all these institutional similarities between Muslim and non-Muslim states, Muslim dynasties did chart new directions. For over 600 years following the establishment of the first Turkic dynasty in Delhi by the Mamluk or Slave ruler, Qutbu'd-din Aibak in 1206, the language of the Muslim ruling elite was Persian. As participants in a Persian-speaking culture that stretched into central and south-west Asia, these dynasties were a conduit for introducing innovations in ruling institutions, as well as distinctive cultural traditions in law, political theory, and literary and religious styles. They also brought practical innovations in mounted warfare, cropping patterns, and irrigation techniques, like the widespread 'Persian' wheel. They fostered urban growth and road networks that encouraged trade within the region and beyond. Arabic-speaking Muslims had been present much earlier in the subcontinent, establishing a kingdom in Sind in the lower Indus valley in 711 as part of the expansion of the Umayyad dynasty based in Damascus. They were also found by the eighth century as traders along the Malabar coast of the south-west, where they settled, intermarried, and sustained distinctive cultural forms forged from their Arab ties and local setting, and in so doing helped link 'al-Hind' to seaborne trade routes. In the years from roughly 1200 to 1500, the movement of goods and peoples through Indian Ocean ports, as well as overland through the Persian-speaking lands, was such that Janet Abu-Lughod has characterized this period as an 'Islamic world system' of economic and political interaction. In this system, the Indian subcontinent played a significant part. Participation in these ruling and trading networks did not require that individuals be Muslims, but Muslim political expansion facilitated the success of the whole.

Another pattern set early in the Sultanate period was the enduring ethnic and linguistic pluralism of both the ruling elites and those ruled. The rulers comprised not only those of Turkic heritage but also Afghan, Persian, and native-born as well as immigrants from afar. Of these the best known was the great Moroccan traveller and memoir writer, Ibn Batuta (d. 1368–9), for whom Arabic legal knowledge was a passport to travel and employment. Ibn Batuta served the Tughluq dynasty of the fourteenth century as chief judge of Delhi; and his memoirs are testimony to the cosmopolitan vitality and variety he encountered. His first encounter with the sultan recorded the court's enthusiasm for travellers:

> I approached the sultan, who took my hand and shook it, and continuing to hold it addressed me most affably, saying in Persian, 'This is a blessing; your arrival is blessed; be at ease; I shall be compassionate to you and give you such favors that your fellow-countrymen will hear of it and come to join you.' Then he asked me where I came from and I said to him, 'From the land of the Maghrib.' . . . Every time he said any encouraging word to me I kissed his hand, until I had kissed it seven times, and after he had given me a robe of honor I withdrew.

The subjects of the dynasties were primarily non-Muslim, designated as *zimmi*, 'protected people', left to their own law and customs. They were, in principle, liable to a capitation tax (*jizya*) but not subject to military conscription. Law, generally, was administered according to the law of the parties or, if they differed, that of the defendant. For most Muslims, that meant Hanafi law shared with central and south-west Asia, while for those of the south, with their Indian Ocean ties to Arabia, law was Maliki. It was accepted here as elsewhere in Muslim polities that administrative law on such matters as taxes would have its own codes apart from the divinely sanctioned *shari`a* norms based on classical Arabic texts. The creativity and vigour of cultural life on all sides was shaped by this pluralism.

For the Sultanate rulers, as for the Mughals who succeeded them, Islamic ambitions focused on extending Muslim power, not on conversion. One clue to the lack of any systematic programme of conversion is that India's Muslim populations were not primarily found in the core areas of Muslim rule. Historians have long asserted that converts flocked to the sufi message of equality to escape the hierarchic discriminations of a Brahman-dominated 'caste' society. There is, however, no correlation between areas of Brahmanical influence and those of substantial conversion to Islam – and the extent of Brahmanical influence in the pre-colonial period, in any case, is increasingly contested. Nor, perhaps surprisingly, did the sufis themselves ever teach that Islam offered social equality. Indeed, however much they may have preached equality before Allah, Muslims have always lived in hierarchic societies.

In areas undergoing agrarian settlement, sufis did nevertheless play a key role as agents of gradual incorporation into the larger cultural and civilizational structures of the day. They received grants of forested land whose clearing they oversaw, and they served as mediators to both worldly and divine powers. Richard Eaton has shown the importance of this process for the two main areas that were to emerge with largely Muslim populations, western Punjab and eastern Bengal. In other areas Hindu religious specialists performed much the same role. In the Telugu region of south-east India, for example, as Cynthia Talbot has shown, the establishment of new temples was associated with agricultural expansion in the contemporaneous Kakatiya kingdom (1175–1324). A second force driving conversion, for individuals or clusters of artisanal or other families, was, according to Susan Bayly, not a desire to escape hierarchy, but rather a desire to seize a strategic opportunity to move upwards within the existing social hierarchy. Intermarriage also contributed to the growth of the Muslim population, as did the choice of individuals or families to follow charismatic teachers. When the first censuses were taken in the late nineteenth century, the Muslim population of British India was roughly one-quarter of the whole.

Historians now discredit not only accounts of forced mass conversion, but also accounts of systematic destruction of temples and other non-Muslim holy places. As in the case of accounts of conversions, reading the Muslim court histories as matters of fact, rather than as literary convention, has misled many scholars. There was, to be sure, destruction of non-Muslim temples and places of worship under specific circumstances, for example while raiding areas outside one's own territories for plunder. The most famous of such forays, perhaps, are those of Mahmud Ghaznawi (d. 1030) into Sind and Gujarat. Mahmud was drawn to the riches of India to secure booty for his cosmopolitan court at Ghazna (in contemporary Afghanistan), in a manner not unlike the raids of Indic rulers who carried away vanquished idols as symbols of their victory along with their booty. The sultans who established permanent courts in north India also destroyed temples during the initial phase of conquest to mark their triumph. The complex of the early twelfth-century Quwwatu'l-Islam mosque, adjoining the great minaret of Delhi, the Qutb Minar, was built on the site of destroyed temples and utilized elements of the earlier structures. The use of 'recycled' elements from earlier structures – as true around the Mediterranean, for example, as for India – was sometimes a declaration of power, sometimes simply expedient use of abandoned debris. Firoz Shah Tughluq (r. 1351–88) chose to adorn his fort built in the mid-fourteenth century, for example, with a column from a millennium and a half earlier, whose builder had long been forgotten, as a way perhaps to assert a link to some ill-defined earlier glory (plate 1.2).

Muslim spiritual and philosophical life in India evolved together with the religious life of non-Muslims. Each was responding to a shared context and, at the same time, interacting with the other's expressions of their respective traditions. No cultural pattern of the Sultanate period was more enduring for the Muslim population than that of sufi devotionalism. Indeed, one of the defining characteristics of Islam in the Indic context throughout its long history is the pervasiveness in discourse and institutions of the sufi tradition. Like the `ulama associated with the courts, the sufi holy men typically adhered to the shari`a, but they also stressed inner realization of the divine presence, the practice of moral and physical disciplines, and the need to submit to the authority of charismatic chains of saintly authority. They served the rulers, yet, to a varying degree, sought to present themselves as distant from the corruption of worldly rule. The founders of the most important sufi lineages, Chishti, Suhrawardi, Qadiri, and Naqshbandi, were central and west Asian in origin, but they flourished in the subcontinent. Sufi teachings were enriched and stimulated by the presence and competition of similar holy men of the Indic bhakti traditions of devotion, spiritual disciplines, and sophisticated monistic philosophies. Bhakti devotion and worship, in turn, flowered as well.

THE EMERGENCE OF REGIONAL KINGDOMS

By the fifteenth and early sixteenth centuries, the Sultanate in the north had given way to a series of regional kingdoms, Gujarat, Malwa, Jaunpur, Delhi itself, and Bengal. In the Deccan and

Plate 1.2   Asoka Pillar, Ferozshah Kotla, Delhi.

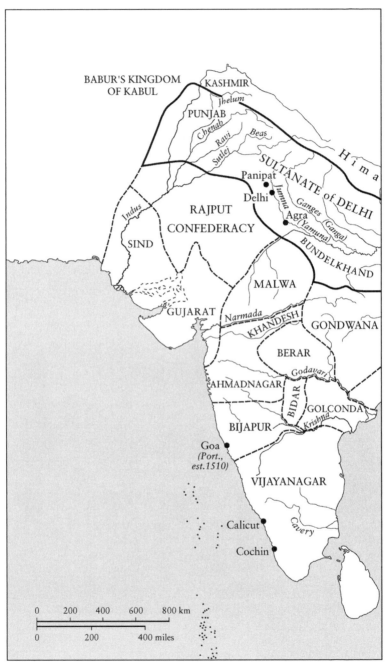

BABUR'S KINGDOM
OF KABUL

KASHMIR

Jhelum

PUNJAB

Chenab

Ravi

Beas

Sutlej

H i m a

SULTÂNATE of DELHI

Panipat

Delhi

Jamna (Yamuna)

Ganges (Ganga)

Indus

RAJPUT
CONFEDERACY

Agra

SIND

BUNDELKHAND

MALWA

GUJARAT

Narmada

KHANDESH

GONDWANA

BERAR

Godavari

AHMADNAGAR

BIDAR

GOLCONDA

BIJAPUR

Krishna

Goa
*(Port.,
est.1510)*

VIJAYANAGAR

Calicut

Cavery

Cochin

0   200   400   600   800 km

0   200   400 miles

Map 1   India *c.* 1500.

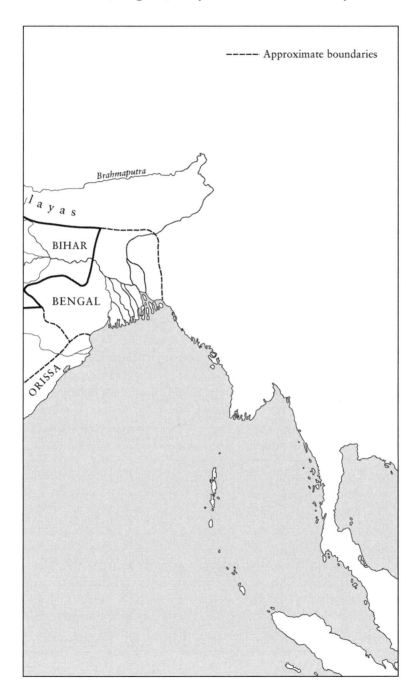

peninsular India, moreover, Sultanate incursions had overturned existing regimes, opening the way for new kingdoms to emerge. Shortly after Muhammad bin Tughluq, whose efforts to expand south were most intensive, withdrew from the capital he had established at Daulatabad in the Deccan, the Bahmanid kingdom, also dominated by Muslims, was established in 1345. After roughly a century and a half, it, like the Sultanate, gave way to more localized powers across the Deccan, and these kingdoms, Bijapur, Ahmadnagar, Berar, Bidar, and Golcunda, persisted as Muslim dynasties from the late fifteenth century well into the Mughal era.

At about the same time as the establishment of the Bahmanids, the kingdom of Vijayanagar, based in Karnataka but soon expanding into Andhra and beyond, was founded by brothers who had served the Tughluqs, probably been Muslim for a time, and who now espoused a strong Shaivite tradition, that of worshipping Lord Shiva, as an ideology that sharply distinguished them from the Sultanate and Bahmanids. That kingdom emulated the military technology of the Sultanate, even employing units of north Indian mounted fighters. Although drawing on earlier models of south Indian kingship, Vijayanagar shared political idioms with the neighbouring states as well. Several kings, including the most powerful, Krishnadevaraya (r. 1509–29), called themselves the 'sultan among Hindu kings', with both the terms 'sultan' and 'hindu' (an Arab geographical term) taken from Muslims. Vijayanagar public buildings drew on the architectural forms of northern building; and even the dress of the king marked him as part of a wider political culture. Vijayanagar's most persistent warfare was with Bijapur, a state whose capital city shared with its opponent's the same name, 'City of Victory'. By the fifteenth and sixteenth century, Hindu inscriptions further suggest a kind of equivalence among the dominant powers of the time, with the leaders of the Bahmanids (or Turks or Mughals) known as *asvapati*, the lords of the horses; Vijayanagar as *narapati*, the lord of men (infantry); and the Gajapatis (along the Orissan coast) as 'lords of the elephants'.

Despite the emergence of political divisions and distinctive vernacular cultures, the first three centuries of Muslim rule fostered long-enduring changes in trading networks, social life, and religious institutions, as well as political strategies, that made for continuity across a broad geographical area. The fifteenth and early sixteenth century in northern India foreshadowed in some ways the regional kingdoms that succeeded the Mughal Empire in the eighteenth century. Both were periods characterized by widespread similarities and connections, despite political divisions, as well as by creative cultural expression in local, vernacular contexts.

Bhakti leaders dating from this period whose teachings and cults persist to the present include Kabir (1440–1518), Guru Nanak (1469–1539), Mirabai (c. 1498–c. 1550), Dadu (1544–1603), Tukaram (1608–1649), and Chaitanya (1486–1533). Like the sufis, the bhakti teachers emphasized the individual's own devotion to the divine. A minor strand, represented by Kabir and Nanak, emphasized worship of a personal God without form. In so doing they distanced themselves from distinctive Hindu and Muslim symbols. As Nanak wrote, 'The gods and goddesses whom you worship and to whom you pray, what can they give? You wash them yourselves; left to themselves they will sink in the water.' Nanak by contrast encouraged a selfless love for God: 'He who is immersed in His love day and night sees Him immanent in the three worlds, and throughout all time. He becomes like Him whom he knows. He becomes wholly pure, his body is sanctified, and God dwells in his heart as his only love.'

More common than worshippers of a formless god were Vaishnavites devoted to Lord Vishnu; Shaivites, devoted to Lord Shiva; and worshippers of the Goddess (*devi*) in her many forms. Vaishnavite worship was focused on the manifestations of Lord Vishnu as either the ideal king, Lord Ram, or as the pastoral Lord Krishna, celebrated as child, cowherd, and lover. This emphasis on individual access to the divine, often coupled with critiques of merely formal ritual, nonetheless accommodated, for the most part, the guidance of Brahman priests, who played a central role in sectarian communities.

Both the Persian and the Indic traditions used erotic encounters to represent the relationship between the human and the divine. By the late fourteenth century, sufi poets were writing in a range of lyric and narrative forms, including the *masnawi* love stories that simultaneously depict a story of human passion and the quest for ultimate truth. These poets composed not only in Persian but also in the vernaculars of north India, and, later, of the Deccan. They drew on the rich vocabulary and resonances of Indic philosophic and religious thought, as well as on a range of poetic conventions characteristic of bhakti poetry. Bhakti poets, in turn, were influenced by the new genres derived from Persian. Muslim chroniclers writing in the vernaculars, like early Arab historians before them, also enriched Islamic traditions by incorporating regional epic and legendary figures into their writings. In the Bengali *Nabi-vamsa* of the late sixteenth century, for example, the deities of the Hindu pantheon were simply understood as Islamic prophets.

In architecture as well the period was one of variety and creativity. To look only at mosques of the fifteenth century, for instance, no one would mistake the brick mosques of Bengal, the almost Gothic wooden structures of Kashmir, the temple-like pillared halls of Ahmadabad, or the massive, pylon-based mosques of Jaunpur for each other; yet all represented a Muslim culture new since the period had begun, now finding expression in a variety of local contexts. One measure of the centralizing Mughal power, which would soon emerge, is the extent to which it was able to achieve a common aesthetic taste, reflected in temples and mosques, palaces and forts, across its far-flung domains (as exemplified in plate 1.5).

THE MUGHAL EMPIRE

In 1526, the Delhi-based kingdom of the Afghan Muslim Lodi dynasty fell to the brilliant military strategy and superior artillery of Zahir al-Din Muhammad Babar (1483–1530) at Panipat, northwest of Delhi. Like the Sultans, the Mughals stimulated a new level of settled agriculture, military capability, and geographic integration. Babar was a scion of both Timur ('Tamerlane', 1336–1405) on his father's side and the Mongol Chingiz Khan (1167?–1227) on his mother's. It was the former lineage the dynasty cherished and it is, thus, an irony of history that since the nineteenth century these rulers have been called by a variant of the latter's name. Babar had longed for his lost patrimony in Samarkand and turned to Hindustan as what seemed poor compensation. Babar bears ready comparison, as the historian Stephen Dale has argued, to contemporary princes of the Renaissance in his self-cultivation and his eclectic interests, from hard-boiled military strategy to the nuances of Turkic and Persian poetry. His own Turkic memoirs, and his daughter Gulbadan's Persian memoirs, are testimony to this image. Gulbadan recounted one of the most famous episodes of Babar's life – the emperor's willing sacrifice of his life to save his sick son:

When his Majesty came and saw how it was, his light-revealing countenance at once became sad and pitiful, and he began more and more to show sign of dread. His Majesty [said], 'Although I have other sons, I love none as I love Humayun. I crave that this cherished child may have his heart's desire and live long because he has not his equal in distinction.' During Humayun's illness his Majesty walked round him. He kept up that going-round, in anxiety and deep dejection. While going round he prayed, saying in effect: 'O God! If a life may be exchanged for a life, I who am Babar, I give my life and my being for Humayun.' That very day he fell ill, and Humayun poured water on his head, and came out and gave audience.

One exquisite later miniature illustrating Babar's memoirs depicts him laying out the kind of formal garden he so loved, at once an aspect of his range of skills and metaphor for the order he aspired to bring to individual and corporate life (plate 1.3). Gulbadan's memoirs, further, offer a rare view into the lives of the court women. In this account they are shown as counsellors and mediators among family members, they dispose of property, and they organize ritual occasions that define social solidarities. When Gulbadan died, the emperor Akbar helped carry her bier.

Babar ruled for a mere four years, and neither he, nor his son Humayun, forced into exile in Persia, did more than establish garrisons to mark the area they controlled. The foundation for an enhanced infrastructure of roads and the beginnings of agricultural surveys was laid by resurgent Afghans, the Surs, who ruled until Humayun, accompanied by Safavid immigrants, regained control of the kingdom in the final year of his life (1555–6). It was Humayun's son Akbar whose half-century of rule established the dynasty as an empire, brought about by conquests that moved the frontiers of Mughal control north to Kabul and Kashmir, east to Bengal and coastal Orissa, south to Gujarat and part of the Deccan and, most important of all, south-west from Delhi to Rajasthan.

Akbar embraced and then built on the Sultanate policy of a diverse and inclusive ruling elite. He sought to incorporate powerful

Plate 1.3 *Babur Supervising the Garden of Fidelity*, by Bishan Das, from
the Baburnama.

indigenous lineages, above all those of the Rajputs, who were confirmed in rights to the revenue of their own domains. He began the dynastic custom of taking Rajput wives (who were not expected to convert to Islam), among them Jodh Bai, mother of Akbar's successor Jahangir (r. 1605–27). The diverse Mughal ruling elites comprised not only differing strands from central Asia, but Persians (who as Shi`a differed in religion from the majority Sunni Muslims), some Arabs, as well as locally born Muslims, Rajputs, together with a few Brahmans and, later, Marathas. The unifying ideology of the regime was that of loyalty, expressed through Persianate cultural forms, not a tribal affiliation (like that of the Ottomans), nor an Islamic or an Islamic sectarian identity (like that of the Safavids). This ideology also encompassed lower-level military and scribal officials, largely non-Muslim.

Loyalty was focused on the person of the ruler, the apex of a pyramid of vertical bonds. Akbar's chief memoirist and publicist, Abu'l Fazl, held up the emperor as a man of extraordinary vitality, universal curiosity, and master of every art. He fostered a new image of the emperor as not only a military and strategic leader, and patron of the holy and learned, but as himself a person of spiritual knowledge and charisma. In Abu'l Fazl's words in his celebrated *Institutes of Akbar*:

No dignity is higher in the eyes of God than royalty, and those who are wise drink from its auspicious fountain. A sufficient proof of this, for those who require one, is the fact that royalty is a remedy for the spirit of rebellion, and the reason why subjects obey. Royalty is a light emanating from God, and a ray from the sun, the illuminator of the universe, the argument of the book of perfection, the receptacle of all virtues. Many excellent qualities flow from the possession of this light: a paternal love toward the subjects; a large heart; a daily increasing trust in God; prayer and devotion. He must see that no injustice is done within his realm.

Akbar and his successors thus claimed a different kind of kingship from that of the Sultans.

The emperor's quasi-divine status was expressed not only in theoretical writings, but also in ceremony, sufi allegiance, artistic allegory, and architectural analogies. Akbar was associated with images of immanent light and human perfectibility cultivated among some Shi'i and sufi thinkers. His teachings, labelled the *din-i ilahi* or 'divine faith', served as a focus for a small number of court disciples who took the emperor not only as their royal but their spiritual master as well. Some few Hindus beyond the Rajput generals were among the inner circle of the elite in Akbar's court. Among them were the architect of the empire's agrarian policies, Todar Mal, and the courtier and confidant, Birbal, whose *bons mots* and humour have come down through history. There were court 'ulama who opposed Akbar's claims, no one more famously than the disaffected Àbdu'l-Qadir Badayuni (*c.*1540–1615), thanks to whose indiscriminate ridicule Akbar was memorialized as an apostate.

Akbar's use of Islamic symbols was not exclusionary, and he welcomed to his new court at Fatehpur Sikri for discussion Brahmans, yogis, Jains, Jesuit priests who travelled up from Portuguese trading enclaves on the south-west coasts, Zoroastrians, and Muslim scholars of every orientation. He, like Jahangir after him, was particularly fascinated by yogis, whose influence on Muslim thought and practice in India has been extensive (and little recognized). Like many intellectuals and holy men in the open climate of this period, Akbar sought shared esoteric or philosophic truths across traditions, as well as disciplinary practices in the pursuit of those truths. He patronized translations into Persian of the Sanskrit *Ramayana* (the story of Lord Ram) and *Mahabharata*, as well as miniature painting representing episodes of the two epics. He abolished the jizya taxes levied on non-Muslims.

Jahangir continued his father's catholic religious interests. He was personally devoted not only to the Qadiri saint, Miyan Mir, but also to the Vaishnava yogi, Gosain Jadrup. He continued the practice of enrolling loyal nobles as disciples, who symbolized their allegiance by wearing his portrait and pearl earrings of servitude. Shah Jahan's claims to legitimacy were made in stone. His architectural achievements include gardens, the planned city of Shahjahanabad (whose 'Red Fort' is represented in Plate 1.1), and, most famed of all, the tomb dedicated to his cherished wife, the Taj Mahal (plate 1.4), all associated with paradisiacal symbols. By this symbolism, Shah Jahan made himself nothing less than the analogue of the divine, his paradise represented in greenery and stone. The Mughals shared such ritual elaborations with other early modern rulers across Eurasia, who in a variety of ways identified their aspirations to unparalleled power with expressions of cosmologically or divinely sanctioned rule.

Plate 1.4 Taj Mahal, Agra, from the Great Gateway (1648).

A further key to Akbar's successes were the administrative reforms that created an enduring framework for rule. There was nothing specifically 'Islamic' about these strategies; they built on Sultanate precedents, and in broad form were shared by early modern agrarian empires across Asia. Nobles were awarded ranks, known as *mansab*, demarcated decimally, and were expected to provide horse-men according to the rank number for the emperor's use. They were appointed to positions in two parallel hierarchies, one with civil responsibilities and one military – thus a check on each other – at levels from district, to province, to centre, throughout the empire. Nobles were assigned the right to collect the assessed tax revenue of pieces of land, *jagirs*, as the basis of their remuneration. By ro-tating these assignments frequently, nobles were incapacitated from building a local base that could challenge Mughal authority. Even a relatively centralized empire like this, however, was limited in its reach into local communities. Mughal officials typically negotiated for delivery of the revenue demand with lineage heads and chieftains, homogenized in Mughal usage as *zamindars* (land-holders).

At the bottom of this hierarchy were the peasant cultivators. Their condition under the Mughals has been a subject of controversy. In his classic study of the Mughal agrarian system, Irfan Habib con-cluded that the cultivating peasantry, though not owners of the land, hence unable to sell it, still possessed a hereditary right of occu-pancy so long as they paid the state's revenue demand. For Habib, the result was an unceasing oppression, as their superiors sought to strip the cultivators of all surplus. Growing in intensity as the seventeenth century proceeded, these exactions precipitated a series of revolts that shook the empire, and in the end helped bring about its downfall. Other historians have pointed out that the existence of extensive tracts of uncultivated land moderated exploitation, as cul-tivators could vote with their feet if the burden of taxation became intolerable. Further, as we discuss below, most agrarian revolts were zamindari-led, and so did not involve the peasantry as the main pro-tagonists. Sustained by an expansive economy, the peasantry were, at the very least, unlikely to have emerged from the years of Mughal rule any worse off than they were at its start.

Generations of modern historians and politicians have blamed Shah Jahan's successor Aurangzeb for undoing the cultural plural-ism and administrative efficiency of the empire. Aurangzeb had contended for the throne with his eldest brother, Dara Shukoh (1615–58); and the two have come down through history as ideolog-ical opponents, Dara, as the 'liberal' and Aurangzeb as the rigid 'con-servative'. Dara was, indeed, an intellectual in the tradition of Akbar, who sought out shared philosophical truths in all religious traditions. He translated the Sanskrit *Upanishads* and wrote a treatise linking sufi and Upanishadic philosophical thought, his celebrated *Majma'u'l-bahrain* (The Mingling of the Two Oceans). To focus on divergent philosophies neglects the fact that Dara was a poor general and leader. It also ignores the fact that factional lines in the succession dispute were not, by and large, shaped by ideology, even though Aurangzeb, not surprisingly, accused his brother of idolatry. It is also worth noting that a major focus of Aurangzeb's reign was warfare directed against other Muslims. Although Aurangzeb encouraged a more narrow and austere Islamic style in courtly culture, that was not the cause of imperial decline.

Aurangzeb shifted but did not fundamentally alter the religious policy of the empire. However much the emperors fostered cultural pluralism, they all, like Aurangzeb, privileged the Islamic. Aurangzeb generously patronized the 'ulama and ordered a compilation of judicial opinions in the *Fatawa-yi 'Alamgiri*. He cultivated an image of himself as a man of personal piety. He patronized Islamic leaders and sites; he restored policies that applied differential taxes on Hindus (not incidentally a source of revenue for his hard-pressed regime); and he favoured Muslims for official employment. Aurangzeb's towering mosque in Benares was an assertion of Mughal power and Islamic strength. But his destruction of temples in Benares, Mathura, and Rajasthan had less to do with iconoclasm, since he continued to patronize other Hindu temples, than with the presumed disloyalty of nobles associated with these sites. The building and patronage of the temples of loyal nobles, like the erection of mosques that enjoyed state support, was regarded as an element in state policy. Temples, like other buildings constructed in the shared imperial architectural style, among them the Rajput-built Hindu temple in plate 1.5, were visible manifestations of Mughal power. Similarly, Aurangzeb's accusation of the Sikh guru, Tegh Bahadur (r. 1664–75), of blasphemy, and his subsequent execution, must be seen in the context of imperial politics. Tegh Bahadur was an active military organizer and proselytizer with family ties to a supporter of Dara; his execution mingled Islamic justifications with imperial politics, as had Jahangir's execution of the fifth guru, on similar grounds, before him. To the end, Aurangzeb depended on

Plate 1.5   Interior of Hindu Temple constructed in the Mughal Style, by
Raja Man Singh, at Brindaban.

non-Muslim courtiers. More than a quarter of the mansab holders
along with his leading general were Hindus.

Did Aurangzeb's very success in achieving the widest expansion
of the empire, as is often argued, sow the seeds of its undoing? He
was determined to expand into the Deccan at any cost against the

Muslim kingdoms that had succeeded the Bahmani Sultanate and against the newly insurgent Marathas, a formidable enemy with their guerilla tactics and strategically placed hill forts. In 1685 his forces took Bijapur; in 1689, Golconda. The core area of the north was neglected as the emperor, his court, and his armies, a veritable moving city as the French physician Bernier's memoirs vividly evoke, remained far from Delhi. The system of co-opting new elites through the award of jagirs ran aground as the pace of need, exacerbated by the debilitating costs of these campaigns, outran the availability of profitable grants. Not only the Marathas, but also Sikh and Jat zamindars, as well as some among the Rajputs, soon challenged imperial rule. These insurgents were, however, kept in check until the end of Aurangzeb's reign.

Clearly, a focus on the personality, or even the policies, of one emperor, whatever short-term problems he may have created, is inadequate in explaining imperial decline. Such a focus fits too easily with the old European theory of Asiatic 'despotism'. Two more persuasive lines of argument suggest long-term transitions, incipient in the seventeenth century, that contributed to accelerating decentralization after Aurangzeb's death in 1707. One, perhaps surprisingly, is that the upstart warriors, Marathas, Jats, and the like, as coherent social groups with military and governing ideals, were themselves a product of the Mughal context, which recognized them and provided them with military and governing experience. Their successes were a product of Mughal success. A second line of argument is economic. Throughout Asia, the economies of the agrarian empires had been fuelled in the seventeenth century by the influx of specie gained from New World conquest, as Europeans sought valued commodities. Asian economies, including that of the Mughals, were increasingly monetized, and cash-crop production, demand-responsive, expanded. Evidence of the vast extent and wealth of the empire remain in the dynasty's monuments, above all those of Shah Jahan. Indian seaborne trade, to be sure, was largely in the hands of Arabs and, from the beginning of the sixteenth century, the Portuguese. English and Dutch trading companies further established themselves in coastal enclaves during the seventeenth century. But the monetization and expanding commerce generated by this trade gave rise, as we shall see in the next chapter, to new Indian commercial and political elites, especially in the southern and eastern coastal areas. The regional states of the eighteenth century can thus be seen as the fruition, not the end, of Mughal rule.

The challenges to Aurangzeb did not come from groups that had been suppressed under Muslim rule and now sought to regain their autonomy. Marathas, Sikhs, Jats, and even Rajputs represented social groups with old names but new cohesion and status. These were not age-old Indian 'castes'. One of the surprising arguments of fresh scholarship, based on inscriptional and other contemporaneous evidence, is that until relatively recent centuries, social organization in much of the subcontinent was little touched by the four normative hierarchic categories (*varnas*) known from Sanskrit Vedic texts: Brahman priests as ritual guardians of social purity; Kshatriya warriors; Vaisya merchants; and Shudra peasants. Nor were 'sub-castes' or *jati* (endogamous groups identified by varna) the building blocks of society. There was, in practice, far more importance given to occupational identities and individual mobility than most commentators since the colonial period have recognized. A major stimulus to the use of the Sanskrit categories appears to have been the claims of aspiring dynasts in the Mughal period who, as parvenu *kshatriya*, in turn identified peasants and soldiery as ranked groups, giving new meanings to old titles that earlier had had only loose regional or occupational meaning. Muslim social hierarchy itself, one might note, also took on new formality, evident by the eighteenth century, with the well-born identifying themselves in terms of four ranked putative descent groups: Sayyid, descendants of the Prophet; Shaikh, descendants of his Companions; Mughal; and Pathan. The category of 'shaikh' was particularly porous in absorbing the upwardly mobile.

What Susan Bayly calls the 'paradigmatic case' of kingly social mobility is that of Shivaji Bhonsle (1630–80), the pivotal figure in the Maratha insurgency that so plagued Aurangzeb in the Deccan. Shivaji was of cultivator background, from peoples known in western India as Marathas or Kanbis. By the sixteenth century, the term 'Maratha' had acquired respectability through its use by the Deccani sultans as they rewarded these communities for their service as soldiers and office holders. Shivaji's father served the states of Bijapur and Ahmadnagar, as well as the Mughals, before unsuccessfully leading a guerilla force against them. Shivaji himself continued as a guerilla fighter. On one famous occasion he pretended to surrender, only to murder the Bijapuri general, Afzal Khan, with a concealed 'tiger claw' as he feigned an embrace. Subsequently, he was roundly defeated by Aurangzeb's Rajput general, Jai Singh, and accepted a mansab in Mughal service, only to defy imperial ritual when he felt slighted by the rank awarded him. Shivaji gained legitimacy from Mughal honours, but he also sought status elsewhere. Under the Mughals, the term *Rajput* had become the symbol of legitimate kshatriya rule, and so Shivaji determined to acquire that status for himself. He recruited a Brahman preceptor from a devotional sect, in the style of a Rajput, and then found Brahmans willing to accept the idea that kshatriya were defined by action, not birth. These Brahmans accordingly provided him with the ritual and genealogical services that legitimized him as a descendent of warrior forebears. In 1679, he had himself installed as king in elaborate Brahmanic ceremonies. Shivaji exemplifies the role of the successful warrior in fostering formalized caste ideals. He welcomed men of skill and loyalty with no regard to birth, but he subsequently built classifications of jati and varna into his courtly ritual and organization.

The Mughal period was thus one of far-reaching political, economic, and social reconfigurations. Cultural life flourished as well in the context of internal pluralism and regional cross-fertilization. Mughal miniature painting and architecture, both with Persian roots but utterly transformed in the Indian environment, endure as the most visible legacies of that brilliant cultural life. Medical systems, the Sanskrit *ayurveda* and the Arabic *yunani tibb* (derived from Greek theories), which share a holistic framework of temperature and moisture, interacted to their mutual enrichment. Music flourished. Fundamental elements in Vaishnavite devotionalism in particular took shape, as the work of poets like Sur during Akbar's reign, and the beloved *Ramcaritmanas* of Tulsidas make clear. The most luminous Islamic thinker of this period, the Naqshbandi sufi Shaikh Ahmad Sirhindi (1564–1624), serves as a reminder that the subcontinent itself has been a centre of Islamic thought and practice. Sirhindi, who criticized imperial cultural policies, was a thorn in the side of the empire, and was even imprisoned for his self-aggrandizement by Jahangir. But his cosmological and philosophical thought had lasting impact not only within the subcontinent but in central Asia and the Ottoman lands as well. The basic openness and eclecticism of the period is illustrated by the incorporation, with the advent of the European trading companies, of new techniques of shipbuilding, horticulture, and even art (for example, in depictions of landscape and perspective). A metaphor of 'stagnation' could not be more misleading.

The flexibility and openness of Mughal institutions is also under-lined if that period is described not, as it long has been, as part of 'Medieval' India or 'Moslem' India, terms that suggest isolation and exoticism, but instead, to use the term now preferred by many his-torians, as 'Early Modern'. Such a description points to a range of transformations that began about 1500 across Eurasia, and not only in Europe where the periodization 'Early Modern' for the sixteenth to eighteenth centuries is standard usage. The historian of Mughal India, John Richards, has identified several of these unprecedented worldwide processes of change, starting with the creation of global sea passages that linked the entire world for the first time. The im-pact of these changes on India, as pointed out above, includes inten-sification of monetization and the expansion of textile production evident already by the seventeenth century. This era also saw popu-lation growth and the spread of the agricultural frontier in India as in many other world areas. India, like other areas of Asia, adopted New World cultivars, among them tobacco, maize, and peppers. The Early Modern period was also an era of centralized states, of which the Mughal was one. And it was a period of technological diffusion, not least in relation to gunpowder. This technology was so important that one historian, Marshall Hodgson, described the great agrarian empires of the period – Ottoman, Safavid, Mughal, Ching – as 'gunpowder empires', not only because of the power available to those able to deploy improved personal firearms and cannon, but because these regimes were stimulated to new levels of bureaucratic control in order to support new military technology.

What then, to ask again, about 'Muslimness'? For roughly half a millennium Muslim dynasties dominated political life in the sub-continent. Both 'Orientalist' views and recent Hindu nationalism have argued that Hindu beliefs and institutions were repressed in these long centuries. In contrast, to reiterate points made above, the very institutions of social organization, as well as new patterns of Vaishnavite and Shaivite worship, emerged precisely in this period.

Islamic thought and practice, above all within the framework of sufi devotionalism, were similarly transformed. The regimes were 'Muslim' in that they were led by Muslims, patronized (among others) learned and holy Muslim leaders, and justified their existence in Islamic terms. But loyalty, not religious affiliation, defined participation, and non-Muslim elites were central to the functioning of Sultanate and Mughal regimes. There were no programmes of mass, much less forced, conversion.

Were the regimes then 'foreign', as is frequently alleged? Certainly, the dynasties were founded by people from outside the current political boundaries of South Asia, and immigrants saw India as 'a land of opportunity'. But cultural areas spilled out beyond current borders, and those within central Asian circuits, or ocean-borne trading networks east and west, arguably had more in common within these areas than with putatively 'national' groupings. What does 'foreign' mean in an era before modern states and passports? How long does it take for those of different origin to be accepted as 'natural' in any given place, especially when indigenous symbolic systems and institutions are, one could argue, themselves changing in interaction with those of the sometime outsiders? The fact that Hindus and Muslims came to see themselves as distinct religious communities, even two nations, is a central fact in the modern history of India. But it is crucial to understand, despite continuities in terminology, how very different communities of the past were from those of today. Pre-modern political regimes fostered upper-class identities that incorporated individuals of diverse regions and religions. The illustrations in this chapter each represent a specific noble to whom a range of allies and subordinates owed allegiance. Each artifact made visible this noble's claim to assert military might, to impose order on the society he controlled, and to act as the apex of subordinates from whom he took service and resources. The contrasting image of self-conscious 'horizontal' communities of Hindus and Muslims, like the image of pre-colonial India as a land of self-sufficient villages, rigid caste hierarchies, and overall stagnation, reads characteristics of colonial society into the pre-colonial past.

2

Mughal twilight: the emergence of regional states and the East India Company

Our time traveller in 1707, especially if he had been misled by European accounts of 'Oriental despots', may well have failed to appreciate the extent to which the Mughal Empire, like other premodern political systems of that scale, operated by a hierarchic distribution of authority among different levels of society. There was no monopoly of military force; there was no monopoly of political authority. The Mughal himself was *shahinshah*, 'king of kings', hence one sovereign among many. Competition to expand geographically was always endemic, as was competition between the vertical levels of the system. It is conflict, as Bernard Cohn has written using the late Mughal period as an example of such systems, that achieves the precarious consensus and balance that allows such political systems to persist. Effective rule required not only resolving competition but also judgment about the conflicts with which to engage. During the first half of the eighteenth century Mughal power contracted, while those who had once been subordinate to the Mughals flourished. Among the new regional powers was a joint stock company of English traders, which, by century's end, was poised to claim the mantle of the Mughals as ruler of the subcontinent.

THE 'FAULT LINES' OF MUGHAL CONTROL

A cogent perspective on Aurangzeb as ruler comes from one Bhimsen, a Hindu Kayastha memoirist, who, in his final decades of service, acted as auditor and inspector for a Rajput noble. Writing at the end of Aurangzeb's life, Bhimsen gives us a 'grass roots' view of what he sees as imperial failure. He was, as John Richards has written, one of many who claimed generations of loyalty to the Mughal regime, men who prided themselves on their devotion and courage as well as their mastery of Indo-Persian courtly culture. As Bhimsen followed his master into the futile battles against the rebellious zamindars and chiefs, he despaired of the difference between earlier Mughal rule and that of the later Aurangzeb:

When the aim of the ruling sovereign is the happiness of the people, the country prospers, the peasants are at ease, and people live in peace. The fear of the king's order seizes the hearts of high and low. Now that the last age [kaliyuga] has come, nobody has an honest desire; the Emperor, seized with a passion for capturing forts, has given up attending to the happiness of the subjects. The nobles have turned aside from giving good counsel.

Bhimsen then went on to make what one might call a sociological point about the disorder he deplored. The zamindars, he explained, had 'assumed strength . . . enlisted armies, and laid the hand of oppression on the country'.

In identifying the upstart zamindars as a key sign of disorder, Bhimsen singled out one of the three crucial 'fault lines' that opened up challenges to centralized Mughal rule. The zamindars were men with local roots, often lineage heads and chieftains, who possessed local knowledge, and control over peasant cultivators. They had amassed power as they grew in wealth during the prosperous seventeenth century, and they had secured recognition, sometimes even including rank and office, from the Mughal authorities. After Aurangzeb's death, as Muzaffar Alam has made clear in several studies, zamindars across northern and central India rose up to resist imperial authority. Rarely did they coordinate their activities. Indeed to the contrary, local chieftains often contested with each other for mastery of the countryside. Some did, however, come together to form cohesive communities able to sustain an enduring challenge to Mughal authority. Among these, the most prominent were the Marathas of the Deccan, the Sikhs in the Punjab, and the Jats south-east of Delhi in the area of Agra.

A second 'fault line' intrinsic to Mughal administration was that of established princely rulers, who had accepted Mughal power but kept authority within their own compact domains, rendering tribute but not subject to Mughal administration. Such territories were typically located in inaccessible or peripheral areas. Some chiefs simply ceased to deliver tribute; some, increasingly, resisted Mughal demands from the strength of their forts. To some extent the Rajputs, who had held full control of their desert homeland even while serving the empire, fit this category. By the late seventeenth century, two of the most important Rajput houses were in rebellion.

The third 'fault line' was that of provincial governors, who were appointed by the emperor in the normal course as administrators over areas where they had no pre-existing local connections, but who then acted autonomously, even while continuing to pay lip service to Mughal authority. This style of breaking away became visible in 1724, when the imperial prime minister, Nizamu'l Mulk, withdrew to Hyderabad, ceased to participate in imperial projects, and even fought against Mughal troops to assert his autonomy. Harsh reality was soon dignified by ceremony, as he was made Mughal viceroy for the southern portion of the empire. The rich provinces of Awadh and Bengal similarly gained *de facto* independence beginning in the 1720s as the local govenors, now called *nawabs*, appointed their own officials, and named their own successors (even if through the 1730s the successor would be confirmed by the emperor). As rulers of quasi-independent states, they diverted to themselves revenues formerly sent to Delhi, engaged in diplomatic and military activity, and withdrew from attendance at court. From appointed Mughal officials, these erstwhile governors had become by mid-century the heads of dynasties of their own.

In addition to these noble and chiefly rebels, the weakening of the empire opened opportunities for the ruthless and ambitious of all sorts. One, who later became a Robin Hood-like folk hero, was Papadu, a low caste Telegu bandit chieftain. In the years after 1700, as John Richards and V. Narayana Rao tell us his story, Papadu, from a toddy tapping (fermented liquor manufacturing) caste, recruited followers from an array of untouchable and ritually low groups to form an army of several thousand. With it he mounted successful assaults against several of the major towns in Telengana. Finally, following a year-long seige of his hill-fort refuge by a combined Mughal and zamindari force, Papadu was captured and killed. Rebellion of this sort, as Richards and Narayana Rao make clear, was not destined for success. As leader of a 'dual rebellion', against both imperial and local chiefly authority, Papadu struck too boldly at the most basic ordering of society, and thus mobilized against him all those with a stake in the established hierarchies of caste and wealth.

These Mughal 'fault lines', especially that of the chiefs and zamindars, have often been viewed as an assertion of the Hindu struggle against alien rule. In the case of the Marathas, Indian nationalists of the later nineteenth century, like the moderate M. G. Ranade, saw Shivaji and his successors through the anachronistic lens of an emerging resistance to British rule and so made them a 'nation' challenging 'foreign' domination. B. G. Tilak, the extremist nationalist, subsequently made of Shivaji a hero of Hindu rule. This theme took on new salience in the 1930s and 1940s as relations between Hindus and Muslims deteriorated in the years leading up to independence, so that Shivaji became a symbol of Hindu resistance to Muslim dominance. Similarly, Sikh resistance to Mughal rule has been interpreted as ideologically motivated. In fact, those in rebellion made alliances on the basis of expediency and did not seek out a religiously unified front. For example, when the Rajput Rajas of Marwar and Mewar rose at the end of Aurangzeb's reign, Prince Akbar, sent to subdue them, instead joined them; he also made overtures to Shivaji's son and successor, before ultimately failing and fleeing for his life. The Marathas were active players in Mughal factional rivalries, paying lip service throughout to Mughal power, often striking deals to share access to contested tracts. Shahu (r. 1708–49), raised at court after his father, Shivaji's son Shambaji, was executed in 1689, accepted the position of Mughal *diwan* (the chief civil administrator) for the core Maratha areas. Certainly, distinctive rituals and ideologies were important to the insurgent regimes, but these did not preclude strategic cooperation and even alliances with Muslim rulers.

THE NORTH-WEST: SIKHS, PERSIANS, AND AFGHANS

An agrarian-based Sikh revolt led by Banda Bahadur offered a major challenge to Aurangzeb's successor, the aged Bahadur Shah (r. 1707–12). The Sikhs, like the Marathas, are an example of the formative role of interaction with Muslim dynasties over many centuries. Guru Nanak himself, the great teacher of loving devotion to a formless God and contempt for worldly structures of power and rank, was of a khatri family that served the Sultanate dynasties. He himself as a young man studied Persian and worked for some ten years in a revenue storehouse for the Afghan Lodi dynasty. Three of his successors were patronized by Akbar, during whose long reign Amritsar emerged as the centre of a virtually autonomous area. The gurus sought worldly as well as spiritual powers. Participation in factional competition for succession at the court in fact cost two gurus their lives. The last guru, Gobind Singh (1666–1708), like other Punjab chiefs, variously used and resisted Mughal rule. Although defeated by Aurangzeb at the end of his reign, Gobind appealed to the new emperor, in vain, for restoration of his lands. With Gobind's death, worldly leadership passed to guerilla chiefs, of whom the strongest was Banda.

Although the Mughals had the support of several Punjab zamindars and lineage heads, only in 1715 did they finally defeat and execute Banda. Many Sikhs then remained quiescent, but a core group took to the hills, plundering and killing. Even they responded, albeit briefly, to the overture of a Mughal jagir and a title to their leader in 1730. Held at bay by their own rivalries, their proximity to the imperial capital at Delhi, and invasions from the north-west in mid-century, the Sikhs were unable to do much more than raid and establish small principalities until the 1760s.

The Punjab, and with it Delhi, experienced devastating blows through every level of society in these decades. No episode more shattered imperial confidence and stability than the attack of the Persian Nadir Shah (r. 1736–47) in 1739, who wrought havoc along his routes and unleashed butchery and brutality that left some 30,000 dead in Delhi alone. His booty, as he returned home, included Shah Jahan's fabled peacock throne. Subsequent years saw a growth of Afghan power, profiting in part from Russian and Chinese expansion that drew Afghans into burgeoning networks of trade sustained in large part by Hindu bankers based in cities like Shikarpur. In 1748 and 1757 the Afghan Ahmad Shah Abdali (r. 1747–73), whose empire reached into Baluchistan, the Makran coast, Sind and much of the Punjab, attacked Delhi. The Delhi area was further challenged from within by the Afghan Rohillas and the Jat zamindars of Agra. The view from the perspective of Delhi, as indeed from much of the Punjab, would have been one of unmitigated chaos and confusion by the mid-eighteenth century.

THE NEW REGIONAL ORDER: 'MILITARY FISCALISM' AND CULTURAL EFFLORESCENCE

The view from Delhi, nevertheless, does not describe India as a whole. Overall, the eighteenth century was a period of gradual population growth, slow rise in prices, urbanization, and the establishment of new markets. Within the zamindar warrior states, as well as within the now autonomous Mughal provinces, the new regional kingdoms were centres of effective state-building, reaching deeply into their populations and building powerful armies. The symbol *par excellence* of the eighteenth century was that of the fort. These comprised not only bastions like the rugged, highly defensible Deccan hill fort of Daulatabad (plate 2.1) asserting a regional power, but, within the regional states, the mud-walled strongholds of a range of local powers. But such fortified redoubts were not the whole story. By mid-century, the ruler of the new Jat kingdom centred at Bharatpur, in close proximity to the core of Mughal power, was sufficiently secure to build a garden palace in nearby Dig (Deeg). Although Raja Suraj Mal's Gopal Bhavan (plate 2.2) was named for Lord Krishna, to whom the rulers were devoted, his use of pietra dura work, along with domes, arches, and pavilions, and formal garden, all recall Mughal imperial style, and so provide a visual reminder of the extent to which those who challenged Mughal power were its products, at times even surpassing in effective administrative control their Mughal predecessors.

The Maratha state in the middle decades of the eighteenth century offers the best example of bureaucratic efficiency in this period. The key architects of this organization were a hereditary line of prime ministers, Chitpavan Brahmans, of whom the first was Balaji Vishvanath (r. 1713–20). Despite factional rivalries, Maratha military might, especially under the *peshwa*, or prime minister, Baji Rao (r. 1720–40), extended the state's reach into Gujarat and Malwa, with raids in the 1730s as far as Delhi, and to Bengal a decade later. At the same time, the state established strong control over

Plate 2.1 Daulatabad Fortress, Maharashtra.

Plate 2.2 Gopal Bhavan, Garden Palace of the Jat rajas of Dig, c. 1763.

rural chiefs, military adventurers, and others who became the intermediaries to deliver the state's share of the revenue. In the Maratha
domains as elsewhere, a prominent feature of the eighteenth century
was the collapse at the local level of separate lines of civil and military authority, in favour of the single figure of the revenue *farmer* or
contractor. The farmer bid to secure the right to pay into the state's
treasury an agreed upon sum for a certain tract of land for a fixed
term of years. He bore the expenses of collection, and he claimed as
his own any additional revenues collected. For the state this arrangement provided a secure income at minimum cost. It often opened
the way to extortion, however, as contractors, unchecked so long as
they filled their contracts, set out to amass personal fortunes at the
expense of hapless cultivators. Yet, where contracts were awarded
for an extended series of years, revenue farmers had an obvious
incentive to encourage agricultural prosperity in the areas under
their control, and the process clearly gave many enterprising and
upwardly mobile individuals an arena for action. The most successful farmers combined military power with cash advances to local
villagers, as well as participation in the trade of the commodities
produced. The forty years when Mian Almas Ali held districts yield-
ing one-third the revenue of Awadh, for example, were looked back
upon by the people in later years as a 'golden age'.

An innovation with far-reaching implications for the working
of the new system of regional states was the recruitment of infantry forces, handling more efficient artillery and deployed with
far greater discipline and effectiveness than the traditional mounted
cavalry of the Mughals. The eighteenth-century states welcomed
European adventurers to train these new units of professional soldiers, who, unlike peasants conscripted by noble overlords for limited periods, were now full-time mercenary troopers. Uniformed,
they were trained to follow orders even under attack. By mid-
century, Hyderabad had contingents of French-led fighters, but
Germans, Dutch, and others found their way to the Indian courts
as well. Plate 2.3 shows the tomb in Agra of John William Hessing (and his in-laws and descendants), who began his career in the
employ of the Dutch East India Company in Ceylon, moved on
to serve the Nizam of Hyderabad, and ended as a colonel in the
service of the Maratha Sindhia commanding the city of Agra. As
the size and style of the tomb suggest, these men, while military

Plate 2.3   Mughal-style tomb of European 'adventurer' John William
Hessing, Agra, 1803.

adventurers, nevertheless adopted many Indian social and cultural
practices.

Mercenary adventurers and infantry contingents were expensive,
for they had to be paid in cash. This new demand on state resources

stimulated novel strategies of governance. These strategies, summed up, in historian David Washbrook's phrase, as 'military fiscalism', created a new relationship between revenue extraction, the military, and financial agents. Building on the gradual monetization and economic expansion already evident in the previous century, rulers increasingly turned for assistance to families of bankers, traders, and revenue intermediaries. Over the years these men had established increasingly broad networks of clients and created financial instruments that enabled them to take up key roles in the political system. In Bengal, for instance, the banking family of the Jagat Seths provided credit to the nawabs, and advances for the selling and moving of crops to zamindars and revenue farmers. By mid-century such financiers had become indispensable to the rulers of many of India's states. At the same time, to facilitate revenue collection, zamindari landholdings were frequently consolidated, and, along with the older lineage heads and chiefs, new men, including court officials, military adventurers, and banking families themselves, emerged as zamindars.

As they grew ever more desperate for funds, some rulers adopted an opposite scheme, that of bypassing intermediaries and collecting directly from the peasantry. This was the solution adopted by the Muslim conquest state of Mysore, founded by Haider Ali in 1761. Haider and his son Tipu Sultan introduced into their state a rigorous revenue management founded upon the encouragement of peasant agriculture and the elimination of zamindars and farmers. In so doing they brought Mysore an enviable degree of prosperity, and the funds to maintain an army of 60,000 men. Yet no more than those who sought succour by borrowing, could the Mysore rulers by their ruthless centralization of power stave off eventual defeat at the hands of those who, as we will see, controlled more resources and a larger army. In the end, 'military fiscalism' did not so much preserve India from conquest as open the way to it.

Recent studies of the Ottoman Empire in the eighteenth century suggest that society in that period underwent a limited transition from 'vertical' to 'horizontal' solidarities. One might imagine, schematically, a 'vertical' ordering of authority as one passing from the emperor to nobles to lesser functionaries to lineage heads, thence to village head and family patriarch. Problems would be solved hierarchically, by turning to the person above for a solution. In a 'horizontal' ordering, by contrast, solidarities among members of the same occupational group, or geographic region, or sectarian or other voluntary association, formed the basis for dispute settlement. The eighteenth-century move to a 'civil society' apart from the state may have been more evident in the Ottoman lands than in the Indian subcontinent. Nonetheless, a somewhat similar transition among such groups as traders, bankers, and networks of religious specialists, cutting across some boundaries of region and even ethnicity, was taking place in India as well.

The new regional states also fostered enduring changes in cultural expression, setting new directions in poetry, art, architecture, music, and religious thought. The Rajput courts in particular established themselves as centres of cultural patronage. Plate 2.4 shows the palace dominating the remarkable new city of Jaipur, laid out by Raja Jai Singh in the 1720s and 1730s on a geometric grid. In the distance is the triangular shape of one of the astronomical devices of the Jaipur observatory, one of three Jai Singh established to measure celestial patterns. The eighteenth-century Rajput courts welcomed artists, including those fleeing the imperial capital, and, along with several states in the Himalyan hills, developed renowned schools of painting, each known for distinctive palettes, facial types, or subjects. Among the most significant subjects taken up were those known as *ragmala*, 'a garland of musical modes', which depicted visually the mood created by a classic musical mode, in this case those associated with episodes of the divine/human love represented above all by the symbol of Lord Krishna. Plate 2.5 depicts the lovers Radha and Krishna as an approaching storm mirrors their mounting passion. The cult of Lord Ram, the ideal king, also flourished in this period. His legendary birthplace at Ayodhya emerged as a pilgrimage centre, its buildings patronized by the Shi`a nawabs of Awadh. Warfare enhanced the popularity, also, of armed ascetic orders of Gosains and Bhairagis, who were often looked to for protection in times of disorder.

Islamic traditions also found new expression in the regional settings. Poets like Shah Abdu'l Latif Bhita'i (1689–1752), writing in Sindhi, and Bulhe Shah (1680–1758) and Waris Shah (b. c. 1730), in Punjabi, produced masterpieces of mystic poetry in the vernaculars

Plate 2.4   Jaipur city palace, with Jai Singh's astronomical observatory
to the left rear.

that reinterpreted local folk stories. Abdu'l Latif used the Kutchi
love story of Sasui searching for her Baluch beloved to tell the story
of the human soul, symbolized as a woman, searching for the divine,
much as in the bhakti poems and paintings of the era. This verse,

Plate 2.5   Ragmala painting of Radha and Krishna, Kulu, early
nineteenth century.

for example, turns on the enduring theme of the poignancy of 'love
in separation':

> I have not met my love but thou
> Art sinking to thy rest, O Sun.
> The messages I give thee, take
> And tell to my beloved one.
> To Kech go, say: 'The sad one died
> Upon the path.' 'Twas not for me

> To meet my love: death supervened.
> I'll die, be nothing utterly
> In separation from my love.

At the Delhi court as well, the vernacular language of Urdu, with its
heavy use of Persian loan words, was adapted to Persian poetic genres by great poets including Mir Taqi Mir (1723–1810) and Khwaja
Mir Dard (1720–85).

One of the most influential figures in Muslim religious life in the
capital was Shah Waliullah (1703–62), the Naqshbandi sufi, whom
many later Islamic movements in modern India would claim as their
forebear. He was part of the scholarly circles based in the Hijaz con-
cerned with setting a new standard of fidelity to the traditions of the
Prophet Muhammad's sayings and actions (*hadith*). Those teachings
found particular resonance in the renewed attention in eighteenth-
century India to devotionalism, across religious traditions, since in
the Islamic case devotion to the Prophet was seen as essential in
the quest for the divine. Hadith served also as an anchor in the
flux of changing political and social circumstances of the period. In
the Punjab and among the Rohillas in particular, Chishti sufis disseminated renewed attention to hadith. This was a period of Shi`a
efflorescence as well. Shi`a-led states, including Bengal for a time,
and, above all, Awadh, patronized the elaborate mourning ceremonies that expressed devotion to the Shi`a *imams*, and supported
the writing and recitation of Urdu-language elegies (*marsiya*).
This poetic tradition was begun by men like Mirza Rafi'ud-din
Sauda (1713–81), who with so many others sought refuge at the
Lucknow court from the mid-century disorder in Delhi.

In the wake of the collapse of authority in northern India, the
climactic encounter in the struggle for mastery took place in 1761,
as Marathas and Afghans marshalled their armies on the historic
field of Panipat, where the Mughal Empire had been won. The battle defined the limits of power for both. The Afghans prevailed
on the battlefield, but they were unable to sustain an empire so
far from Afghanistan, and so withdrew. Maratha power, from its
base in Poona had over the preceding decades extended its reach
far to the north and east. Following the defeat at Panipat, further
advance stopped and the Marathas split into four increasingly separate states. Each was dominated by one of the newly ascendant

Maratha military houses, and each, although loosely linked to the peshwa in Poona, possessed its own geographic base: the Gaekwad in Baroda, Sindhia in Gwalior, Holkar in Indore, and the Bhonsle in Nagpur.

THE RISE OF THE ENGLISH EAST INDIA COMPANY

As a new system of regional states emerged, the English East India Company was amassing strength for what was to become a successful challenge to all of the others. Founded on 31 December 1600, and chartered by Queen Elizabeth, the English company was one among several European trading ventures that sought to tap the riches of the 'East'. Central to the enduring strength of the Company was its organization as a joint-stock enterprise. Individuals could not hope to trade on their own so far from Europe while the English Crown, unlike that of Portugal, did not care to commit its resources to so uncertain an undertaking. The joint-stock organization allowed merchants to share the risk of trade, and enabled them to raise further funds as needed. The access to resources provided by the company structure made the English a formidable competitor as they confronted India's indigenous merchant families. The Company gained further strength from its possession of centralized direction, through a 24-member Court of Directors, the stability of an archive, and a staff recruited for their specialized skills. As we shall see in subsequent chapters, it was in its engagement with India, not in England itself, that Britain developed many of the institutions of the 'modern' state, among which none was to be more crucial than the joint-stock corporation.

Granted a monopoly of Britain's Asian trade, and the right to arm its vessels in order to fend off interlopers, the Company sought entry into the hugely profitable spice trade with the islands of the East Indies. There, however, they encountered a better organized and financed rival, the Dutch East India Company (VOC). They quickly determined to centre their trading operations in India instead. This decision created both economic and political problems for the Company. Apart from Malabar pepper, which formed the bulk of the Company's earliest cargoes, India possessed no spices. To make matters worse, the Indians had no interest in the

Plate 2.6 Painting of *The East Offering its Riches to Britannia*, by Spiridion Roma, 1778, at the East India House, London.

commodities England had available for sale, most notably woollen goods, so that, against the reigning principles of mercantilism, and to severe disapproval at home, the Company had to export bullion to pay for its Indian purchases. Furthermore, unlike the Dutch, who easily overwhelmed the petty rajas of the archipelago, the English in seventeenth-century India confronted the Mughal Empire at its height. Hence there could be no thought of conquest. Only as humble petitioners for favour could the English hope to gain access to the Indian market. The Mughals welcomed the English to offset the predominance of the Portuguese, and later of the Dutch, as did Indian merchants, who relished the opportunities afforded for profitable trade.

The East India Company during the seventeenth century, nevertheless, created for itself a secure and profitable trade. In place of the lucrative but limited trade in spices, the English developed markets in Europe for a variety of Indian produce, including indigo (a blue dye) and saltpetre (used for gunpowder). Most valuable, however, were fine quality hand-loomed Indian textiles. With the growth of a consumer economy in a prospering Britain, after 1660, the demand for Indian fabrics, such as chintz, calico, and muslin (all words of Indian origin), increased rapidly. As would be demonstrated time and again, the modern consumer possessed an almost insatiable desire for the luxury goods of the tropical, and subsequently, colonial world. The Company's imports from India to Europe, worth some £360,000 in 1670, tripled in value over the subsequent thirty years, and then doubled again to reach nearly 2 million pounds by 1740. The 1778 painting, *The East Offering its Riches to Britannia* (plate 2.6), indicates the array of Asian ports which supplied valuable goods, from tea to textiles, to Britain.

Sustaining this trade was a grant awarded in 1617 by the emperor Jahangir to Sir Thomas Roe, James I's ambassador to the Mughal court. Under its terms the English were allowed to establish factories at selected Mughal ports, most notably Surat in Gujarat. These 'factories' were not (in contradistinction to our current usage) sites of manufacture, but rather warehouses where goods were collected by resident agents, called factors, until they could be loaded aboard ship. Although the Company's naval prowess encouraged the Mughals to grant such trading rights, for the Mughals had no navy of their own, still the Company, not allowed to fortify its factories, remained wholly dependent on the goodwill of the Mughal authorities for their trading enterprise. These exports generated customs revenues, especially in Gujarat and later in Golconda, where in 1678 Dutch and English *specie* import met the paybill of 17,000 cavalrymen; and they brought wealth to merchants and weavers. The historian Om Prakash has estimated that the overseas demand generated some 80,000 jobs, primarily in weaving, in Bengal alone. The major beneficiaries, however, were the local merchant entrepreneurs who gave out advances to weavers, and supplied commodities to the European companies. Until the coming of British supremacy, competition between rival European companies secured a reasonable return for Indian producers.

By the 1660s, as Mughal power began to falter, the Company found its factories, especially that in Surat, raided twice by Shivaji, increasingly vulnerable, and so turned to a policy of armed defence. This brought the Company into conflict with the Mughal authorities, who inflicted a humiliating defeat upon them in 1686. Nevertheless, by 1700 the Company had secured the three 'presidency' capitals – of Madras, Bombay, and Calcutta – from which its authority was subsequently to expand into the interior. Though only tiny footholds on the Indian coast, these three cities, secured by powerful fortifications, such as Fort St George, Madras, pictured in plate 2.7, grew and prospered. Indian merchants flocked to them, seeking security for their persons and property in increasingly unsettled times. The English further sought to reassure Indians by disavowing any effort, of the sort practised by the Portuguese Inquisition and French Jesuits, at conversion to Christianity. Throughout the eighteenth century missionaries were refused residence in the English settlements.

Bombay, an island with a magnificent harbour, was secured in 1661, in a manner comparable to the alliances forged between Akbar and the Rajputs, as part of the dowry of a Portuguese princess who married King Charles II. As the Company shifted its operations there from Surat, Parsi merchants and artisans, Zoroastrians of Iranian origin, came along with them. For the most part the Company's officials lived a communal life within the forts, from where they dealt with the Indian brokers and merchants, settled outside, who

Plate 2.7   Fort St George, Madras, *c.* 1750.

procured textiles from weavers in the countryside by the provision of cash advances. These presidency capitals were not established with the objective of colonial conquest. The number of Company personnel posted to each never exceeded a few hundred, while the forts were guarded by ill-trained soldiers, some 300 in Madras, recruited from the streets of London.

The Indian trade participated in a larger worldwide trading arena. So-called 'Guinea' cloth, exported from India to West Africa, was used to purchase slaves for West Indian plantations, while in Southeast Asia Indian textiles provided the medium of exchange for the spice trade. Throughout the seventeenth century and the first decades of the eighteenth, the English had to contend with powerful rival trading companies, who, like themselves, established fortified posts along the coast of India. By the 1680s the long-established Dutch had been joined by the Danes and by the French at Pondicherry, a south Indian enclave they retained until 1950. As the Mughal Empire weakened following the death of Aurangzeb, and the trade grew ever more profitable, so too did the temptation to gain an advantage over one's rivals by political means. In 1717 the British secured from the emperor Farrukhsiyar the valuable boon of duty-free export of their goods from Bengal. The French, however, as late-comers had the most to gain from intervening in local politics.

The occasion was the War of the Austrian Succession in Europe (1744–8). This war inaugurated some seventy years of conflict between Britain and France, and with it a new kind of warfare in which these two European powers contended for mastery around the globe, in America and India as well as Europe itself. Increasingly, this rivalry was propelled by a modern nationalist enthusiasm which caught up peoples as well as dynasties. In India, the French governor-general François Dupleix (1697–1764) saw in the recurrent disputes over succession among Indian princes, among them Arcot and Hyderabad, an opportunity to advance French interests. He devised the strategy of offering one contender in such a dispute the support of French troops; in return, once in power, the client prince awarded the French favourable commercial terms at the expense of the British. At the same time, Dupleix moved directly against the British, successfully beseiging Madras in 1746. These achievements moved the Pondicherry merchant Ananda Ranga Pillai to make of Dupleix an ideal Indian ruler:

When [the name of Pondicherry] is uttered, her enemies tremble, and dare not stir. All this is owing to the ability, readiness and luck of the present governor, M. Dupleix. His method of doing things is not known to anyone, because none else is possessed of the quick mind with which he is gifted. In patience he has no equal. He has peculiar skill in carrying out his plans and design ... and in assuming a bearing at once dignified and courteous towards all.

In none of this was there any sense that Dupleix was a 'foreigner' whom an 'Indian' ought to oppose. Rather the French, like other Europeans, were simply assimilated into the shifting array of local powerholders.

This challenge to their interests provoked an immediate British response. They regained Madras by the 1749 treaty that ended the war, and they set out to turn the tables on Dupleix by playing the same game. In short order they had placed their client on the throne of Arcot, and Dupleix was soon recalled in disgrace. Despite Dupleix's insights into the precariously balanced eighteenth-century Indian political order, with the opportunities it afforded for manipulation, the French, preoccupied with dynastic quarrels in Europe, simply did not possess the resources to contain their rivals in India. Above all, as latecomers to India, they had never developed the close ties with Indian merchants and intermediaries that sustained the British, with the result that the French India trade, on average about half that of the English Company's in value, had by mid-century sunk to a mere quarter of that of their rival's. For Britain, by contrast, not only was the Company a major player in domestic politics, but popular opinion, especially in the country's port cities, saw in trade, and in empire, the way to secure Britain's greatness. 'Rule Britannia', a marker of the new patriotism, was first sung in 1740. The figure of Britannia, seated on a rock abover her Asian tributaries in the Spiridion Roma painting (plate 2.6), visibly represents as well this growing sense of national identity, which set Britain apart from an Asia seen as a collection of cities and regions.

The four years of war from 1744 to 1748 made visible, for the first time to Europeans, the power of disciplined infantry in Indian warfare. A few hundred French or British soldiers, firing in volleys from a square formation, could now hold off thousands of Mughal cavalrymen. A contingent of European troops were thus worth a great deal to an Indian ruler. Critical too to European success was the fact of national loyalty. Although Europeans often took service as adventurers with Indian states, they would never fight against their own countrymen, or change sides in the middle of a battle, as Indians, motivated not by an equivalent 'Indian' nationalism but by more parochial loyalties, frequently did. The Seven Years' War, from 1756 to 1763, pitting Britain once again against France, made apparent for all to see the implications of this 'military revolution'.

THE CONQUEST OF BENGAL

From the early eighteenth century onwards, the trade of Bengal had grown ever more profitable to the East India Company. By 1750, this rich deltaic province, the outlet for the trade of the entire Ganges valley, accounted for 75 per cent of the Company's procurement of Indian goods. Dean Mahomet, an Indian in Company employ who later emigrated to Britain, described Dacca (Dhaka) in these terms:

Dacca is considered the first manufactory in India and produces the richest embroideries in gold, silver, and silk...Provisions of all sorts are exceedingly cheap and plentiful in Dacca: the fertility of its soil, and the advantages of its situation have, long since, made it the centre of an extensive commerce...Here is also the residence of a grand Nabob, who, at his accession to the throne, conformable to an old custom, something similar to that of the Doge of Venice on the Adriatic, enjoys a day's pleasure on the river, [in a barge] sheathed with silver.

Bengal's wealth was thus at once made to appear nearly boundless, and made familiar by evoking Italy's canal-laced 'mistress of the seas'. It is not by accident that the figure representing Calcutta in *The East Offering its Riches* is placed at the centre of the painting with the richest gift, that of a basket of jewels and pearls. From such images came an enduring picture of India for the British.

Determined to extend their profits, the British in Bengal had by mid-century begun systematically abusing the right to free trade awarded them by the emperor. Free trade passes were sold to Indian favourites, and extended illegally to participation in the internal trade in grain and other commodities. In 1756, on the outbreak of war, to deter French attack, the British began extending the fortifications of Calcutta. All this the young Nawab Siraj-ud-daula, who had recently come to the throne of Bengal, rightly saw as a challenge to his authority. Hence in June 1756 he marched on Calcutta, defeated the garrison, and imprisoned those who were unable to flee. Some forty or more of those imprisoned, confined in a small airless room, died overnight of suffocation. Although the nawab had not ordered this mistreatment of his English prisoners, which was an act of negligence on the part of his officers, nevertheless the incident, exaggerated as the 'Black Hole' of Calcutta, reverberated down the years as evidence for the British of Indian cruelty and barbarism.

To avenge this humiliation, the British turned to Colonel Robert Clive (1725–74), who had already distinguished himself in the wars in the south. An expedition mounted from Madras retook Calcutta in February 1757, and secured restoration of the Company's trading privileges. Not content with this victory, Clive entered into a conspiracy with a group of merchant bankers headed by Jagat Seth, at odds with the new nawab over his financial exactions from them, to overturn Siraj in favour of a more pliable ruler. Together they fixed upon the disaffected general Mir Jafar, who promised the British lavish payments in return for their help in placing him on the throne. The result was the famous battle of Plassey, on 23 June 1757. Militarily the battle was a farce, Mir Jafar's troops standing aloof as Clive routed Siraj's forces. The consequences of the encounter, however, were to be momentous.

Although Mir Jafar was made nawab after Plassey, he was, and was visibly seen to be, a puppet maintained in power by Clive and his army. The cash payments alone were staggering. The British received some 28 million rupees, equivalent to 3 million pounds sterling, of which nearly half went to private individuals, including Clive himself. The Company secured the revenue collecting rights over several districts, and an unimpeded trading access to the countryside. To be sure, Clive did not intend conquest, nor did the Company's directors at home. The Company's servants in India, determined to amass fortunes for themselves, refused any check on their rapacious activities. In the process, as they lived ever more extravagantly, they became known as *nabobs*, from the Mughal term *nawab* (governor). For its part, the Company too sought ever more funds for its trading operations. Significantly, after 1757 the Company ceased the shipment of bullion to Bengal. Instead, in a dramatic turn in Britain's economic relationship with India, it used the province's internal tax revenues to finance the purchase of the goods it annually shipped to England. Bengal was, Clive assured the governor of Madras, 'an inexhaustible fund of riches'.

Nawabi sovereighty was most visibly demeaned as the British took over for themselves the trade in a range of valuable commodites, notably salt, betel nut, tobacco, and saltpetre. These, as Sudipta Sen points out, were the 'Nawab's prestige goods' endowed with the signs of the ruler's authority. In 1760, the hapless Mir Jafar was replaced, following another round of presents, by Mir Kasim. Unwilling to countenance the continuing British plunder of his kingdom, Mir Kasim sought to retrieve his authority over at least the northern part of Bengal and adjacent Bihar. In so doing he provoked what was to be the final confrontation, for the British, their appetite for wealth and power whetted, would accept no constraints. By 1764 the battle lines were drawn, between Mir Kasim, allied with the Nawab of Awadh and the Mughal emperor on one side, and the East India Company on the other. On 23 October of that year, at Buxar, in a hard-fought contest unlike that of Plassey, the British made themselves the masters of eastern India.

No longer able to keep up the pretence that they were mere traders, in 1765, by a treaty with the Mughal emperor, in return for an annual tribute the Company secured the *diwani*, or revenue collecting rights, for the provinces of Bengal, Bihar, and Orissa. Legally, this made the Company the emperor's deputy, as revenue minister, a position they retained until 1858. The administration of justice, or *nizamat*, was left to the nawab. In form Bengal remained a Mughal province. In fact, however, it was wholly under the control of the East India Company, for neither the emperor in Delhi nor the figurehead nawab exercised any independent authority over the region. Still, however, the British vacillated. Reluctant to abandon a profitable trade for the uncertain advantages of rule, Clive as governor determined to leave the actual collection of the revenues in the hands of the nawab's officials. But mistrust of these officials, combined with the Company's insatiable need for funds, above all for its fast-growing army, led the British in 1772 to 'stand forth' as diwan. A new era was about to begin.

What, one must ask, impelled a 150-year-old trading company suddenly to embark on a career of conquest? And how were the British so easily able to carve out a state for themselves among the contending powers of post-Mughal India? As neither Clive nor the Company had devised a coherent plan, much was the product of circumstance. The Seven Years' War provided a convenient occasion. Although France was not able after Dupleix to mount a serious challenge to Britain in India, still the war, with the patriotic sentiment it stirred up, justified military adventure around the globe. Clive's 'heroic' exploits in Bengal complemented, or so it seemed, those of James Wolfe in Quebec. Then there was simply the importance to the Company of the Bengal trade, together with, on the other side, the threat its size, and the privileged position of the British, posed to the nawab. Conflict, if not inevitable, depended on a restraint neither party was likely to exercise indefinitely. In addition, there was the sheer greed of the resident British. Once the opportunity to secure 'Nabob' wealth presented itself, there could be no holding back. Clive himself, after all, set the example. As he told the House of Commons in 1772, he was 'astonished at his own moderation' when he left India with an immense fortune, including the jagir of an Indian district worth £28,000 annually. The Company, for its part, initially hesitant, fearful of the spiralling costs of Clive's adventurism, became reconciled to empire once its fiscal advantages to themselves, above all in financing their Asian trade, became apparent. Indeed, the Company used its new-found wealth to construct a palatial headquarters for itself in London, for which it commissioned, as its centrepiece, the ceiling painting of the *East Offering its Riches* discussed above.

As it moved into Bengal, the Company took advantage of those strategies of 'military fiscalism' that were key to success in the political system of eighteenth-century India. Among these were a titular obeisance to the Mughal emperor in Delhi, utilization of trade monopolies in such goods as saltpetre that local nawabs had developed, the deployment of a disciplined professional infantry (which Europeans pioneered in India), and close ties with newly powerful banking and financial groups, such as the Jagat Seths, whose autonomous position gave them an unprecedented importance within the political system. More generally, one might argue, with David Washbrook, that the mid-eighteenth century witnessed a 'conjuncture' of two thriving commercial worlds, that of India and that of Western Europe. India and England, as part of the 'Early Modern' world, that is, had been simultaneously shaped by an interconnected trading system. Far from juxtaposing a 'progressive' Europe with a declining 'traditional' India ripe for conquest, such an argument finds the key to the European penetration of India precisely in its accessibility and its flourishing economy.

But why did the English East India Company succeed so spectacularly in India when others, European and Indian, did not? Much of the answer lies in Europe. An island nation for whom overseas trade was vital, Britain was committed to securing its Indian interests at all costs. Control of the seas, in an era in which export trade brought the greatest profit, gave Britain an edge over all rivals. For

India, the eighteenth century thus offers a dramatic contrast with the Mughal agrarian order of the seventeenth, when overseas commerce was of secondary importance. Furthermore, although the industrial revolution was not yet underway, the British economy had already become suffused with a dynamic commercial ethos sustained by secure private property rights. In India the British could hold out to indigenous mercantile classes, first in the presidency capitals and then in the countryside, as local rulers did not, the attractive prospect of freedom from arbitrary exaction. Part of the reason for Britain's success too lies, quite simply, in the fact that after 1757, by its conquest of Bengal, the East India Company had gained control of India's richest province. This gave it the resources to dominate the other players in the continuing contests among India's regional states. With a larger revenue base, the Company could field a larger army than its Indian rivals, and organize a more efficient state structure. As a result, even though the British state in Bengal was forged, in large part, from the same elements of 'military fiscalism' as other states throughout the subcontinent, it could over time subdue them all one by one.

3

The East India Company Raj,
1772–1850

In 1772, determined at last to put an end to the chaos and fiscal disorder its intervention had precipitated in Bengal, the Company's directors appointed Warren Hastings, a man with a distinguished record of diplomatic and commercial service in India, as the first governor-general of the company's Indian territories. Subordinating the other presidencies to a new capital established in Calcutta, Hastings set about the task of creating an ordered system of government for British India. Hastings's thirteen years at the helm of government were far from untroubled. Indeed, throughout his years in office he had to contend with a divided council in Calcutta whose majority opposed his every move, while after his return to England his actions were made the subject of an embittered impeachment trial in the House of Commons. As a spectacle, for Hastings was ultimately acquitted, the trial dominated British public life for years. Nevertheless, Hastings laid an enduring foundation for the British Raj in India. This chapter will begin by examining the structures of governance established by Hastings, and his successor Lord Cornwallis (1785–93), in British-ruled Bengal. It will then ask how and why the British went on to conquer the entire Indian subcontinent in the first two decades of the nineteenth century, and it will conclude by assessing the relationships that grew up between what was known as the 'Company Bahadur', as though it were a Mughal grandee, and its Indian subjects in the years up to 1850.

FOUNDATIONS OF COLONIAL RULE

When Hastings took office, the East India Company's agents knew nothing about India apart from the requirements of trade, and they almost never ventured outside their coastal enclaves. With rare exceptions, among them Hastings himself, they knew no Indian languages. Within the existing British Empire, furthermore, rule over a vast indigenous population such as that of India was unprecedented. With the partial exception of Ireland, Britain's previous imperial expansion, in the West Indies and North America, had involved the dispossession of the native peoples in favour of settlers from Europe and Africa. Hence, as they confronted their new responsibilities in India, the British found themselves sailing in wholly uncharted waters. Their difficulties were further enhanced by the reluctance of the Company's agents in India to abandon their profitable trading activities for the uncertain advantages of government. Linked to the appointment of Hastings as governor-general, therefore, was the first of a series of Regulating Acts, which endeavoured to subordinate the Company to the British Government, and to impose upon its agents the obligation of ruling, as Edmund Burke, the Whig statesman and political philosopher, put it in the debates over Hastings's impeachment, as 'trustees' for the people of India. This subordination took institutional form in 1783 with the creation of the Board of Control, whose president sat in the British Cabinet.

From the outset the British rejected, as inappropriate for a conquered land, their own system of government, or even that of the American colonies, which had representative assemblies under a royal governor. This decision was reinforced by a conviction of India's enduring cultural difference from Britain. As Hastings described his 'plan' to the directors in 1772, the objective should be to 'adapt our Regulations to the Manners and Understandings of the People, and the Exigencies of the Country, adhering as closely as we are able to their ancient uses and Institutions'. This was, however, easier said than done. Were the English meant to rule India 'despotically' as they believed was customary practice in the 'Orient'? Were they arduously to reconstruct the administrative system of the Mughal Empire? Were they to search out supposed legal principles which had 'continued unchanged from remotest antiquity'; or were they to follow in the footsteps of their immediate predecessors, the Nawabs of Bengal? Both principle and practice were at stake as the British debated these questions. On one thing, however, the British were agreed. They could not avow a preference for 'despotism', for a commitment to the 'rule of law', in their view, defined them as a 'civilized' nation, and so alone could give legitimacy to their Raj. Yet colonial rule by its very nature could not help but create its own version of the 'despotic'.

Two fundamental convictions shaped Hastings's jurisprudence. One was that, as the historian Bernard Cohn has written, there existed in India 'a fixed body of laws, codes that had been set down or established by "law givers" and that over time these had become corrupted by accretions, interpretations, and commentaries.' Hastings saw his task as that of restoring these 'original' texts in all their purity, and so freeing the British from dependence upon Indian legal scholars trained in Sanskrit or Arabic. Hastings further believed that there existed distinct and separate codes of law for Hindus and for Muslims. In civil suits regarding marriage, inheritance and the like, he wrote, 'the Laws of the Koran with respect to Mahomedans, and those of the Shaster with respect to the Gentoos [Hindus] shall be invariably adhered to'. This insistence on a fundamental difference between 'Hindu' and 'Muslim' reduced a variety of sectarian communities characterized by distinct customs and practices to two, each defined through its textual tradition. In so doing Hastings inaugurated the practice of seeing these categories as central to the organizing of Indian society; and this, in turn, helped shape how Indians constructed identities for themselves in subsequent years.

The 'recovery' of these so-called 'ancient' usages was no easy task. Indeed, the arduous process of compilation made clear the artificially contrived nature of the whole enterprise. In 1776 Hastings convened a panel of Sanskrit legal scholars (*pandits*) to compile a 'Code of Gentoo Laws'. The pandits, as N. B. Halhed described their work, first 'picked out sentence by sentence from various originals in the Shanscrit [*sic*] language' legal decisions on different topics. Then, as no Englishman at the time knew Sanskrit, these passages were 'next translated literally into Persian' and from that tongue they were rendered into English by Halhed himself. Within a decade the jurist Sir William Jones had mastered the Sanskrit language and so set in motion the 'Orientalist' scholarship which was to make accessible to all the ancient past of India. The insistence upon a 'fixed' body of law, necessary if the British were to administer Hindu law, inevitably privileged Brahmanical texts over local usages that varied by caste and region, and gave Brahman pandits, attached to the courts as 'law-finders' until 1864, an unprecedented role in decision making. The whole, complementing the earlier growth of Brahman political power, brought about the 'Brahmanization' of Indian law. Legal procedure was further transformed by the introduction of English case law, in which individual suits were brought to trial before a judge, in place of traditional procedures based on mediation and consensus.

Hastings also took the first steps towards the establishment of a distinctively colonial form of executive governance – that of the 'Collector' in charge of a district. Mughal precedents existed for such an administrative structure, which made it attractive in Hastings's eyes, but the Mughal system had ceased to function under the Bengal nawabs. Hastings was further hampered by the lack of trained British personnel. As Clive had observed as early as 1765, when the British first took over the diwani, 'To trust these collections upon which our security and credit depend to the management of the Company's servants totally unacquainted with the business would have been a dangerous and at this time would have been termed a criminal experiment.' Hence revenue administration during the Hastings era had to be left, for the most part, to the old Indian officeholders. Change was to come only under Lord Cornwallis, who, untainted by his defeat in America, came to India with a mandate for reform. Frustrated, baffled, and angry at the 'intricacy and confusion' of the district accounts left in Indian hands, Cornwallis displaced all senior Indian officeholders in favour of Company servants. Making the Indians scapegoats for the credulity and complicity in misrule of the English, Cornwallis averred that, 'Every native of Hindostan, I verily believe, is corrupt.' This was to be the start of a policy of racist exclusion in employment that was to characterize the Raj almost to its end.

As the name makes clear, the collector's primary function was the collection of taxes. His reputation depended, in large part, on his ability to bring in regularly the full amount of his district's assessed demand. However, the collector also, as magistrate, controlled the police, and often, as judge, decided cases in court. The hinge figure at the heart of the government, the district collector was responsible to a hierarchy of British bureaucrats above him, and supervised the work of an array of Indian subordinates below. These men, while responsible for the actual work of revenue collection, and sometimes able to manipulate for their own advantage naïve or inexperienced collectors, exercised no independent authority, and had no opportunity for promotion. The Cornwallis reforms, by the payment of high salaries, a monopoly of senior positions, and guaranteed pensions, secured for the Company's civil servants, now debarred from private trade, a reputation for incorruptibility and impartiality. The last reform was that of Lord Wellesley (1798–1805), who founded the College of Fort William at Calcutta (1802) as a place where incoming civil servants were taught local languages prior to taking up their appointments. At the same time, the Company directors established a college at Haileybury in England (1804) to provide fledgling civil servants, required to spend two years there, with the rudiments of a general education before out going to India. Thus was created the famed 'steel frame' of Indian administration, the Indian Civil Service, in which the British, and many Indians, took great pride. As the Indian Administrative Service, it survived the Raj, though with its powers reduced to accommodate a democratic politics. Plate 3.1 shows a district magistrate during a tour of the countryside in 1965 as he reviewed, village by village, rights to land still recorded on a cloth map of holdings.

The establishment of the civil administration on 'a most equitable, solid and permanent footing' was complemented by the organization of an efficient military. Britain's initial campaigns, ousting the French and toppling the Bengal nawabs, required but little military force. Defending Bengal against attack, and subsequently conquering the whole of India, was another matter. A force sufficient for this task could not be composed of scarce and expensive Europeans. Hence Clive himself, in the aftermath of Plassey, had begun recruiting Indian soldiers, known as *sepoys* from the Persian *sipahi*, to fight for the Company. Rejecting as unreliable those who had served the nawab, Hastings established the

Plate 3.1   District magistrate reading out to assembled villagers owner's
names written on a cloth map of village holdings to confirm property
rights, Faizabad, Uttar Pradesh, 1965.

Company's recruiting base among the high caste Hindu peasantry,
primarily Rajput and Brahman, of the eastern Gangetic plain, from
Awadh to Bihar. Anxious to avoid social upheaval, Hastings, and
his successors, took care to accommodate caste and religious sen-
sibilities in the army. Common messing was avoided, overseas service was not required, and Hindu festivals such as the Ram Lila secured official recognition in the cantonments. This encouragement
of high caste ritual status, however, left the government vulnerable to protest, even mutiny, whenever the sepoys detected infringe-
ment of their prerogatives. During the later eighteenth, and early
nineteenth century, the army grew rapidly in size. Some 100,000
strong in 1789, the Indian Army expanded during the Napoleonic
wars to 155,000 men, with a cavalry arm as well as infantry, making it one of the largest European-style standing armies in the
world.

The sepoy army was, of necessity, a mercenary force. Loyal service was secured in part by regular pay and the prospect of a

pension – uncommon in other Indian armies – and in part by the development of regimental pride. Such pride, fed by victory in the field, took visible shape in the sepoy's red coat and the discipline enforced on the army. The autobiography of one soldier, Sita Ram, tells how he was inspired to enlist by a visit from his uncle. 'He [the uncle] had such a splendid necklace of gold beads, and a curious bright red coat, covered with gold buttons; and, above all, he appeared to have an unlimited supply of gold *mohurs*. I longed for the time when I might possess the same.' Once enlisted, Sita Ram encountered the drill field. 'The parade ground was covered by parties of six or eight men, performing the most extraordinary movements I had ever seen, and these to orders of a language of which I did not understand a single word. I felt inclined to laugh, and stood astonished at the sight. However a violent wrench of my ear by the drill havildar [sergeant] soon brought me to my senses.' Sita Ram served faithfully in the army for over forty years, but, like all sepoys, he had no hope of rising into the officer corps, a jealously guarded European preserve.

Along with restructuring the government, Hastings set in motion what was to become a decades-long enterprise of mastering India's geography, history, and culture. Driven in part by an Enlightenment enthusiasm to know, and thus to classify and order, everything under the sun, a study of India also advanced the interests of India's new rulers. As Hastings explained straightforwardly to the directors in 1784, 'Every accumulation of knowledge and especially such as is obtained by social communication with people over whom we exercise dominion founded on the right of conquest, is useful to the state . . . it attracts and conciliates distant affections; it lessens the weight of the chain by which the natives are held in subjection; and it imprints on the hearts of our countrymen the sense of obligation and benevolence.' Hastings's major institutional creation was the Asiatic Society of Bengal. Founded in 1784, under the leadership of Sir William Jones, the society dedicated itself above all to study of the religious and cosmological texts of Indian antiquity. In so doing these British scholars, working closely with the Sanskrit pandits to whom they were always deeply indebted, elaborated a history for India, much as was being done for the nations of Europe itself at the same time.

Central to this history was the momentous discovery of a past, through shared 'Aryan' linguistic ties, that linked India with Britain itself. As Jones wrote, between Sanskrit, Greek, and Latin there existed 'a stronger affinity than could possibly have existed by accident'; hence all three had 'to have sprung from some common source'. Thus there came into view the widely dispersed family of related languages that had spread outwards from central Asia in prehistoric times. More generally, by their studies Jones and his successors made of 'Hinduism' a great religion and repository of ancient wisdom, while India itself was given a glorious past comparable to that of Greece and Rome. Archeological discoveries in the first decades of the nineteenth century reinforced this conviction of India's ancient greatness. The decipherment of the Brahmi script, for instance, revealed that India had enjoyed a long period of Buddhist predominance under such rulers as those of the Mauryan dynasty. The history of the pillar shown in plate 1.2 is instructive. As indicated in chapter 1, the fourteenth-century sultan Feroz Shah erected it at his court. But he had no idea what the column signfied or who had carved it. Only after the discoveries of the early nineteenth century was this pillar, with others like it across northern India, associated with the hitherto unknown Buddhist emperor Asoka Maurya (c. 268–33 BC). Asoka's rule was subsequently imagined as an era of amity and non-violence, and in the twentieth century was celebrated by Gandhian nationalists.

Such a sympathetic approach to Indian learning, though inspired by an Enlightenment search for correspondences and connections between cultures, should not, as the historian Thomas Trautmann comes perilously close to doing in his description of it as a 'love story', be allowed to obscure British belief in the superiority of their own civilization. Unlike European histories of 'progress', the arc of India's history, as even Jones described it, declined from ancient greatness into 'sordid priestcraft' and 'superstition'. Such a trajectory not by chance helped legitimate Britain's conquest. Jones too, despite his belief that India had much to teach the West in literature and philosophy, still conceived that in scientific reasoning the Indians were 'mere children'. The tension between the supposedly pristine Hinduism of the past and the 'corrupt' present can be sensed in these lines by Halhed:

Ages *have* been, when thy refulgent beam
Shone with full vigour on the mental gaze:
When doting superstition dar'd not dream,
And folly's phantoms perish'd in thy rays.

Hence it is not surprising that, as Britain's self-confidence grew through the era of the Napoleonic wars, the sympathetic 'Orientalist' assessment of India's civilization slowly withered. As a result, as the years went by, Jones's ties of language gave way to a theory of biological race in which those of presumed Aryan descent in India, regarded as degenerate from long centuries of mixing their blood with that of the land's indigenous peoples, shared little with their European 'cousins'.

In the more mundane realm as well there existed a tension between the abstract categories that the British brought to India with them, and the incorporation of Indian systems of information. As the historian David Ludden has written, for men like the late eighteenth-century map maker James Rennell, 'the real India experts were those scientists and trained administrators who worked and travelled in the countryside and observed local conditions.' Local knowledge, and local ways of understanding, from the outset shaped how the British made India their own. The British inserted themselves into the networks of Indian newswriters and postal services; placed agents in princely courts; and collaborated, as they surveyed the countryside, with locally influential landholders and informants. Village boundaries were demarcated, for instance, not by the British alone but by 'treaders' under the watchful eye of the community. As C. A. Bayly has argued, 'the colonial information order' was erected 'on the foundations of its Indian precursors'.

The insistent demand for a more 'scientific' understanding of India, however, meant that over time abstract institutionalized knowledge increasingly displaced the earlier 'indigenous networks of knowledgeable people'. The detailed surveys of Colin Mackenzie and Francis Buchanan in the years after 1800 visibly marked out the new order. Though remaining dependent on native assistants, both men voraciously inquired into all aspects of Indian life. From the sketch of the ruined temple depicted in plate 3.2, to lists of crops and castes, and histories of local families, the work of these men, though unsystematic, presaged the authoritative gazetteers and censuses of

Plate 3.2　Detail from *A Company Officer about to Sketch a Ruined Temple, c.* 1810. Note servants carrying chair, writing instruments, and easel.

the later Victorian era. Exemplary of the new information order was the Great Trigonometrical Survey. Begun in 1818, this survey sought to map the entire country on the basis of a detailed triangulation, using baselines measured with steel chains. The 'great meridional arc' that resulted, 1,500 miles from south to north, by far the most extensive geodetic survey undertaken anywhere in the world at the time, vastly exceeded any military or revenue requirements of the Company. Its achievement, as Matthew Edney has noted, was a triumphalist articulation of British mastery, at once scientific, rational, and imperial, over India's landscape. Such a reliance on maps and statistics, however, as they isolated the British from informed Indian opinion, left them vulnerable to panics, fear, and in 1857, a massive uprising that took them by surprise.

Early colonial life, above all in the presidency capitals, in similar fashion set British and Indian apart, yet brought them together in a shared intimacy. In both Calcutta and Madras the fort – a reminder that colonial rule depended on guns – provided the core from which the city expanded outwards. Madras possessed a clearly demarcated 'Black Town' given over to Indian commerce and residence. The British themselves, as they spilled out of the confines of the fort after 1770, developed garden suburbs dotted with large Palladian mansions. Much as did the fort itself, this pattern of settlement made visible the coming into being of a new colonial order. Calcutta, with a population of some 200,000 by the 1780s, including over 3,000 European residents, by the end of the century was sharply divided between the pillared and porticoed European mansions of Chowringhee and the densely settled Indian sectors of the city to the north.

Although the English residents of these cities, often wealthy nabobs, elaborated a lavish lifestyle, lack of resistance to tropical disease brought many of them to an early grave. In such sites as the Park Street Cemetery, Calcutta, they erected towering monuments to announce their claim on immortality. The modern-style cemetery open to all, as it came to replace the old parish burial grounds, provides another instance of an institution pioneered in India, and then later adopted in Europe. During the late eighteenth century nabobs and common soldiers alike customarily lived openly with Indian mistresses, called *bibis*. These relationships defined a domesticity at odds with that of Britain, though common in distant colonial lands. Unlike those of the Dutch East Indies or Portuguese Goa, however, by the 1790s, with the Cornwallis reforms, in India such relationships came increasingly under attack for their presumed immorality, and their complicity in what were seen as the 'corrupt' practices of the Hastings era. The nabobs themselves always confined their adoption of Indian customs and clothing to their private lives. They never allowed the pursuit of pleasure to challenge their conviction of their own racial superiority. As a result they rarely accepted as fully 'British' the children born of their Indian bibis. Stigmatized as 'half-castes' or Eurasians, those of mixed race were denied entry into government service by Cornwallis in 1793. Over time they came to form a community, unlike the mixed 'indische' elites of Java, uncomfortably placed between British and Indian, and disdained by both.

With moral reform came racial estrangement. Increasingly, though with a time lag in more distant areas, British men in India were expected to live modestly in a bungalow with a British wife, wear British dress, and refrain from social intercourse with Indians outside their official duties. Historians have sometimes alleged that this estrangement was the product of the appearance in India of large numbers of English women, called *memsahibs*, who enforced a bourgeois domesticity upon their men. In fact, British racial distance fed upon the arrogance bred by conquest, as well as the spread from the early nineteenth century of evangelical religion and a moralizing liberalism. British women, as the embodiment of British racial purity, simply made visible in the domestic realm this new racial order.

In recent years historians have sought to minimize the extent of the changes brought about by the imposition of colonial rule in eighteenth-century India. Between the Company's state in Bengal, it is said, and other post-Mughal 'country' powers, there was little to choose. Much, certainly, of the old persisted. The British had long insisted, in the writings of men like Alexander Dow, that despotism, or the unchecked will of the ruler, defined the Mughal–Indian political system. Despite their repudiation of despotic rule, the British from the start found themselves caught up in it. At the heart of the charges brought against Hastings by Edmund Burke, for instance, as exemplified by his rough treatment of the Begams of Awadh and the Raja of Benares, was that as governor-general he had acted the part of an Indian rather than a proper British ruler. In later years, especially in the person of the district collector, the ideal of the benevolent despot, imagined as someone ruling Indians in their own best interest, remained attractive. In other ways too the Company embraced indigenous practice. Throughout its years of governance, the Company acknowledged the suzerainty of the Mughal king in Delhi. Their coins bore his profile, while Mughal Persian remained the official language until 1835. The Company also actively patronized Hindu and Muslim religious institutions as their predecessors had done.

Still, by 1800 the foundations had been laid for a new political order. Hastings's reforms looked ahead to the novelty of what Radhika Singha has called 'a despotism of law', while the new Oriental scholarship gave Indians a new perspective on their country's past. From the management of Hindu temples to the precepts of the criminal law, everyday practices became increasingly rule-bound, and so lost their previous flexibility in application. Above all, the British had created an army of unprecedented size. The range of the Company state, its monopoly of physical force, and its capacity to command resources, as C. A. Bayly has written, 'set it apart even in its early days from all the regimes which had preceded it'.

CONQUEST AND SETTLEMENT

The arrival of Lord Wellesley as governor-general in 1798 ended a quarter-century during which the British had existed as one among several Indian 'country powers'. Spurred on by a new vision that saw the British Empire encompassing the entire subcontinent, Wellesley inaugurated twenty years of military activity that made the Company by 1818 master of India. Complementing Wellesley's conquests-at-arms was the elaboration of an aggressive imperial enthusiasm. Much of this was the product of events in Europe. Thoughout these years an embattled Britain confronted Napoleon, whose armies triumphed not only in Europe but in 1798 in Egypt, the gateway to India; and the patriotism stirred up by this desperate struggle easily spilled over into a conviction of Britain's right to rule whatever territories its armies might conquer. Something of this defiant spirit may be found in Lord Valentia's defence of Wellesley's magnificent new Government House in Calcutta, criticized for extravagance by the Company's directors:

The Head of a mighty Empire ought to conform himself to the prejudices of the country he rules over; and the British in particular ought to emulate the splendid works of the Princes of the House of Timour, lest it should be supposed that we merit the reproach which our great rivals the French have ever cast upon us, of being alone influenced by a sordid mercantile spirit. In short, I wish India to be ruled from a palace, not from a counting-house; with the ideas of a Prince, not with those of a retail-dealer in muslins and indigo.

Wellesley first moved against Tipu Sultan in Mysore. Implacably hostile to the British, backed by a powerful army of infantry and

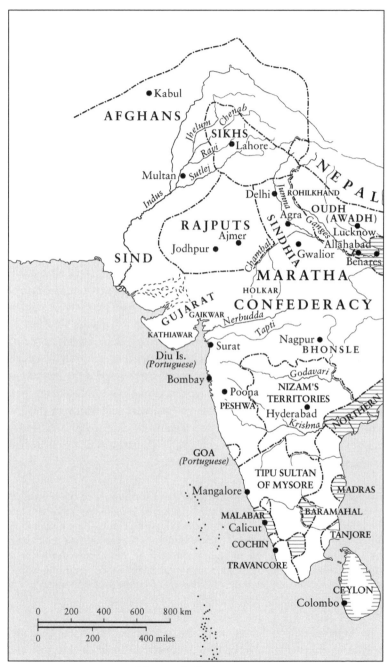

Map 2   India in 1798.

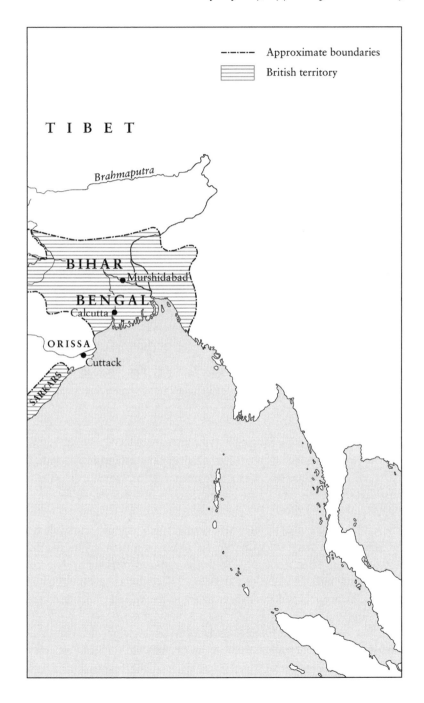

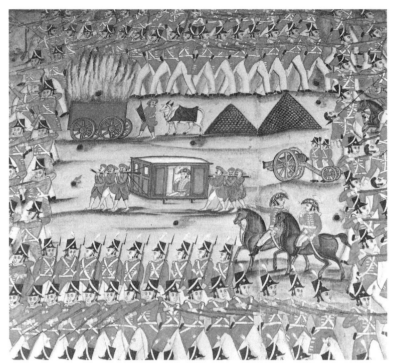

Plate 3.3 Detail from *The Battle of Polilur 1780*, by an unknown Indian artist, *c.* 1820.

artillery supported by an extensive light cavalry, Tipu had fought the British to a draw in the 1780s. Plate 3.3, by an unknown Indian artist, shows the last stand of a beleagured British force as it sought unsuccessfully, despite its disciplined rows of soldiers, to hold off Tipu's troopers. Although a conquest state similar in many ways to that of the East India Company's own, Tipu's Mysore, surrounded by British territory and unable to secure support from distant revolutionary France, simply did not command sufficient resources to hold out indefinitely. For the British, Tipu was the model of an 'Oriental despot', and his defeat in 1799 provoked great rejoicing in Britain.

In the first years of the new century Wellesley extended the frontier of British India northwards in the Ganges valley, and began the process of incorporating the Marathas into the empire. Although by the end of the eighteenth century the Maratha 'confederacy' had lost whatever coherence it had once possessed, its various baronial chieftains, each embedded in his own regional base, still possessed substantial resources. Mahadji Sindhia, for instance, established at Gwalior near Agra, built up in the 1780s a powerful military machine supplied with ordnance from his own factory. Nevertheless, far removed from their home base in Maharashtra, these chieftains were wholly dependent on fragile alliances with local elites and European adventurers, while their divisions and dissensions opened up opportunities for the British to play one off against the other. By negotiating the treaty of Bassein (1802), Wellesley neutralized the peshwa at Poona (Pune); and by his campaigns in the north, which led to the 1803 conquest of Delhi, he checked the ambitions of the Marathas in that region. But the struggle for supremacy in central India was not resolved. Only in 1817, as the British sought to contain the Pindaris' bands of irregular cavalry who roamed throughout central India levying plunder, was the final battle joined, as the Marathas were seen as the Pindaris' patrons. The following year much of Gujarat and Maharashtra were added to the Company's domains, while the defeated Maratha chieftains were reduced to the status of 'protected' princes wholly dependent on the British.

Substantial further acquisitions came about through the working of the subsidiary alliance system. Devised in Clive's time, these alliances, between the Company and Indian princes, were justified as a way of securing Bengal from attack by deploying its troops within states friendly to it. The prince on his side secured protection against his enemies, external and internal, and agreed to meet the cost of the troops and to accept a British resident at his court. By this arrangement the prince could be sure of a powerful ally, while the British could meet their enemies at a safe distance from their own territories, and share with others the cost of maintaining their expensive army. Among those drawn early into this net of obligations were the rulers of Arcot, Awadh, and Hyderabad. In its workings, however, this seemingly equitable arrangement led only to British conquest, and to Indian bankruptcy.

The imperatives of 'military fiscalism', as we have seen, had driven India's princes, from the mid-eighteenth century, into the arms of bankers and financiers as they endeavoured to finance expensive armies. Alliance with the British did not resolve, but only exacerbated, this financial squeeze, for the British demanded large sums rigorously and relentlessly every year. As they sought revenue to meet these subsidiary payments, princes were driven to ever more desperate expedients. The classic case is that of Awadh, allied with the British from 1765. There the incessant demand for revenue, by pitting nawab and Rajput chieftain against each other, destroyed the fragile political system in which the mutual weakness of each had secured a certain stability. Impoverished local chieftains found themselves driven into revolt, while great revenue contractors, such as Almas Ali Khan, enriched themselves at the expense of the state. Attempts to ratchet up the revenue inevitably brought down upon the hapless nawab British complaints of misgovernment and oppression, while, deprived of funds for his own purposes, his own soldiers in arrears, he was drawn ever deeper into debt.

Outright defiance, such as that of the Awadh Nawab Wazir Ali in 1798, only led to even more forceful intervention as the British manipulated court factions to secure a more pliable ruler. Wellesley secured a temporary resolution of the crisis in 1801 by the drastic expedient of annexing half of Awadh to British India, which brought an end to the subsidy demands. This cession, of rich lands to the west and east of Awadh's central core, however, left its rulers more strapped for funds than ever, and increasingly at the mercy of armed landholders (*taluqdars*), who defiantly consolidated power in the countryside. From 1815 onwards, abandoning all attempts at government, the nawabs retreated into their courts, where they patronized literature, music, and dance with a refined luxuriance that won for them only the contempt of the British. The elephant procession and ornate architecture of Lucknow shown in plate 3.4 illustrate something of the princely style of life, as does Satayajit Ray's compelling film, *The Chess Players*. The 'decadence' and anarchy of which the British so frequently complained, and which they used to justify Awadh's annexation in 1856, were, in large measure, their own creation.

With the final defeat of the Marathas in 1818, the subsidiary alliance system ceased to serve its original purpose, that of buffering

Plate 3.4 *City of Lucknow*, 1824, by J. Ackerman.

the British from their enemies. A large number of states nevertheless remained in existence, among them the sprawling domains of the nizam of Hyderabad, and more were formed from among defeated rulers who were allowed to retain their thrones. Even in the changed conditions of uncontested supremacy these states served useful purposes. Dry and hilly areas that produced little revenue, from the Rajasthan desert and Himalayan foothills across central India, were more economically administered by local rajas than by an expensive British staff. Loyal princes could help dampen discontent in British India, as was to be demonstrated by the assistance of India's princes during the crisis of 1857. The continuation of princely rule also helped the British veil their power behind that of rulers whose ceremonial and ritual authority remained visibly intact. The magnificence of princely courts, with the gifting and patronage activities that they sustained, kept alive ties between prince and subject, and obscured from both the loss of the state's former independence.

The system of 'indirect rule' was carefully patrolled by the British. States were not allowed to possess an independent military force, nor to engage in diplomatic relations with each other. Central to the system's functioning was the 'Resident' posted at the prince's capital. Residents actively intervened in succession disputes; they formed alliances with state diwans, or prime ministers, often outsiders but men close to the state's bankers and revenue officials; and, as time went on, through the appointment of carefully selected tutors, they endeavoured to train heirs to adopt Western notions of 'progressive' government. To the frustration of the British, efforts to reform princely governance rarely met with much success. Disdaining the innovations of their rulers, which brought them no benefit, princes preferred instead the solace of indigenous music and the arts.

The first two decades of the nineteenth century also saw the beginnings of a fundamental transformation in India's economy, and in Britain's relationship to it. Throughout its first decades of rule the Company continued still to see itself as primarily a commercial body, purchasing its 'Investment' of Indian piece goods for the British market and developing new markets for such commodities as raw cotton and opium in China. The opium trade, in particular, was to prove highly remunerative. Its production tightly regulated by advances to growers, the opium was sold by the Company to

British traders who smuggled it into China. The profits from its sale at once sustained the Company's always precarious finances and relieved Britain from the need to export bullion to pay for Chinese tea, in increasing demand, with other luxury goods, like sugar and chocolate, in Britain's burgeoning consumer market. By the 1830s opium provided up to 15 per cent of the Indian Government's total revenue. Although the Company from the 1790s endeavoured to insure that Indian marketplaces and fairs were open to all-comers, free trade was always subordinate to the fiscal and military needs of its burgeoning empire.

As the new century proceeded, British private merchants, spurred on by the industrial revolution and the hope of new markets in the East, challenged the Company's trade monopoly. A responsive Parliament ended its Indian monopoly in 1813, and that to China in 1833. At the same time the balance of trade between Britain and India began to shift. By 1815 Indian textiles and other artisanal commodites could no longer compete in Britain, or on the world market, with British machine-made goods. Within a few years British textiles began to penetrate the Indian market, initiating the development of a classically 'colonial' economy, importing manufactures and exporting raw materials, that was to last for a century, until the 1920s. Yet the integration of India into the world capitalist order remained halting and incomplete. The fate of indigo, a blue dye popular in Europe which generated substantial export income for India throughout the later Company period, is revealing. Grown by European planters, who secured the crop by cash advances to peasant cultivators, often supplemented with coercion, indigo remained always a precarious source of wealth. Markets in Europe were unpredictable, and subject to boom and bust fluctuations, to which planters in distant India were acutely vulnerable. The creditors who sustained production were equally at risk. Market crashes in 1827, and again in 1847, precipitated massive banking failures that reduced funds available for years afterwards.

Although new opportunities in commercial agriculture brought advantage for some, the loss of overseas markets for artisanal produce was devastating, especially for skilled weavers in the great weaving centres, such as Dacca and Murshidabad. In the countryside weavers managed to survive by taking advantage of cheap imported thread, but those who had relied on hand spinning for subsistence were often driven back into agriculture. At the same time the rapid decline in the number of Indian courts, lavish spenders on luxury goods and armaments, reduced demand for many commodities. The disbandment of these courts also forced on to the land large numbers of former militiamen and retainers, which in turn further adversely affected artisanal production.

Overall, although the period of straightforward plunder of the country's riches had come to an end, the East India Company during the early decades of the nineteenth century did little to set India on a path of economic growth. To be sure, many of the obstacles were structural. Unlike contemporary Britain or the United States, where canal networks were built to provide easy access to the interior, India could rely only on its rivers, and primarily on the Ganges, for the transport of bulk commodities. While this generated wealth for river towns such as Mirzapur, it left the rest of the country outside the orbit of the export economy. The lack of infrastructure, of banks as well as roads, deterred direct overseas investment, with the result that the only available British capital was that provided by the accumulation of private wealth within India. Indeed, far from investing in India, the resident British commonly took their money home with them by investment in secure Company bonds. This 'drain' of wealth was complemented by the Company's withdrawal of funds to cover what it called the 'Home Charges', including pensions, debt service, and the cost of maintaining the Company's offices. In later years, these payments were to provide a highly visible target for nationalist accusations of British economic exploitation.

From the later 1820s into the 1840s India was also hammered by economic depression, involving a fall in the value of the rupee, and a contraction in the supply of silver. Although partly the result of a worldwide silver shortage, the situation was exacerbated by the Company's policy of deflationary finance, as it sought to trim its budget deficits. Throughout, the heaviest burden India had to bear was that of the land revenue demand. Essential to the support of the army and the administration, these payments, rigorously collected in cash, lay at the heart of the British impact upon the Indian countryside.

As the British initially knew nothing of Indian rural society, their first attempts at revenue management, under Hastings, involved a series of disastrous experiments in leasing and auctioning the right to collect taxes. Matters were made worse by the devastating famine of 1770, in which up to a quarter of Bengal's population may have died, and which reduced the province's available assets for years to come. By the eighteenth century the British had come to believe that private property in land alone ensured stability and progress in society. At the same time the physiocrats in France were arguing that land was the basis of all wealth. Hence in 1776 Philip Francis, on the Bengal council, put forward a plan for a 'rule of property' for Bengal. As Francis wrote, 'if private property be not once for all secured on a permanent footing, the public revenue will sink rapidly with the general produce of the country.' Such ideas conformed with the eighteenth-century Whig belief in the importance of a hereditary landed aristocracy. The zamindar, according to this vision, was an Indian version of the English gentleman-farmer; once his property rights were secure, he would be as enterprising as his English counterpart. The scheme took legislative shape in 1793, under the Whig grandee Lord Cornwallis, when the Bengal Permanent Settlement, with enduring consequences for the region, vested in the province's zamindars a full proprietary right in their estates with a revenue assessment fixed in perpetuity.

Unfortunately, the Cornwallis settlement wholly misconceived the position of the zamindar, with the result that its outcome bore little resemblance to Francis's expectations. In India, prior to the coming of the British, the bundle of rights associated with property were not concentrated in a land 'owner', but rather dispersed among all those, among them the peasant cultivator, the zamindar, and the government, who had an interest in the land. For his part, the zamindar collected 'rent' from the peasantry, and, after deducting a share for his own maintenance, passed on the remainder as 'revenue' to the state. He could sell or transfer only his own revenue collecting rights, not the land itself, for that did not belong to him. Under the new land system, by contrast, the peasantry found themselves reduced to the status of tenants without rights, while the zamindar as proprietor found his entire estate liable to sale in case of default in paying the taxes assessed on it. As the high and inflexible British demand could not at first easily be met, estates rapidly came on to the market. It has been estimated that up to one-third of the estates in Bengal changed hands in the twenty years after the 1793 Permanent Settlement. The purchasers were those familiar with the institutions of the new regime and who had prospered under it, especially Brahman and Kayastha employees of the Company and of the old zamindars.

Neither the old owners nor the new, however, had much interest in acting the part of the 'improving' English landlord. It was never feasible to sweep away the existing cultivators in order to introduce costly 'improvements'. Hence the Bengal zamindars rapidly became a class of rentiers, who, as the rural population rebounded from the period of famine, lived increasingly comfortably from the rents they extracted from their tenants. These they often had to share with intermediary tenure holders, such as *jotedars*, who directed agricultural activity in the villages. But cultivation remained, as before, a matter of subsistence cropping across a myriad of tiny paddy fields, in contrast to the consolidation of holdings characteristic of the contemporaneous 'enclosure' movement in Britain.

Discouraged, the British after 1800 sought an alternative to reliance upon zamindars. This took the form of the *ryotwari* settlement pioneered by Thomas Munro in the lands taken from Mysore. Under this form of settlement property rights were awarded to the peasant cultivator (*ryot*). This change of policy was not wholly a matter of choice, since the Mysore wars had effectively destroyed the class of agrarian magnates across large areas. Still, Munro, a product of the Romantic movement then spreading across England, idealized the simple life of the peasant, whom he wished to rule with as little disruption of his old ways as possible. Implemented throughout most of Madras and neighbouring Maharashtra during the 1820s, much in the ryotwari system was nevertheless an exercise in self-delusion. Dominant village elites often intercepted settlement rights, and so denied tenurial protection to the lowly cultivator with the plough. The British at the same time abandoned the idea of permanency in assessment. Anxious to secure a share of the increased produce as the country prospered, everywhere outside Bengal they retained the right to revise assessments every twenty or thirty years. Its demands pitched always at the highest level society could bear, the land revenue system generated an enduring discontent that erupted into rebellion throughout much of the north in 1857.

With the settlement of the revenue demand went a larger determination to 'settle' all of India's people in a visibly fixed location on the land. The eighteenth century, as we have seen, was an era marked by incessant movement – of herders and pastoralists, of armies and yogis. This process continued into the early nineteenth century, as raiding groups such as the Pindaris moved through the ill-defined and ill-patrolled borders of India's states. In the Company's view, such activities posed a political threat to its own monopoly of coercion, and brought economic loss as well, for these wanderers eluded its network of taxation. Much of this effort of 'sedentarization' was directed against the tribal people of central India. Forest dwellers, often hunter-gatherers who periodically raided into the areas of settled agriculture, these tribals, such as the Bhils of Khandesh, were subjected to a series of armed incursions during the 1820s. Bhil raids, as the historian Ajay Skaria has written, 'were treated by British officials not as occasions for negotiations but rather as acts of aggression on territory on which they had exclusive sovereignty.' The tribal peoples were subsequently either confined to the forest, but deprived of control of its resources, which were now to be 'scientifically' managed, or encouraged to abandon their 'wild and wandering ways' for cultivation. One of the tasks of the Khandesh Bhil Agency was to extend loans to tribes in order to make them take up settled agriculture.

In similar fashion, groups such as the Banjara carriers, whose pack animals had accompanied eighteenth-century armies, together with herders such as Gujars and Bhattis, found their grazing grounds restricted by assessment of waste lands and the creation of private property rights, while their employment opportunities declined with the disbandment of armies. Those who persisted in wandering found themselves the objects of suspicion, and began to be stigmatized as 'criminal tribes'. Such suspicion fuelled one of the most famous episodes in the history of British India – the campaign against *thagi* (thuggee), which gave the English language the word *thug*. Notorious for their secrecy, their presumed devotion to the blood-thirsty goddess Kali, and their custom of ritual murder of travellers by strangling, thags fed British fears, and fantasies, of an exotic India beyond their reach. Hence the British created an imagined conspiracy, in which diverse bands of highway robbers were forged into a fraternity of criminals by birth and profession, and the force of the colonial state was then unleashed upon it. In the sweeping arrests that followed, the ordinary procedures of the criminal law were set aside. But the 1839 announcement of the 'extirpation' of thagi set off an orgy of self-congratulation. The British could now conceive of India as a pacified land, composed of a law-abiding, tax-paying peasantry.

TRADITION AND REFORM: INDIAN SOCIETY UNDER THE COMPANY

Thomas Macaulay, law member of the governor-general's council, wrote in 1834 of the young Charles Trevelyan, his future brother-in-law:

He is quite at the head of that active party among the younger servants of the Company who take the side of improvement . . . He has no small talk. His mind is full of schemes of moral and political improvement, and his zeal boils over in his talk. His topics, even in courtship, are steam navigation, the education of the natives, the equalisation of the sugar duties, the substitution of the Roman for the Arabic alphabet in the Oriental languages.

These sentiments expressed the expansive optimism of an era in which it seemed that the barriers of custom and tradition everywhere would give way easily before the power of British liberal ideals. Britain, after all, had vanquished Napoleon; and, the only industrialized nation, it had made itself the 'workshop of the world'. In evangelical Christianity it believed itself the possessor of a 'saving' religion to be shared with all people. For its advocates – from Adam Smith and Jeremy Bentham on to James and John Stuart Mill – liberalism was not just a philosophy of governance suited to England. Its precepts defined not 'Western' civilization but civilization itself. In India, liberals confidently saw their task as that of stripping off the shackles of 'despotism', 'priestcraft', and 'superstition' that left its people, as James Mill wrote in his *History of British India* (1818), 'the most enslaved portion of the human race'.

Inevitably, liberals did not join Orientalists in venerating the achievements of India's ancient past. As Macaulay wrote, in a phrase that has reverberated down the years, 'the entire native literature of India and Arabia' was not worth 'a single shelf of a good European library'. For the liberal, England's superiority was unquestioned. Yet it was not racial or even environmental in character. Indians, like anyone else, could be transformed through the workings of law, free trade, and education. As Macaulay insisted in his 1835 'Minute on Education', Britain's mission was to create not just a class of Indians sufficiently well versed in English to help the British rule their country, but one 'English in taste, in opinions, in morals and in intellect'. In time – though not, of course, in the near future – an India so transformed would become independent, but it would embody 'an imperishable empire of our arts and our morals, our literature and our laws'.

Lord William Bentinck as governor-general (1828–35) began the process of implementing the reform agenda. This was not to be an easy task. Funds were always scarce, while Bentinck was anxious not to antagonize Indian opinion by moving too fast. Among his first acts was the 1829 abolition of *sati*. With its immolation of a living woman on her husband's funeral pyre, this act, rather like British public executions, catered to an English obsession with death as spectacle. Although English observers in the eighteenth century had valorized sati as an heroic act of romantic self-sacrifice, by Bentinck's time it was seen as emblematic of India as a land of a barbarous and blood-thirsty faith. Above all, for the British sati testified to the moral weakness of Indian men, who lacked the masculine strength to nurture rather than to degrade their women, and so to the consequent need for Britain to stand forth to protect them. Although responding to outraged liberal and evangelical opinion, Bentinck nevertheless took care to solicit Indian support, above all from a panel of Brahman pandits whom he enlisted to assure him that the practice was not required by 'scripture'; and he represented his action as that of an enlightened Hindu ruler. Despite its visibility, sati was not in fact, with at most some 800 cases annually throughout Bengal, widely practised. Indeed, one European resident of Calcutta in 1780 wrote vividly about the horrors of sati, but then reported that she had 'never had the opportunity of witnessing the various ceremonies, nor have I ever seen any European who had been present at them'. Hence prohibition of sati could satisfy the liberal reforming impulse without risk of triggering an upheaval. Other, more widespread practices, such as that of female infanticide among the Rajputs of northern India, the British tiptoed gingerly around.

Central to the liberal credo was education. From Hastings's time, the Company had supported Sanskrit and Arabic education, through colleges established in Benares and Calcutta. As opinion began to shift, this policy came under attack from the so-called 'Anglicists', who insisted that Western subjects and the English-language should form the basis of study. The Anglicists' victory, in 1835, propelled by the powerful rhetoric of Macaulay's 'Minute', was followed by the establishment of government schools in India's major cities, though not in the countryside, and no attention was given to primary education. No government-run schools existed at the time in England, where education was controlled by religious denominations. Here, as with the contemporaneous trigonometrical survey, the separate cemetery, and the subsequent introduction of competitive examinations for the Indian Civil Service, the institutions of the modern state took shape in the colony, which can be seen as something of a laboratory of administrative practice, before making their way back to England. That education was not meant simply to produce clerks is visibly represented in such structures as the college at Patna shown in plate 3.5, whose elegant neoclassical architecture represented a vision of the civilized modern world.

Even before Bentinck's arrival Indians had begun the process of coming to terms with the new Western culture associated with British rule. Private European and Indian initiative had in 1819 led to the foundation in Calcutta of India's first English-language institution of higher learning, the Hindu College. By the 1830s several thousand Indians were studying English in that city alone. Few, however, were prepared to adopt as their own the ideas associated with men like Macaulay, for that would have involved the wholesale repudiation of their culture. Most famous of those who did so were the Young Bengal group, based in Hindu College, and associated with the enthusiast Michael Derozio (1809–31). Defiantly eating beef and drinking whiskey, these young men derided 'irrational' Hindu customs; some few among them, including Derozio, converted to Christianity.

Most Indian thinkers, as they confronted the powerful ideas of the 'West', sought to achieve some balance between 'tradition'

Plate 3.5   Façade of Patna College, *c.* 1837.

and 'reform', between a richly textured culture that still sustained them and the excitement of new ways. In assessing the various movements which grew up it is essential to avoid simplistic dichotomies. 'Tradition', in both Hinduism and Islam, as we have seen in chapter 1, possessed its own vitality; while 'reform' could take many shapes. In areas away from the immediate environs of the presidency capitals, movements of reformed practice were little influenced by the West, and so followed customary channels into the colonial period. Hindu devotionalism remained attractive, especially to upwardly mobile groups seeking to distance themselves from tribal or low caste origins. Most prominent, perhaps, was the movement founded in Gujarat by Swami Narayan (1780–1830). Rejecting much of Brahmanical ritualism in favour of a Vaishnavite devotionalism, Swami Narayan drew followers from displaced nomadic and warrior communities, and so helped further the process of agricultural settlement.

The most significant Islamic movement of the early nineteenth century was that asssociated with the reformist ideas, discussed above, of Shah Waliullah. Expounded by his son Shah Abdul Aziz, who translated the Koran into Urdu, Walliullah's ideas spread widely among the Muslim elite of northern India. For many Muslims, a reform of Islamic practice, with a closer adherence to the precepts of the Koran and hadith, and the purging of much saint worship from sufism, was coupled with the aim of restoring an ordered political and social life. Although Western knowledge, usually through Urdu translations of scientific works, found a home in the Delhi College, founded in 1792, Western learning had little role to play in a regeneration which sought its principles from within the Islamic tradition. The most charismatic of these reformers was Sayyid Ahmad Barelvi (1786–1831). During the 1820s Sayyid Ahmad preached throughout the Gangetic plain, drawing supporters from among hard-pressed Muslim weavers and artisans. In 1829, drawing on his earlier experiences as a trooper in the army of the Afghan ruler of Tonk, he set out to establish a state of his own. To do so he organized, from the Afghan frontier, a campaign against the Sikh state of Ranjit Singh. Unable to secure support among Afghans little interested in Islamic reform, Sayyid Ahmad's small band of followers proved no match for Ranjit's army, which drove him into the Himalayan foothills, where he died fighting. Sayyid Ahmad's memory lived on, however, to inspire subsequent Islamic uprisings along the frontier, and to frighten the British with imagined 'Wahabi' conspiracies.

A range of other revolts unsettled British India during the years of Company rule. Some joined religious rhetoric with class antagonism. In 1821 Shariat Allah (1781–1840) returned from two decades in Mecca to preach a purified Islam. By the 1830s he had gained a large following among the rural population of eastern Bengal for what became known as the Faraizi movement. His followers' refusal to pay customary levies to support Hindu temples and festivals gained for the movement the enmity of the province's Hindu zamindars. Shariat Allah's son Didu Miyan organized the Faraizis to assert directly the rights of cultivators and artisans against Hindu landowners and moneylenders and British indigo planters. For several decades the Faraizis took a leading role in organizing agrarian protest activities throughout eastern Bengal.

A number of revolts sought to contest the monopoly of coercive force that the British determined to secure for themselves. These were usually led in the plains by zamindars and by tribal chieftains in the hills and jungles. The poligars of the far south, for instance, put up a fierce resistance to the Company's forces during 1800–1, while such forest peoples as the Bhils in the 1820s, noted above, and the Santals of western Bengal in 1855, fought to preserve their tribal ways. These revolts did not succeed against the might of the Raj, but they testify to the depth of enduring, if rarely effectively organized, discontent that accompanied the imposition of British rule over India.

Among those who sought to come to terms with the new Western learning, by far the most influential was the Bengali scholar Ram Mohan Roy (1772–1833). Learned in Sanskrit, Arabic, Persian, and English, employed for some years at the turn of the century by the Company and its officers, Ram Mohan endeavoured to create from the ancient Upanishadic texts, with their monistic philosophy, a vision of a rationalist and monotheist 'modern' India. Breaking with devotional Hinduism, he responded sympathetically to the monotheism of Islam and the ethical idealism of Christianity. Ram Mohan found Christian doctrine, however, especially the divinity of Christ, incompatible with his search for a 'rational' religion. Such speculative reasoning confounded the Christian missionaries who, with the end of restrictions on missionary preaching, were now arriving in India to convert the 'heathen'. Ram Mohan's faith was close to that of the deistic Unitarians with whom he corresponded in Bristol and Boston. To propagate his beliefs he founded a society called the Brahmo Samaj in 1828. Something of the dignity and confidence with which he approached the English is evident in the portrait, shown in plate 3.6, painted at the end of his life in England, where he was received with honour.

Ram Mohan's social and political programme, whose central values he described as 'improvement' and 'enlightenment', drew him to the liberals clustered around Bentinck. With them he supported English education and the abolition of sati. Indeed, calling upon the government in 1823 to promote 'a more liberal and enlightened system of instruction, embracing mathematics, natural philosophy, chemistry and anatomy, with other useful sciences', Ram Mohan provided arguments Macaulay was subsequently to adopt. But, unlike English liberals, he did not repudiate the Hindu past. To the contrary, rather like the Orientalists of an earlier generation, he saw in the ancient 'scriptures' a 'pure' Hinduism upon which

Plate 3.6   Ram Mohan Roy (1772–1833).

he could ground his rationalist faith, and from which he could challenge, as not 'properly' Hindu, the latter-day practices of idolatry and sati. Such a return to the earliest texts to provide a secure footing for reform was to be a continuing feature of Hindu reform movements.

With such views went also an acceptance of Orientalist notions of India's 'decline' from a glorious past, and the singling out of the medieval Muslim rulers as prime agents of that decline. Such a theory of India's past inevitably exacerbated the emerging divide between Hindu and Muslim. Even the liberally minded Ram Mohan described the centuries of Muslim rule as a time when 'the civil and religious rights' of India's 'original inhabitants' were 'constantly trampled upon'. For writers not steeped in these notions, by contrast, such as Mrityunjay Vidyalankar, whose 1808 history of Bengal was commissioned by Fort William College, changes of dynasty spoke only of the failings of individual rulers, whose replacement, when they ceased to follow *dharma* (good conduct), no matter whether by Muslim or even by Briton, could not but be for the common good. The protagonists of such a history were gods and kings, not peoples or nations.

Ram Mohan Roy attracted the support of the influential Tagore family, headed by one of India's first capitalist entrepreneurs, Dwarkanath Tagore; his son Debendranath (1817–1905) refounded the Brahmo Samaj after Ram Mohan's death. Still, Ram Mohan's radical views provoked intense controversy among Calcutta's educated elite. Known as the *bhadralok* (respectable people), these were merchants, clerks, government employees, rentiers, and the like, mostly of upper castes, who had prospered under the British. Among their number, especially as patrons of the new learning, were the monied purchasers of estates sold during the upheaval surrounding the Permanent Settlement. For the most part these men were unwilling to follow Ram Mohan Roy in repudiating so ruthlessly so much of contemporary Hindu devotional practice. The conservatives led by Radha Kanta Deb, who founded the Dharma Sabha (1830) to rally support for Hinduism, have often been denounced as hide-bound reactionaries opposed to progress. Yet these men shared much with Ram Mohan Roy. Deb, for instance, was an active patron of the Hindu College, and supported English education. They opposed Bentinck's abolition of sati not simply from a desire to see the practice continue, but out of an objection to the colonial government's interference in Indian domestic and family life. Such objections to British-sponsored reform were to recur, with increasing vigour, among nationalists at the end of the century.

Bhadralok opinion was shaped not only by principled disagreements, but by social factions, called *dals*. These linked various caste groupings together under leading figures such as Tagore and Deb, who adjudicated disputes among their members on issues of caste status and pollution. Membership in a dal, as S. N. Mukherjee has shown, often influenced positions taken on the issues of the day. Another distinctive Bengali forum for discussion was that provided by *adda*, informal gatherings for conversation in the homes of patrons of culture and literature. Formalized public debate was, however, a novelty in early nineteenth-century India. Translation and publication of texts in Indian languages, as well as support of local scholars, had been a feature of Fort William College from its establishment. The result was a 'print culture' not so different from that which was growing up in Europe at the same time. As tracts were printed and texts circulated, educated Indians, even though excluded from the government of the country, created for themselves a public arena where the issues of the day were discussed. Regardless of the positions taken by their organizers, the existence of public meetings, pamphlets, and voluntary societies announced the coming of a new 'modern' India. From its origins in Calcutta, this style of public activity spread to the other presidency capitals, and then, more slowly, into the interior, where debates with Christian missionaries provided some of its liveliest moments. Nevertheless, especially by comparison with the freer climate in Britain, the reformist vision remained always constrained by its colonial context.

The governors-general who succeeded Bentinck, the Whig Lord Auckland (1836–42), the Tory Lord Ellenborough (1842–4), and the old general Lord Hardinge (1844–8), were less committed to reform. Auckland restored support to Oriental learning, while in the final settlement of the upper Ganges valley in the 1840s such men as James Thomason sought to temper the British commitment to individual ownership by a policy of joint settlement with village communities. Such settlements rarely included all residents of the village, and partition of holdings was permitted, but their adoption, accompanied by an idealization of the self-sufficient Indian village community, marked a backing away from the universal enforcement of individual property rights.

During these years slowly unfolding events on India's north-western frontier triggered the Company's last conquests. Through the first four decades of the nineteenth century, as the Company expanded its territory up to Burma in the east, and Nepal in north, the frontier to the west remained stable. Pulling together the disparate Sikh tribes, and incorporating Muslims as well as Sikhs, Ranjit Singh created in the Punjab a prosperous state with a disciplined army of some 20,000 infantrymen and 4,000 cavalry. As the British had no wish to tangle with this powerful force, and Ranjit carefully avoided attacks on British territory, only with Ranjit's death in 1839 did the Company become involved in the lands along and beyond the Indus.

The first step forward was in the lower Indus. Attractive both for its control of the trade along the river, which British fantasies imagined as a 'highway' to Central Asia, and the access it provided to Afghanistan, Sind was conquered between 1839 and 1842 by the headstrong Charles Napier. The first Afghan War followed, as the British sought to make this mountainous region a 'buffer' state to counter the growing Russian advance towards the Hindu Kush from the north. The opening gambit in what was to become the 'Great Game', the war was a disaster for the British. Trapped in Kabul, the British Indian force was wiped out, with only a single survivor, out of some 15,000 men, left alive to tell the tale. Abandoning the attempt to subdue Afghanistan, the British next turned to the Punjab. Disputes among the Sikh chieftains, and within its army, opened up opportunities for intervention which led to the first Sikh War in 1845 and the installation of a British resident in Lahore. Among those who sought advantage by supporting the British was the Hindu raja of Jammu, Gulab Singh. His reward was the lush mountain kingdom of Kashmir, with an almost wholly Muslim population. Thus was the stage set for what was to become, a century later, the most embittered and enduring conflict between the two successor states of the Raj.

The years from Hastings's time to the mid-nineteenth century brought about a momentous set of changes for India. Above all, the East India Company, in the 1770s a fledgling state among other equally powerful regional states, had by 1850, with the conquest of the Punjab, brought the entire Indian subcontinent under its control to form a vast Indian Empire. Under the Company's government a beginning had been made, especially with the encouragement of commercial agriculture, towards transforming India's economy to serve the needs of the larger world-capitalist order. A system of law and property rights had been instituted. Various plans for social reform had been enunciated. New ideas, of India's past and of its possible futures, began to circulate among the educated. Yet in no way was this a straightforward process of 'modernization'. Many 'reforms' existed only on paper or were confined to tiny urban elites. Others had the effect of binding Indians more tightly to the soil, as warrior aristocracies were turned into landlords and wandering pastoralists forced to become peasant cultivators. Indian commercial and banking elites had profited with the British from the new opportunities of the colonial era, as exemplified by such collaborative ventures as Carr Tagore & Co. Yet they found themselves by mid-century, with almost the sole exception of the Parsis in Bombay, driven out of the export sector into less remunerative inland trade or on to the land. South Indian temples, once great sources for the redistribution of wealth, found their assets taxed and, shorn of government patronage, their management constantly scutinized for 'corrupt' practice.

Other changes tied Indians more closely to rigidly defined notions of what was taken as their own 'tradition'. Texts, not local custom, now mattered, with the result that Brahmans lengthened a growing dominance over a society increasingly stratified by the prescriptions of caste, which alone the law recognized. Thus new property laws sought to release individual energies, only to be immediately hedged round with concessions to British defined 'customs' of caste and tribe. Women, once able to inherit property, found themselves excluded by a British determination to uphold 'Hindu' law. These various 'traditions', of hierarchy and ritual distinction, were, to be sure, not invented by the British. But they now began to press upon Indian society in rigid and unaccustomed ways. A renewed commitment to reform had to await the coming, in 1849, of a more energetic governor-general, and, a decade later of Crown rule.

4

Revolt, the modern state, and colonized subjects, 1848–1885

The revolt of 1857–8, which swept across much of north India in opposition to British rule, has conventionally been taken as the dividing point that marks the beginning of modern India. Historical periodization is, however, always somewhat arbitrary. With greater distance from the colonial period, when the searing chaos of the uprising was understood either as 'Mutiny' to the colonial rulers or as the 'First War of Independence' to many nationalists, it is possible to focus on substantial, long-term transformations rather than on a single event. Such an emphasis, moreover, places India in the context of changes taking place in the larger world, not just in terms of events and personalities in India itself. Far from modernity 'happening' in Europe and then being transplanted to a country like India, many of these changes took place in relation to each other.

Modern technological changes, among them canals, railways, and telegraph, were introduced into India within years of their introduction in Europe. Changes essential to the modern state, including the unification of sovereignty, the surveying and policing of the population, and institutions meant to create an educated citizenry were also, broadly speaking, introduced during the same period in India and in parts of Europe. Indeed, certain modern practices and institutions were either stimulated by the Indian experience or originated in India itself. Municipal cemeteries, as noted above, appeared in India before they did in England; the same is true of English literature as a curricular subject, and of state-sponsored scientific and surveying institutions. The colonial relationship with India was essential, moreover, as Gauri Vishwanathan recently argued, to one of the fundamental characteristics of modern states, namely the practice of state secularism. At the same time, new religious organizations in both India and Britain shared the common pattern of an unprecedented involvement of the laity. In both countries too, the spread of electoral politics was accompanied by debate over the place of religion in public life. Above all, the economic lives of both countries were profoundly, and increasingly, intertwined.

The date 1848 as starting point for the 'modern state' in India is a reminder, however, of a key difference in the nature of the state in India. In Europe during 1848 a wave of protests swept across the continent demanding expansion of the suffrage and other political reforms. In Britain, the Chartist movement, gaining support from economic depression and the limited expansion of suffrage brought about by the Reform Act of 1832, brought the working classes on to the streets in an effort to secure political power for themselves. The opportunities for a public voice and public life varied greatly among regions in India, but even in Bengal, where modern voluntary associations and publications were most widespread, relatively few voices could be raised to demand such political reforms before the end of the century. In politics, as in economic life, an authoritarian colonial state constrained Indian aspirations.

Most historians now agree that the rigidities introduced by colonial policy decisively shaped, even distorted, modernity in India. This approach offers a corrective to what was too easily described during the colonial era as the 'blessings of British rule', namely the pacification and unification of the country, legal codification, the use of the English language, public works, and a range of social reforms. Critics of European modernity, among them Britons as well as Indians, even at the time saw the dark side of these changes, among them racism, militarism, and the economic exploitation that was part of the colonial relationship. What coloured those 'blessings' above all was a mentality that discounted Indian abilities and aspirations to self-rule, an attitude the historian Francis Hutchins termed the British 'illusion of permanence'. British rule in the 1830s and 1840s had been founded in Enlightenment notions of universal human destiny and expectations of progress, although, to be sure, even then an authoritarian strain was evident in evangelical and utilitarian reform. But by the 1870s the mood was different, above all in an explicitly authoritarian attitude among colonial officials. They were, for the most part, convinced of an essential difference between British and Indian that justified indefinite control of political power by a 'superior race'.

DALHOUSIE: THE UNIFICATION OF SOVEREIGNTY AND NETWORKS OF COMMUNICATION

At the end of the nineteenth century, John Beames recalled his early days as a wet-behind-the-ears civil servant in the late 1850s:

But Adams [his superior] had told me as we walked along that the work was so heavy he could hardly get through it, so I suppose he had no time for teaching beginners. My stock of available knowledge consisted of Persian and Hindustani... Of law and procedure I, of course, knew nothing... I said as if by instinct, 'Call up the first case'... Both these people spoke Panjabi, of which I could not understand one word, but the sarishtadar [chief clerk] translated it into Hindustani as they spoke, so I got on wonderfully well... I next began to learn Panjabi, for which purpose I engaged an old Sikh priest... Like most Panjabis of those days the good Bhai was a kindly, simple-hearted old child... They are a fine, manly race... There was no law in the Panjab in those days. Our instructions were to decide all cases by the light of common sense and our own sense of what was just and right...
[Elmslie, his Haileybury classmate and now colleague] and I were in the saddle by five in the morning and worked on horseback for two or three hours, riding about inspecting police-stations, roads and bridges and public building under construction, tree-planting, ferry-boats, settling disputes about land and property between villagers, and such like business. Or we would walk with our horses led behind us through the narrow lanes of the ancient town, accompanied by a crowd of police officers, overseers, and others giving orders for sanitary improvements, repairing roadways and drains, opening out new streets, deciding disputes and a variety of similar matters... Hard work as usual filled up the day.

Beames's recollections illustrate pervasive attitudes that shaped British rule in India from mid-century. A paternalist self-assurance, with a commitment to material progress and hard work, were as true of James Ramsey, marquis of Dalhousie, who served as governor-general from 1848 to 1856, as they were of the young John Beames in the Punjab countryside. Dalhousie arrived in Calcutta with a two-pronged vision that set in place significant elements of the framework of what turned out to be the remaining century of British rule. Dalhousie was committed, in the first place, to unifying British sovereignty both territorially and legally. And he was convinced of the importance of new networks for communications and transportation in India as well.

Dalhousie's arrival coincided with the Second Sikh War in 1848–9, which brought about the annexation of the rich, strategically critical, province of Punjab, and so extended the Raj up to the Khyber Pass. Dalhousie also reluctantly, but effectively, prosecuted a military campaign in Burma in 1852, responding primarily to commercial interests, and annexed lower Burma (as a prelude to Dufferin's final annexation of the whole country in 1886). Under Dalhousie's direction, the administration of the Punjab was entrusted to a coterie of like-minded officers under the strong direction of two brothers, John and Henry Lawrence. In the tension between rule through codification and system on the one hand, and enlightened despotism on the other, the 'Punjab School' tilted to the latter. Driven by confidence in the 'man on the spot' and a belief that they alone could bring order and prosperity to a contented peasant society, Punjab officials enjoyed a wider range of discretionary authority than was true elsewhere. The power entrusted to Beames, at age twenty-three with no experience, is telling. The Jallianwalla Bagh massacre of 1919, evidence of the tragic side of such official power, is telling as well.

A second dimension of the push to unification was an effort to curtail princely sovereignty. The modern state could not tolerate, from Dalhousie's perspective, the nested sovereignties and fluid boundaries characteristic of earlier regimes. At the very beginning of his administration, Dalhousie wrote, 'I cannot conceive it possible for any one to dispute the policy of taking advantage of every just opportunity which presents itself for consolidating the territories which already belong to us, by taking possession of States that may lapse in the midst of them.' In so doing Dalhousie hoped to gain, he continued, security, financial resources, and the promotion of the 'best interests' of those thus ruled. By 'lapse' Dalhousie meant the death of a ruler without a natural heir in any state created by or dependent on the British. He thus chose not to recognize the widespread custom of adoption to secure an heir. By this device, Dalhousie secured possession of seven states in seven years, in central India, Bengal, Rajasthan, and the Punjab hills. Among them were Satara and Nagpur, both significant Maratha states, and Jhansi, whose woman ruler would soon take to battle. Dalhousie also used the justification of 'lapse' to terminate pensioners' subsidies, among them that of Nana Sahib, the adopted son of the Maratha peshwa of Poona. Dalhousie's final annexation was that of Awadh (known under the British as Oudh) in 1856, richest state of all, not by the 'doctrine of lapse' but on the grounds of persistent misgovernment. He even sought (checked by demurrals at home) an end to the titular rule of the Mughal at Delhi, as whose servant, legally, the Company continued to operate. Whatever 'feudal' façades were to be created in the aftermath of 1857, the British were to insist upon the principle of unified sovereignty, including a monopoly of military force, held firmly in British hands.

The second prong of Dalhousie's vision was his embrace of the new technologies that were transforming the West. They were to prove essential to the cultural, political, and economic integration that would emerge both within India and between the colony and the metropole. The railway, the telegraph, the postal service, and improved steam transport together transformed the imperial system of the late nineteenth century. The potential of the railway for India was clear to Dalhousie, who had worked with Gladstone at the Board of Trade in London during the railway fever of the 1840s. He was convinced that the railway would be the key to the spread of British power and civilization. Above all, it would extend the market for British manufactured goods, and secure access to raw materials such as cotton needed by British industry. The railway would also serve military interests. As Dalhousie wrote to the Court of Directors in 1853, it would allow the concentration of military strength as needed 'in as many days as it would now require months to effect'. Dalhousie oversaw the beginning of railway construction, starting with two lines from Howrah (Calcutta) and Bombay. To reach his first posting, in 1859 Beames rode the train from Howrah to the end of the line, only a little over 100 miles at that point; most of the rest of the way he perched on top of his luggage on a horse cart, taking some twenty-four days in all to reach the Punjab. By the end of the century this was a journey of under three days by train.

The building of the railway offers a window into the working of the British Raj in India at mid-century. The project was funded by British capital, raised for multiple companies who operated in different locations. The Company, and after 1858 the Crown, guaranteed the investors, virtually all British, a 5 per cent (or in some cases 4.5 per cent) return, absolutely risk free. This was the first transfer of British capital to India, for the Company, and earlier private investors, had financed their activities through funds raised in India itself. The railway profits, which could have financed India's own development, went instead into the pockets of investors in Britain. The building of the railways, furthermore, provided a market for British goods. Rails, locomotives, rolling stock, and other manufactured goods and even, at times, British coal and Baltic firs creosoted in England, were exported to India. This meant that a major public works project that might have served as a 'leading sector' to generate 'multiplier effects' for India's industrialization had no such effect. The layout of the track supported the extractive and market focus of British economic interests, linking the hinterland to the colonial port cities and those cities to each other. The 'classic' shape of a colonial economy, with market crops like cotton, jute, and tea exported in return for cloth and other manufactured goods, was only possible because of the railway.

The railway was, on the whole, well built at reasonable cost. One limit to its effectiveness came from the disjunctures resulting from track of differing width, with both metre gauge, built as a cost-saving device to accommodate lighter use, and broad gauge. But the cost of moving goods fell dramatically; the value of the railway in providing famine relief was critical; and countless individual Indians enthusiastically took to train travel, for example to visit family members and pilgrimage sites, all results only barely imagined when the first track was laid.

Although limited in its impact to specific areas, Dalhousie energetically encouraged extension of irrigation canal systems. His years in office saw the completion of approximately 500 miles of the Ganges Canal, a source of irrigation water for a vast hinterland, with all the disruptions, both positive and negative, that such a resource brought. In the long term, the most obvious negative consequence was to be salinization of vast areas as the excess water drew salt on to the surface of the irrigated land. The telegraph linking the chief centres of India was completed during Dalhousie's term. Comprising some 4,500 miles of line, it made possible rapid transmission of information on politics, security, trade, and industry, as well as the personal messages of ever more individuals. The cable linking Britain and India (its development spurred by the revolt of 1857) was laid in 1865, a year before the link between Britain and the US. Indeed, the first attempt at an underwater cable at all was probably one stretched across the Hooghly in Calcutta in 1839.

In 1854, moreover, a government postal service was established, bringing to India the same 'penny post' introduced in Britain some fifteen years earlier. Mail could now be sent, the cost to the sender, any distance within the country, at the same low cost. This facility served not only individuals, including people in remote villages (who often depended on literate letter writers and readers clustered outside office buildings), but was indispensable to the communications and fundraising of the voluntary societies, organizations, and publishers emerging in this period. Some indication of the variety of mail delivery services utilitized even in twentieth-century India can be seen in the set of stamps shown in plate 4.1 issued on the occasion of the coronation of the King-Emperor George VI. The mid-century years also saw significant improvements in steamship design with the faster, safer iron hull and the high-pressure engine. Although there is no clear turning point in the introduction of these innovations, one landmark date was in fact 1848, when the Peninsular and Oriental bought the first iron steamers for their Indian Ocean routes. In the 1830s an exchange of letters between Britain and India could take two years; by 1870, with the opening of the Suez Canal, a letter could reach Bombay in only one month.

Dalhousie thus set in place the legal underpinnings of a unified state, with defined boundaries, and individual subjects on whom that state would impinge. He had substantially advanced, moreover, the technological infrastructure that would transform the everyday experience of both state and subjects in myriad ways. The revolt of 1857 seemed to call the very presence of the British into question. What it did not do was reverse these changes.

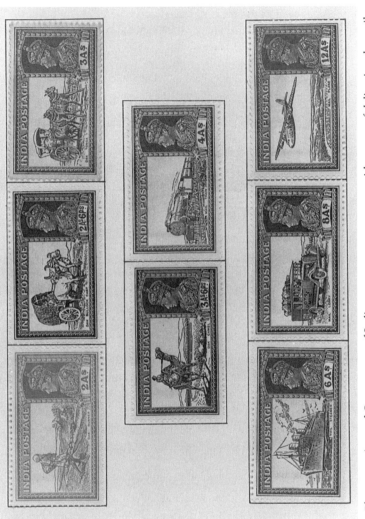

Plate 4.1 A set of Government of India postage stamps, 1937, with scenes of delivering the mail. The four lower value stamps, labelled 'dak', show human and animal carriers, while the higher values depict mechanized 'mail' transport.

1857, CROWN RULE, AND THE AFTERMATH OF REVOLT

Throughout 1857, and into 1858, northern India was caught up in a rebellion that shook the Raj to its foundations. As the unrest subsided, an Indian official serving the Raj, Sayyid Ahmad Khan (1817–98), sought its causes:

I believe that there was but one primary cause of the rebellion, the others being merely incidental and arising out of it. Nor is this opinion either imaginary or conjectural. It is borne out by the views entertained by wise men of past ages: and all writers on the principles of Government agree in it ... It has been universally allowed that the admittance of the people to a share in the Government under which they live, is necessary to its efficiency, prosperity, and permanence. [Moreover,] [t]he Natives of India, without perhaps a single exception, blame the Government for having deprived them of their position and dignity and for keeping them *down* ... What! Have not [the British ICS officers'] pride and arrogance led them to consider the Natives of India as undeserving the name of human beings ... What! Was not the Government aware that Natives of the very highest rank trembled before its officers, and were in daily fear of suffering the greatest insults and indignities at their hands?

Raised in a family close to the Mughal court, by 1857 Sayyid Ahmad had spent twenty years in Company service. He was conspicuously loyal during the uprising, evacuating the European residents from the town of Bijnor, where he was serving, and even taking charge of the district on behalf of the British for some time. His essay, written in Urdu and subsequently translated into English, evoked great interest on the part of the British. He correctly insisted, contrary to British wishful thinking at the time and after, that the Revolt was not merely a mutiny on the part of disgruntled soldiers. It was, rather, he argued, a response to multiple grievances. Among these were British cultural policies, the severity of revenue assessments, and the degradation of landed and princely elites, notably the recently exiled nawab of Oudh. Above all, Sayyid Ahmad faulted the insolence and contempt for Indians evinced by the British, and insisted on the importance of a consultative process that would include them. If it was this key issue of British and Indian relations that precipitated the revolt, it was, ironically, to be in the very intensification of racial distance that the uprising would find its most enduring legacy.

The revolt began with a military mutiny, borne of festering grievances among the soldiers of the Bengal Army. There had been discontent at assignments to Burma, resulting in the 1856 General Services Enlistment Act requiring sepoys to serve wherever posted. There was dissatisfaction with pay and the limited opportunities for promotion. The annexation of Oudh unsettled the high-caste sepoys from that province, who formed one-third of the Bengal Army. And, as the proximate cause, there was the new Lee Enfield rifle, whose use required soldiers to bite off the end of each cartridge – widely reputed to have been greased with pig or cow fat, polluting to both Hindus and Muslims. When sepoys refused to load the rifles, they were publicly humiliated, even expelled from service. On 10 May 1857, in the hot Indian summer, the sepoys posted to Meerut in north India, who had seen eighty-five of their colleagues led off in chains the previous day, rose up in the night, massacred the English residents of the town, and marched on Delhi. There they sought to raise anew the standard of the Mughals under the aged emperor Bahadur Shah, whose name ('the valiant') belied his real achievement – as a poet. As sepoys elsewhere flocked to the rebel cause, the British lost control over a broad swathe of north India, from Bihar to Punjab, as well as pockets of central India. In some areas it took them a year to fight their way back.

Within weeks, taking advantage of the space opened up by the dispossession of the British, disaffected groups in the countryside, landlords and peasants, princes and merchants, each, for their own reasons, took up arms. There was never any coherent strategy for ousting the British from India. The Mughal emperor, the Queen-Regent of Oudh, the Maratha chief Nana Sahib, and others claimed leadership of the uprising. To be sure, a religious rhetoric was often adduced to justify opposition to what was seen as a corrupt moral order, but there was no unifying ideology of any kind. Some rebels, indeed, sought no more than their own immediate advantage, and so settled down, like Devi Singh, the 'King of Fourteen Villages' in Mathura, to plunder the wealthy and prosecute quarrels with their neighbours. 'Loyalty' and 'rebellion' were always fluid concepts. The participation of one magnate in the uprising often encouraged his rivals to throw in their lot with the British in hopes of gaining an advantage should the tide of war turn.

It is important to differentiate between events in the recently annexed province of Oudh and those in the older more settled districts. The revolt in Oudh, as Rudrangshu Mukherjee has forcibly argued, took on the shape of a 'popular' movement, with all classes fighting on behalf of their sepoy kinsmen and deposed king Wajid Ali Shah. Most prominent among the revolt's supporters were the taluqdari landlords, aggrieved by the loss of villages during the 1856 land settlement, who, from the security of their mud forts, rallied their followers, kinsmen, and tenants. Although many among the peasantry had won title to their lands in 1856, to the dismay of the British they threw in their lot with their former landlords – to have boldly confronted them would have been foolhardy – and together they marched on Lucknow to join the seige of the tiny British garrison there.

The revolt in the adjacent North-Western Provinces was of a different sort. There, the response to the uprising was shaped by the experience of fifty years of British rule. As the historian Eric Stokes demonstrated in a series of careful local studies, those rural magnates who had profited from the commercial opportunities brought by the British tended to be loyal, even smothering the sparks of unrest among their tenantry, while those who had lost wealth and consequence often took advantage of the engulfing anarchy to join the revolt. Where tightly knit cultivating communities, especially Jat and Rajput brotherhoods, held the land, they often rose without magnate leadership to protest the heavy differential revenue assessments laid upon them. The revolt in the North-Western Provinces can thus usefully be described as a 'post-pacification' revolt, where long festering but diffuse grievances erupted, by contrast with the 'primary resistance' of the Oudh revolt, where a recently deposed royal family provided leadership. In this way it is possible to link 1857 to uprisings elsewhere that took place in the early stages of colonialism, and to distinguish it from the modern, nationalist protests that followed.

Many remained loyal throughout, and in so doing secured the ultimate defeat of the revolt. Not least among these were soldiers from the recently conquered Punjab, who felt no affection for the Bengal sepoys who had defeated them. In addition, neither the Bombay Army nor the Madras Army rebelled, so insuring that southern

India remained quiet. Among the most visibly 'loyal' were those, like the Bengali intelligentsia, who had had Western education, together with Bengal's zamindars, tied to the Raj by the Permanent Settlement that secured their prosperity. India's ruling princes too, in contrast to those among them who had lost their thrones, almost invariably calculated that their interests were best served by supporting their British rulers. Even among the rebellious Oudh landlords, many hedged their bets by sending emissaries to the British camp, and so in the end survived with their lands intact.

The revolt in the three northern cities of Delhi, Lucknow, and Cawnpore (Kanpur), and the Maratha-led uprising in central India, drew the greatest attention on the part of the British. Troops were massed in Bengal to move up the Ganges, with Benares and Allahabad retaken within little more than a month after the initial outbreak. On the march British troops, and even civilians, unleashed indiscriminate terror, ravaging the countryside and killing randomly. This racial savagery continued throughout the fighting, despite the governor-general Lord Canning's effort – earning him the sobriquet 'Clemency Canning' – to curb such behaviour in the so-called Clemency Proclamation of July 1857. In the most extreme example of Indian violence, the garrison at Cawnpore surrendered to Nana Sahib who, despite his promise of safe passage, rained fire on them as they attempted to board boats; British women and children were also massacred, some 400 in all. Delhi was retaken in September thanks to reinforcements from Punjab. Bahadur Shah was exiled to Burma, the royal sons murdered. In Lucknow Sir Henry Lawrence, the new chief commissioner, secured both Europeans and Indians in the well-fortified Residency before succumbing himself in July. The garrison and their dependents were not liberated until November, and the province itself was not fully recovered until well into 1858. The Maratha leaders, the Rani of Jhansi, who was to fall in battle, Nana Sahib, and Tantia Topi, prolonged the fighting in central India, although with the fall of Gwalior in June 1858 the fighting was effectively over.

On 2 August 1858 the British Parliament passed the Government of India Act, transferring all the authority of the East India Company to the British Crown. The Company had come to seem a mere shell, its trade monopoly long since gone, even the patronage power of appointment (of which John Beames was one of the final examples) revoked in favour of competitive examination in 1853. Shared Company and parliamentary control at home, and nominal subservience to the Mughal in India, appeared as outdated anomalies profoundly implicated in the revolt's heavy cost in British lives and revenue.

The pattern of twenty-year charter reviews now gave way to regular parliamentary scrutiny of Indian affairs. A cabinet member, the Secretary of State for India, advised by a Council of India, was given authority for the government of India. In India supreme authority was vested in the Viceroy, the title assumed by Governor-General Canning when Queen Victoria proclaimed these changes to the 'Princes, Chiefs, and People of India' in November 1858. The viceroy was to be advised by an executive council (originally set up with exclusively British membership in 1853), now expanded for legislative purposes by up to twelve new members, of whom half were to be 'non-official', that is, not employed by the colonial government. That small step began the progress of political arithmetic common throughout the Empire as over time the number and level of councils; the number of members of each body; the proportion of official and non-official, appointed and elected, members; the opportunity to advise on subjects presented or initiate discussion or even have legislative power in some or another sphere, all lurched forward in fits and starts. This constitutional reform was a response to the pleas of Indians like Sayyid Ahmad for consultation, bringing in this case the voice of carefully selected Indian aristocrats to the viceroy's ear. The change to Crown rule also ushered in an elaboration of bureaucratic and technical structures, a change taking place in Britain as well in this period, from police and sanitation to forestry and finance. This last was a subject of immediate attention given the financial costs of the revolt.

Victoria's proclamation further responded to presumed causes of the revolt. In a reversal of Dalhousie's policy, the proclamation guaranteed the princes their titles. No longer were limits put on adoptions: princely 'rights, dignity and honour', as well as control over their territory, would be respected. This meant that about one-third of the people of India were, until the end of the Raj, to remain under the 'indirect rule' of some 500 princes. The government would endeavour, moreover, to promote 'the peaceful industry of India, to promote works of public utility and improvement' in the expectation of the 'social advancement that can only be secured by eternal peace and good government'. And the proclamation explicitly repudiated any 'desire to impose our convictions on any of our subjects' and enjoined 'all those who may be in authority under us' to abstain from interference with Indian religious belief or worship. 'Due regard' would be paid to 'the ancient rights, usages, and customs of India'.

The theory of rule enunciated in this proclamation contained an implicit contradiction. On the one hand, there was the language of a feudal order that stressed the role of hereditary leaders. By so doing the British sought, for the most part successfully, to make of India's princes and large landlords a conservative bulwark for the Raj. On the other hand, the proclamation also expressed a conception of politics associated with British parliamentarism and the liberal political theory of such men as Macaulay. Its inauguration inevitably would undermine the hereditary rulers. In 1859, Lord Canning undertook a series of tours, holding courts, called 'darbars' in superficial emulation of Mughal practice, to recognize not only loyal princes but also landlords, among them the large landlords of Oudh, now invested with honours and titles as aristocratic bulwarks of British rule. In Bernard Cohn's words, already incipient was 'a social order . . . established with the British Crown seen as the centre of authority, and capable of ordering into a single hierarchy all its subjects'. No reversal of Dalhousie's policy, Canning's incorporation of the princes marked the completion of his predecessor's search for a unified sovereignty over India.

A corollary of this new order was a centrally important assumption about the very nature of India: that it was a land made up of a congeries of peoples diverse in their culture, society, and religion, and that the foreign ruler alone peacefully contained that diversity. This assumption was most evident in the military policy that emerged after the revolt. At its heart was a pseudoscientific theory of 'martial races', by which particular categories of people were singled out for military service on presumed grounds of innate physical and moral characteristics which made them the best fighters. These groups comprised above all the loyal Punjabis – Sikhs, Jats, Rajputs, and, in due course, Punjabi Muslims – along with Pathans and Nepali Gurkhas. By 1875, half of the native army was Punjabi, with far-reaching implications for the history of that region. Regiments were now, moreover, ethnically mixed in the expectation that cultural difference would prevent collusion. Only British officers were placed in control of artillery. The proportion of British personnel was substantially increased. At the time of the revolt, British soldiers comprised barely one-sixth of the Bengal Army; now the proportion of British to Indian was targeted to be one to two or three.

The uprising intensified British racism. Suspect sepoys were blown from cannons. Delhi was sacked and monuments wantonly destroyed or appropriated to military use. Coupled with the trial for treason and exile of the emperor, the previous regime and its rulers were effectively 'desacralized'. Muslims were initially prime targets of British distrust as 'fanatics' who would try to restore Muslim rule. Within two decades, however, Muslim aristocrats came to be seen, like the princes, as pillars of loyalty, a role not uncommon in authoritarian settings where 'minority' loyalties are cultivated. In this transition Sayyid Ahmad Khan played a central role. In Aligarh in 1875 he established the Anglo-Muhammadan College, an English-style institution that cultivated gentlemanly skills and conservative politics intended to produce the kind of people appropriate to the loyal consultative regime he had advocated in 1858.

The British never conceived of the rebel leaders as honourable opponents, but rather lumped them all together as 'disloyal', and treated them accordingly. Nana Sahib's murder of British women in particular stirred a fierce hatred. This act left an enduring legacy in Victorian paintings and mass market novels filled with lurid accounts of rape and mutilation that threatened the 'purity' of British womanhood. John Beames, travelling to Punjab two years after the revolt, wrote of his passage through Cawnpore:

The fading daylight lasted long enough to enable me to take a hurried glance at the ghastly place; a desolate, sandy waste it then was. The dreadful well [where the bodies of women and children were thrown] was marked by a few boards, the walls of the roofless houses were riddled with shot and tottering; ruins, flies, evil odours and general misery and distress were all one could see . . . [a] horrible place.

Plate 4.2   Memorial well, Cawnpore, photograph 1903.

The well was soon commemorated by a marble memorial, shown in plate 4.2, designed by the Italian sculptor Marochetti. This photograph, part of a set of stereoscopic views, was meant to remind the British at home of the sacrifices they had endured in India. Cawnpore was a major centre on what emerged in the late nineteenth century as a kind of 'mutiny tour' for British travellers, who travelled from the Lucknow residency, the one place in the Empire where the Union Jack after the revolt was never lowered; to Cawnpore; to the Delhi ridge. The 'mutiny' offered the British a cleansing sense of heroism and self-assertion, a confirmation of moral superiority and the right to rule. Henry Lawrence's tomb in Lucknow, in accordance with his wish, identified him only as one 'who tried to do his duty'.

THE STRUCTURING OF THE RAJ: SECURITY, SANITATION,
ORDERING SOCIETY

The fear and racism evident at the time of the revolt took visible shape in the decades following, as the British created separately demarcated spaces for themselves. In cities these areas were labelled 'civil lines', with associated 'cantonments' for the military. In mountainous regions they established 'hill stations' that served as summer refuges not only for individuals but for the colonial governments. The building of these areas went hand in hand with an increased number both of settled families, their presence made easier by improved communications of the day, and of British military personnel. These spaces communicated racial difference as well as the threatening disorder and 'putrid air' understood to characterize the old cities. They represented, moreover, as part of lived experience, an association of British culture with the 'modern' in contrast to the older sections of the city seen as 'medieval' or 'traditional' – always the necessary foil to modernity. The 'colonial city' was predicated on such duality.

This concern with the disorder of old urban centres confronted Europeans at home at the same time, where it was stimulated by rapid urban growth, breakdown in sanitation, and alarming epidemics. Disease was attributed to the 'miasmic' theory of atmospheric impurities produced by decomposing matter and damp in overcrowded settlements. The theory was specious; the remedies – drainage, removal of refuse, a safe water supply, and, ideally, less crowding – were sound. The 1842 Chadwick Report had spoken of the lower classes – in a language that would have served equally well for the old cities of India – as a population 'short-lived, improvident, reckless, and intemperate, and with habitual avidity for sensual gratification'. In India, however, such judgments were mapped on to 'race'; and whatever official action was taken privileged European interests. The earliest sanitary concerns focused on the military, whose poor health was clear from the fact that in 1857 the death rate among British soldiers, as in the Crimea a few years before, was higher from disease than from battle.

A useful illustrative example of the way health and safety drove urban design can be found in the city of Allahabad, capital of the North-Western Provinces (known as the United Provinces (UP) after its unification with Oudh in 1902). Allahabad was always one of the great pilgrimage centres of the subcontinent, celebrated for its location at the confluence of the Ganges and Jamuna rivers, as well as the mythical Saraswati. The city's population varied during the course of the year, swelling in the winter month of Magh when pilgrims converged, and even more so every twelfth year, when holy men and throngs of believers flooded into the city from all over the country. The British feared itinerancy in all forms so that Allahabad seemed a particularly dangerous site for health and safety. The Mughals, recognizing the strategic location of the city, had had a presence there, and Akbar's fort, overlooking the river, remained. The old city had two or three main streets, but from these a labyrinth – as the British saw it – of narrow streets led off to distinct neighbourhoods, some still with gates fastened at night. The houses, mixed together with shops and warehouses, looked inwards and were densely built. There were several markets for grain and fodder. With the establishment of sanitary commissions and municipal councils, efforts were made to improve sanitation in the old city, but resources were disproportionately directed towards its European areas.

The rail line, in Allahabad as elsewhere, was seen as the main strategic defence for the European population, and so, as it cut through the city, formed a barrier between the civil lines to the north, laid out in 1858 immediately after the revolt, and the old city. In the civil lines area, existing villages were removed and replaced with paved streets and covered gutters, set out on a grid pattern and lined with newly planted avenues of trees. Population density was very low, with European residents living in 'bungalows', a distinctive colonial housing style meant to provide ventilation and protection from heat, in plots that could be as large as 10 acres (plate 4.3). The civil lines contained the buildings around which European colonial society revolved: government offices, the club, polo field, church, and shops. Social life – visiting, balls, certain sporting events, social drinking – were modelled on upper-class behaviour and were exclusively European.

The military cantonment, again laid out on a regular grid, was directly north of the old city and, to further reassure the European

Plate 4.3   Bungalow, Civil Lines, Allahabad, photograph 1866. Note the encircling verandah, where visitors were entertained and business transacted with Indians, and the bungalow's placement in the centre of a large secluded compound with curving entry drive.

civilian population, immediately adjacent to their residential area. Two settlements buffered the margin between European and 'native'. One was a settlement of Eurasians or 'Anglo-Indians', near the railway station. Anglo-Indians, a living denial of racial difference, were often seen as an embarrassment to the British, but a niche for them was found in railway employment in the expectation that their loyalty could be relied upon. The second colony was that of Bengalis, whose numbers grew in 'up-country' cities and towns as their literacy gave them an advantage in government employment. It was, of course, impossible to tie a tight cordon around European society, and servants, traders, and others both entered and lived in the areas intended for Europeans, and many sites – from government offices, to educational institutions and asylums, commercial places, and the frequent Masonic temple – were places of defined and limited interaction between races.

Beames was posted in 1869 to a small coastal town in Orissa. His description of 'our small society' suggests the make-up of the European population after the revolt. He was the magistrate and collector (the chief official of the district). In addition, the English population included 'a Joint Magistrate, a doctor, a Superintendent of police, an Engineer, a Harbour-master, and an Inspector of Telegraphs . . . also two police Assistants and a Deputy Magistrate'. Other Europeans were missionaries, in this case not English but American Free Will Baptists and a Belgian Jesuit. The latter lived, as Beames saw it, like a native fakir, and he raised money to build – to the admiration of officers of the Public Works Department – a church, school and dormitories, and a nunnery. That Beames mentions officials employed in medicine, police, engineering, telegraphs, and public works points to the expanded technical bureaucracies that emerged in the late nineteenth century. Although he draws vivid vignettes of the colourful Europeans he encountered in his career, Indians appear but rarely.

Beyond their separate urban residential areas, the British sought further distance from what they saw as a disease-ridden land by escape to the Himalayas in the north and Nilgiri Hills in the south, a pattern begun even before the revolt for convalescent troops. In 1865, John Lawrence as viceroy made Simla, some 50 miles into the hills and 900 miles from Calcutta, the regular summer capital of British India. Missionaries and princes in turn created what were known as 'hill stations' of their own in such places as Mussoorie and Kodaikanal, Murree and Mount Abu. Women and children often came to the hills for several months while men perforce stayed behind, visiting whenever they could. Fear of specific disease was in the end less important than a range of anxieties about the dangers of life in India, among them fear of degeneration brought on by too long residence in a debilitating land. The hills were meant to reproduce England. Lord Lytton, arriving as viceroy in a rainy Ootacamund in the 1870s rhapsodized over 'such beautiful *English* rain, such delicious *English* mud'. In the hills, in place of the civil station of the plains, were English cottages and country houses, gardens of English flowers, English fruits and vegetables, a bandstand, and a mall, its buildings often half-timbered to reproduce an English country town. There were many hill schools, but European children, whenever funds permitted, were sent home for schooling. The colonial British themselves returned 'home' to retire.

As the British distanced themselves from Indian society, they sought, ever most insistently after the upheaval of 1857, to order and control it. Among the institutions forged in these post-revolt decades were the Survey of India, founded in 1878, and the Census of India, first taken in 1871. After the revolt, new regulations required that newspapers and journals be registered (see the number in the upper left-hand corner of plate 4.4), and copies of books and pamphlets had to be transmitted to the government. The systematized Hindu and Muslim civil law codes, rigidifying and simplifying practice, were finally enacted into law in the 1860s. People who moved had always been suspect; now pastoral and other itinerants were associated with 'criminality', and defined as 'criminal tribes'. Late nineteenth-century British ideology elaborated an array of pseudoscientific 'racial' differences, not only those of the criminal tribes, but also the notion of 'feminine' races (above all the feeble and spineless but clever Bengalis), as well as the 'martial' races discussed above. India was in sum a 'living museum' where ancient customs, habits, and practices endured up to the present.

The most important identity for Victorian anthropologists of India was 'caste', taken as a concrete, measurable 'thing' that could be fitted into a hierarchy able to be ascertained and quantified in reports and surveys. The increasing systematization of caste was closely connected with the use of photography, whose 'exact' images complemented the search for scientific precision. 'Characteristic specimens' could exemplify precise measures of physiognomy, dress, and manners. The first major compilation of such photographs was *The Peoples of India*, published by the Government of India in 1868 in eight volumes. The picture of the Banjaras, for example, nomadic herdsmen and traders, shown in plate 4.5, was accompanied by a description of them as having 'a reputation for perfect honesty', but they were later relegated to the status of 'criminal tribe', a reminder of the fantasy that passed for exactitude. The caste 'system' is thus one of the countless parameters of life in India that is a product of modern change, as are other aspects of social life, not least the powerful position of princes, magnates, and gentry, bolstered

Plate 4.4 *The Lytton Gazette*, Urdu newspaper.

by administrative action then, and now too often identified as 'traditional'.

Such measuring and categorizing of peoples, places, and cultures in order to make the country's inhabitants 'legible' to its rulers

Plate 4.5 'Brinjara and Wife', from J. Forbes Watson and J. W. Kaye,
The Peoples of India, 1868.

was a worldwide phenomenon, a product of late nineteenth-century modernism, not a function solely of colonialism. Nevertheless, in a colonial setting like that of India limitations on an administrative ordering of society, above all from an independent 'public' and from representative institutions of government, were exceptionally weak. The quest for security after 1857 only strengthened this authoritarian imperative.

'NATURAL LEADERS' AND THE LANGUAGES OF MODERNITY

Keshab Chandra Sen (1839–84) was the third generation of an elite Bengali family associated with the commercial and cultural milieu intertwined with colonial rule. His grandfather had been a friend of Ram Mohan Roy. Sen himself had studied at Hindu College, and he spent his short life in exuberant (and in the end divisive) proselytizing for the Brahmo Samaj. A gifted orator with fluent English, he travelled throughout India, nurturing branches of the Samaj in areas as far as Bombay, above all in places where Bengalis in government service and trade had settled. In 1877, shortly after Victoria had assumed the title of Empress of India, he gave a speech in Calcutta:

Loyalty shuns an impersonal abstraction . . . We are right then if our loyalty means not only respect for law and the Parliament, but personal attachment to Victoria, Queen of England and Empress of India [Applause] . . . Do you not recognize the finger of special providence in the progress of nations? Assuredly the record of British rule in India is not a chapter of profane history, but of ecclesiastical history [Cheers] . . . All Europe seems to be turning her attention in these days toward Indian antiquities, to gather the priceless treasures which lie buried in the literature of Vedism and Buddhism. Thus while we learn modern science from England, England learns ancient wisdom from India.

It is perhaps not surprising that Keshab Chandra was one of many figures of like background who spoke, as he did here, in what was for the most part the language of British liberal politics. But the key words in the short paragraph quoted – 'loyalty', 'law and the Parliament', 'personal attachment', 'the progress of nations', 'modern science', and 'ancient wisdom from India', were, in the quarter-century from about 1860 to 1885, to be utilized by other, less Westernized, individuals as well. Such concepts structured discourse in a variety of settings, including the newly important municipalities, and in a variety of genres, not only in English but in the vernaculars, where newspapers and journals, public speaking, debates, petitions, tracts (like Saiyyid Ahmad Khan's on the revolt), and novels were shaping many Indian languages into their modern forms.

The event that stimulated Sen's lecture, the announcement of a new title for Victoria, took place twenty years after the great revolt. Making Victoria 'Empress' was intended to create a new bond between Britain and her chief imperial possession, one that Disraeli as Conservative prime minister imagined would be not only politically useful domestically, but welcome to what was presumed to be the Indian temperament. The title was announced at an 'Imperial Assemblage' orchestrated by the viceroy Lord Lytton (1876–80). It was held in the old Mughal capital of Delhi to underline the imperial motif, and was intended above all to recognize and solidify bonds with princes, rural magnates, and urban notables. They were now regarded, in a phrase that became common at this time, as the 'natural leaders' of their people, able to command the loyalty of those below them, and themselves loyal to the British. For the assemblage, Lytton fabricated a medieval vision of the viceroy as monarch surrounded by his loyal vassals, even presenting the princes with banners emblazoned with European-style coats of arms tailored to each recipient. Later assemblies (in 1903 and 1911) were called durbars in imitation of Mughal usage, and were organized in what was thought to be a more 'Indian' mode that emphasized Indian difference from Europe, not similarity. As Lytton proclaimed in 1877, such gatherings were meant to make visible an empire 'multitudinous in its traditions, as well as in its inhabitants, almost infinite in the variety of races which populate it, and of the creeds which have shaped their character'. At such events the language of 'feudalism' almost wholly pushed aside that of 'liberalism'.

In addition to such assemblies, the British sought to bind India's 'natural' leaders to themselves through the granting of awards, titles, and various privileges, as well as through inclusion in the municipal governments that became increasingly important in this period. In addition to the princes, these favoured 'leaders' now included urban notables. Municipal boards were dominated by government administrators, with the district collector as president, but they also began now to include nominated 'non-official' members. There were two incentives to enhance the role of municipal boards. One was the increased financial pressure produced by the revolt, together with inflation resulting from shifts in the value of silver (the standard for the rupee), and enhanced military and other expenses. There was, for example, pressure both from the military and from manufacturing interests in England to spend more money on irrigation, roads, and railways. There were also demands for strictly municipal needs, among them sanitation ('conservancy'), new police charges (put in place by an act of 1861 that created a public police force), and a whole range of improvements common to Victorian cities and deemed appropriate for the empire as well – schools, parks, markets, fountains, clock towers and the like. These costs were now to be assumed locally, by such means as octrois, income and property taxes, and licence fees, with the police 'as the first charge on all such funds'.

Secondly, liberal imperialists wished to make the municipalities into schools for political education. There were many ironies in this position. First, of course, the 'liberal' view inevitably emphasized the 'backwardness' of Indians, who in this evolutionary understanding of human history needed education to overcome, above all, their lack of the unity England was taken to enjoy. Secondly, it juxtaposed the two inherently contradictory languages of politics implicit in the 1858 Proclamation. Municipal councillors were to be the voice of 'public opinion'. This concept had emerged in Europe and was understood to be the assembled opinion of those unfettered by obligations to hereditary elites or communities, in principle a voice autonomous of the state. This voice, in a second weighty phrase, would express 'the public good'. But the councillors were, of course, chosen precisely because they were loyal to the state, not autonomous. Moreover, they won recognition as the presumed representatives of specific communities. For such councillors, to enter the municipal board was to make a public statement of deference to the government. It meant in large measure supporting the goals of British civil servants, and it typically entailed furthering civic needs through personal philanthropy. It also, typically, provided opportunities that would benefit particular groups. The municipal boards were the kernel that would later flower into legislative assemblies and other representative bodies embodying the same contradictions.

Indians were expected to develop universal loyalties and were criticized for parochialism, yet in colonial institutions they were given incentives to identify with particular religions and castes.

When elections to the municipalities were introduced under Lord Ripon (viceroy 1880–4), the nominated seats, as Narayani Gupta has shown, were typically used to 'balance' the representation of communities, above all that of Hindus and Muslims. Despite the extremely diverse elements that comprised them, these two groups were now lumped together and conceptualized as 'majority' and 'minority'. Articles in Delhi's long-running *Lytton Gazette*, a bi-weekly Urdu journal of news and essays named in honour of the viceroy (see plate 4.4), often reflected the inherent tension in colonial ideology. In one issue the paper celebrated the 1877 assemblage, with its emphasis on 'feudal' loyalties, yet identified its purpose, using the language of modern civic consciousness, as *rifaah-i`am*, 'the public good'. It claimed as well to speak for 'public opinion', `awam ki khahish`.

Another way of contesting the British emphasis on the differences among Indians was to insist upon the participation of Indians throughout the country in a larger Hindu culture. Vasudha Dalmia's study of the literary figure Harischandra, for instance, shows him constructing an incipient Hindu 'public'. In an early editorial in English entitled 'Public Opinion in India' (1872), he wrote:

Unless there be a general desire to shake off the trammels of superstition, the regeneration of India cannot be aimed at. Let the religion of India be the religion that can govern the millions of her subjects without any let or hindrance. Let the dark shadows of sectarianism be vanished by the rays of Western civilization . . . and let the unity be the basis of that grand superstructure of national improvement which every civilised nation has in its possession.

Harischandra thus used modern concepts of progress and 'national improvement' to infuse an old term, that of 'Hinduism', with new roles and new meaning.

THE ENGLISH-EDUCATED

The assemblage of 1877 was the first public recognition by the colonial government of the role of journalists, and the invitations to the event provided an occasion for journalists from across the country to meet. These men, including many who published vernacular-language papers, were among what was emerging as a critical mass of English-educated elites throughout India. They were in part the product of Sir Charles Wood's Education Dispatch of 1854, further evidence of Dalhousie's modernizing impulse that had also set in place the first three Indian universities, one in each presidency capital, inaugurated in the fateful year of 1857. That act stimulated the foundation of private colleges and had also provided for grants-in-aid that encouraged the foundation of schools.

Three points must be made about this early cohort of the English-educated. First, they were representatives of the old professional elites in each region. This fact would have long-term consequences throughout the country as non-elites, for example non-Brahmans in the west and south, saw the disproportionate opportunities afforded to the tiny percentage of Brahmans who had secured a Western education. Secondly, English created linked men from across India who shared no other spoken language. This was a necessary element in the forging of political ties and movements, as English, the cosmopolitan language, would prove to be in colonies throughout the world. A large proportion of the English-educated, moreover, would have experience of regions outside their own in the course of careers in government, law, or journalism, a further force for unity. Third, the English-educated, better understanding the new idiom of liberal politics, would soon provide competition to the 'traditional' notables. Once electoral politics were introduced, they were the ones who most frequently stood for election.

Not surprisingly, they often used the values of liberal discourse to contest a range of British policies. In Lytton, for example, they found much to criticize, including the very holding of the assemblage in a time of widespread famine. Lytton had, moreover, introduced legislation severely curtailing the vernacular press in the very year after the journalists had gathered. A year later he abolished the revenue tariff to secure unimpeded entry into the Indian market for Lancashire cotton textiles. His forward policy in Afghanistan was unpopular both in India and at home, and so contributed to Disraeli's downfall in the British elections of 1880. The outcome was the appointment of the Marquis of Ripon as viceroy by the liberal Gladstone.

The Western-educated class welcomed Ripon who, in keeping with liberal sentiments, repealed the Vernacular Press Act of 1878 and, in his resolution of 1882, established a framework for local self-government with partially elected boards. Ripon's term, however, was blighted by the controversial Ilbert Bill, advanced by the law member of his cabinet to check the anomaly that while Indian members of the civil service could, as judges, try cases involving Europeans in presidency capitals, they could not do so in the countryside. The resulting outcry against the measure among Europeans in India showed the depth of British racial sentiment and offered unintended lessons in the power of 'public' opinion. The issue was resolved by allowing Europeans brought to trial to request a jury of whom half were Europeans; this new policy was now to prevail in the presidency capitals as well. Beames articulated the larger issues at stake when he wrote, describing his own opposition to the Ilbert Bill, 'It is intensely distasteful and humiliating to all Europeans... it will tend seriously to impair the prestige of British rule in India... it conceals the elements of a revolution which may ere long prove the ruin of the country.' The ceiling on Indian advancement in the governance of their own country had again been made clear. Despite the promises confirmed in the Queen's Proclamation of a non-discriminatory recruitment to the civil service, admission to the ICS became harder, not easier, in these years. Examinations were held only in London, not in India, and the maximum age for taking the examination was lowered in 1878 to nineteen. Under such restrictions no more than a tiny handful of Indians were even able to compete.

THE VERNACULARS

The second half of the nineteenth century was a significant period in defining and shaping the modern Indian languages like Bengali, Hindi, Urdu, Marathi, and Tamil. Missionaries, Orientalists, government officials, and, above all, the speakers of these languages transformed them through new uses. Influential vernacular publications were often the product of the new middle class where the 'feudal' and the 'liberal' coexisted, each changed by the other. Many of the quotations in this chapter are examples of the new genres that shaped the vernaculars: the treatise (Sayyid Ahmad Khan), the public address (Keshab Chandra Sen), newspapers (*Lytton Gazette*, Harischandra), and, below, the novel (Nazir Ahmad). The vernacular novel in particular became a vehicle for exploring such issues as new class tensions, the choices of the educated classes, and the socialization of girls within the family. Nazir Ahmad's popular novels in Urdu, the official language through the Gangetic valley and Punjab, dismiss the old princely order in favour of the new culture of British India:

'Prosperityville' was a rather small north Indian princely state. Although it could yield some 500 or 600 thousand rupees a year in revenue, an in-experienced youth sat on the throne. Sycophant counsellors and dissolute favourites seized the occasion . . . With a camaraderie like the Freemasons, they all knew about 'Prosperityville'. So Kalim ('the Talker') kept hearing about it too, and longed for 'Prosperityville' the way a pious mystic longs for heaven. So, doing double time, he arrived at 'Prosperityville' . . . On the way, he began composing a poem in praise of the prince hoping it would win him favour . . . But a few days earlier the situation had turned upside down. News of the maladministration of the state had reached the [British] Resident, and he had . . . deprived the prince of all his power and entrusted the affairs of the state to a 'committee' composed of a few loyal oldtimers, with Nawwab Wide-awake K. B., the chief of Pleasant Town, as chairman.

This early novel, *The Repentance of Nasuh*, written in 1874, was one of the most popular books ever written in Urdu. Nazir Ahmad (1830–1912) came of a well-born Delhi family, and was educated in the Arabic and Persian tradition, but also in modern learning at Delhi College before the revolt. He worked for the Department of Public Instruction, translated the 1861 Indian penal code into Urdu, and rose to be a deputy collector in the North-Western Provinces. He seems to have taken as his model for this book Daniel Defoe's *The Family Instructor, Part I*. The book opens with Nasuh, stricken by epidemic, dreaming that he is being called before the Last Judgment, a court which, not surprising given his background, looks like the British cutchery, but, the author notes in contrast, remarkable for the absence of personal interventions and pleading. When Nasuh is spared from illness, he sets out to reform his life and the life of his family. The novel communicates that only in the context of British India is true religion – i.e. modern, reformed religion – possible. Nasuh's sons Alim and Salim find employment in British government service and in the newly 'scientific' field of indigenous medicine; Kalim, the third son, however, is a metaphor for the old life of

Plate 4.6 *A Husband Slaying his Westernized Wife*, Kalighat painting, Calcutta, *c.* 1880, by Nirbaran Chandra Ghosh. Note the purse and umbrella that are meant to signify Western ways.

aristocratic court culture, the world of poetry and pigeons. In the quote above, Kalim leaves British India for what will be an untimely end in a princely state. Only the British resident and the wise 'natural leader', an aristocrat recognized by the British title 'Khan Bahadur', offer any hope of honest government and right values. A second of Nazir Ahmad's successful novels, which takes up the issue of the reformed woman, is discussed in chapter 5 below.

When Wajid `Ali Shah, the last nawab of Oudh, left for exile he is said to have sung a poem in which he took on the persona of the bride leaving her natal house for the home of her husband – 'Oh father, my home is becoming foreign to me.' The poem appropriated a genre of Indic folk poetry, the bride's lament, to the sophisticated structures of Urdu verse. To the cognoscenti of Urdu, it was not only an empirical song of exile, but also the song of the soul ever seeking the Ultimate. Nazir Ahmad has Nasuh burn Kalim's library of poetry, for such verse was as 'decadent' to him as it was to British critics of the nawab. The new vernacular texts, then, were not untouched receptacles of 'traditions', but were critical in creating and communicating the new. In novels like Nazir Ahmad's and in the Bengali writings of Bankim Chandra and Rabindranath Tagore, discussed in the chapter that follows, the values of a new middle class were being reshaped, internalized, and rendered local, not 'foreign'. The vernaculars were, furthermore, critical in creating new publics, at once modern and, as part of that modernity, linked by language to identities that were both regional and religious.

The Kalighat paintings of this period, like the one from about 1880 reproduced as plate 4.6, are, however, a reminder that changes were sometimes seen with humour and satire. These paintings, inspired by English paintings and watercolours of the late eighteenth century, took shape at a Calcutta pilgrimage site, where there existed a market for vibrant, elegantly modelled figures of the gods. By the late nineteenth century these paintings had begun to satirize the new middle class, symbolized here by markers of the modern outer world, the handbag and umbrella. In this case they also mocked the new gender relations of the Indian bourgeoisie. As with the new vernacular literature, such paintings further indicate how Western models were transformed as they were incorporated into an Indian context.

5

Civil society, colonial constraints, 1885–1919

The decades that spanned the turn of the twentieth century marked the apogee of the British imperial system, whose institutional framework had been set after 1857. At the same time, these decades were marked by a rich profusion and elaboration of voluntary organizations; a surge in publication of newspapers, pamphlets and posters; and the writing of fiction and poetry as well as political, philosophical, and historical non-fiction. With this activity, a new level of public life emerged, ranging from meetings and processions to politicized street theatre, riots, and terrorism. The vernacular languages, patronized by the government, took new shape as they were used for new purposes, and they became more sharply distinguished by the development of standardized norms. The new social solidarities forged by these activities, the institutional experience they provided, and the redefinitions of cultural values they embodied were all formative for the remainder of the colonial era, and beyond.

Yet it was only to be in the 1920s that the British recognized the hollowness of their long-held assumption that self-rule for India would be pushed off into an indefinite future. The viceroys who presided over the final decades of the century – Dufferin (1884–8), Lansdowne (1888–94), and Elgin (1894–9) – were, in Percival Spear's phrase, 'imperial handymen' all. Unshaken by the fissures revealed in the Ilbert Bill controversy and imagining a future like the past, they endeavoured to secure the economic interests of empire, establish secure borders, and provide a government of limited responsibilities. Curzon, as viceroy from 1899 to 1905, by his driven brilliance in seeking those very same ends, precipitated a public furor that energized the till then quiescent Indian National Congress, which was to lead India to independence. The succeeding decade was one of public action and government response, including, under Minto as viceroy (1906–10), a modest expansion of Indian participation in governing councils. Through the First World War, however, the Indian role in governing was limited to providing manpower almost exclusively at the lower levels of government, to service in the army, and to consultation on the part of loyal elites. This continuity with the earlier colonial period sat uneasily on a society experiencing change in every dimension of social, political, and cultural life.

A GLOBAL IMPERIAL SYSTEM

Dadabhai Naoroji (1825–1917), later to be remembered as the 'Grand Old Man of Indian Nationalism', a graduate of Elphinstone College, Bombay, was a mathematician who for half a century argued for the rights of Indians as British subjects. He was the first Indian elected to the British House of Commons, where from 1892 to 1895 he set out India's interests with his characteristic clarity of vision and elegant prose. He expressed with eloquence the values of several generations of elite Indians, as they engaged in a shared language with their colonial rulers over the question of their country's governance, as the following excerpt shows:

In this Memorandum I desire to submit for the kind and generous consideration of His Lordship the Secretary of State for India, that from the same cause of the deplorable drain [of economic wealth from India to England], besides the material exhaustion of India, the moral loss to her is no less sad and lamentable . . . All [the Europeans] effectually do is to eat the substance of India, material and moral, while living there, and when they go, they carry away all they have acquired . . . The thousands [of Indians] that are being sent out by the universities every year find themselves in a most anomalous position. There is no place for them in their motherland . . . What must be the inevitable consequence? . . . despotism and destruction . . . or destroying hand and power.

Naoroji judged British claims of 'govern[ing] India for India's good' nothing more than 'purest romance'. In 'the drain', he identified a critical component of an economic system that fundamentally secured Britain's economic position in the larger world. Each year, funds were transferred to England to liquidate the old Company shares; to pay off debt on secure and profitable capital investments (notably those for the railways); and to provide funds for the operation of the India Office, the purchase of stores for India, and for pensions. That burden, Naoroji argued, contributed to the often oppressive taxation demanded of the peasantry. It was dramatically enhanced when the value of silver (the standard on which the rupee was based) declined against the pound sterling, in which payments had to be made, at the end of the century. Defenders claimed these transfers were fair value for services provided; others, including a handful of British critics, saw it as taking away resources that otherwise would have been used for internal investment within India. The favourable balance of trade with India, to which the revenue flow contributed, enabled Britain to meet its trading deficit with other nations. The issue was a persistent goad to Indian political aspirations.

By 1913 India had become the chief export market for British goods, including textiles, iron and steel goods, machinery, and other products reflecting Britain's industrial strength. India, in return, supplied Britain with critically needed raw materials including cotton, indigo, jute, rice, oil seeds, and tea. By the end of the nineteenth century, India's commercial agriculture tied it to markets and forces beyond its borders in ways that affected the economy as a whole and the lives of millions dependent on it. Far from moving away from an agricultural towards an industrial base in these decades, in all probability the proportion of those dependent on agriculture grew slightly to over 70 per cent. The vicissitudes of dependence on export crops is nowhere clearer than in the case of cotton, whose exports to Britain increased in value almost three times between the mid-1850s and the mid-1870s (because of the American Civil War), only to drop to about a ninth of that level by 1900. Indigo virtually disappeared as an export crop by World War One, as synthetic dyes replaced it, while jute and tea emerged as major cash crops in those same years. The latter were dominated by British business interests, who benefited from favourable arrangements for land and capital. Commercial agriculture, though it provided income to peasant growers, in many areas drove out the sturdy, low-quality grains that had provided staple

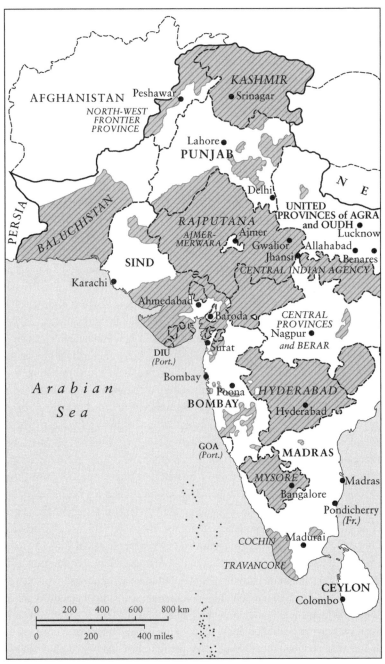

AFGHANISTAN

NORTH-WEST
FRONTIER
PROVINCE

KASHMIR

Peshawar

Srinagar

Lahore

PUNJAB

PERSIA

BALUCHISTAN

Delhi

N
E

UNITED
PROVINCES of AGRA
and OUDH

Lucknow

SIND

RAJPUTANA
AJMER-
MERWARA

Ajmer

Gwalior

Jhansi

Allahabad

Benares

CENTRAL INDIAN AGENCY

Karachi

Ahmedabad

Baroda

CENTRAL
PROVINCES

Nagpur

and BERAR

DIU
(Port.)

Surat

Bombay

Poona

BOMBAY

HYDERABAD

Hyderabad

*Arabian
Sea*

GOA
(Port.)

MADRAS

MYSORE

Bangalore

Madras

Pondicherry
(Fr.)

COCHIN

Madurai

TRAVANCORE

CEYLON

Colombo

0   200   400   600   800 km

0   200   400 miles

Map 3   The British Indian Empire, *c.* 1900.

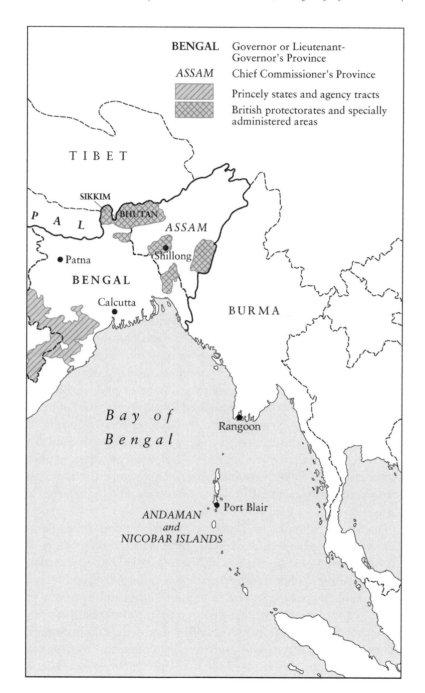

BENGAL   Governor or Lieutenant-
Governor's Province

ASSAM   Chief Commissioner's Province

Princely states and agency tracts

British protectorates and specially
administered areas

TIBET

SIKKIM

BHUTAN

ASSAM

● Patna

Shillong

BENGAL

Calcutta

BURMA

*Bay of
Bengal*

Rangoon

Port Blair

*ANDAMAN
and
NICOBAR ISLANDS*

foods, and in so doing made peasants dependent on food grown else-where. One success story was the large-scale development of 'canal colonies' in the Punjab, where assured water on newly cultivated soils made possible a vast expansion in the output of wheat, sugar cane, and maize. Commercial cropping characterized an increasing proportion of production for internal consumption as well as the export market.

Commercial agriculture was made possible by the transportation infrastructure provided above all by the railway. By the end of the century India possessed the fifth longest railway system in the world. The pre-eminence of British export interests was clear in a layout that focused on routes to the ports and a rate structure that disad-vantaged inland transport. Bombay's neo-Gothic Victoria Terminus, completed in 1887, a popular subject for painting and photogra-phy (plate 5.1), was architecturally similar to railway terminals in London and Melbourne, and so made visible India's central posi-tion in the larger imperial system. The rail lines also, however, made possible the beginnings of Indian-owned industry. This was associ-ated in particular with two families, the Tatas and the Birlas, both based in areas of India where British business interests were less de-veloped than in the east. In 1877 the Parsi Jamsetji Tata founded the Empress Mills in Nagpur, followed by other mills in Bombay and Ahmedabad, and in 1907 he added Tata Iron and Steel in Bihar. The Birlas, of the Marwari clan originating in Rajasthan but ac-tive by the end of the century in trading across the north, similarly moved into textiles and steel during World War One. Both families succeeded by developing products that did not compete with British manufactures, for example in low-count cotton and in yarn for the China market.

The value of India to Britain extended beyond these direct economic advantages. India served at the turn of the century as the centre itself of many aspects of Britain's global imperial system. One of the most important was as a source of indentured labour for Britain's tropical colonies. Indenture had begun as a way to replace black labour in the cane fields after the abolition of slavery in the late 1830s, but it increased with the growing British demand for sugar. Confronted with land fragmentation and agricultural uncertainty from the 1870s, Indian villagers proved increasingly

Plate 5.1   Great Indian Peninsular Railway Terminus (Victoria
Terminus), Bombay. The structure joins an exuberant Venetian Gothic
design with Indian ornament and detail by the Indian students of
Lockwood Kipling, the poet's father.

willing to accept a period of overseas labour. Indentured Indians
went to Jamaica and Trinidad, British Guiana, Mauritius and Fiji,
Natal, and Malaya. Others went to Burma, Ceylon, and along the
East African coast of Kenya, Zanzibar, and Uganda. Plate 5.2 shows
Indian workers in the 1890s building the railway that made possible
development of the new British possessions in East Africa. Between
1911 and 1920, however, indenture was brought to an end in each of
these areas as voices were raised in protest at its continuance. Among
these were the viceroy Lord Hardinge (1911–16) as well as nationalists, including Madan Mohan Malaviya (1861–1946), the founder

Plate 5.2 Indian workers on the Uganda railway, c. 1898. Sikhs and other Punjabis were recruited for the construction of this railway line in Britain's new East African colony.

of Banaras Hindu University (1916). Nationalists found in this overseas migration both a heightened image of imperial exploitation that brought shame to India, and, at the same time, as Indians took up residence around the globe, a vision of 'Greater India', a nation beyond its borders, that recalled images of ancient glory. Engagement with the plight of diaspora Indians, as we shall see with Gandhi, was a critical stimulus to Indian nationalism.

The Indian Army, in similar fashion, was deployed, at the cost of the Indian tax-payer, to protect trade routes and secure imperial interests from China, most notably during the 1900 Boxer rebellion, to East and South Africa, and to the Middle East. British officials themselves, along with Indian police and secretarial staff, especially technical personnel in such areas as forestry and public works, whose skills were honed in India, found employment in other areas of the Empire. Indigenous Indian trading groups also expanded their operations into British colonies around the Indian Ocean. Among these were the Muslim Isma`ili community who followed the Aga Khan, with trading networks particularly in East Africa, and the Madras-based Nattukottai Chettiars, whose control of credit was indispensable to the development of commercial agriculture in British Burma and Ceylon. There were, finally, benefits to Britain from its possession of India that defy measurement, such as its role in enhancing national pride and, in generating that shared emotion, masking Britain's own hierarchies of gender and class. In 1900 Curzon said, 'We could lose all our [white settlement] dominions and still survive, but if we lost India, our sun would sink to its setting.'

NEW CLASSES, NEW COLLABORATORS

In Kipling's literary masterpiece *Kim* (1901), India is populated by a congeries of distinct, often colourful groups, each with its presumably unchanging characteristics. The central figure, Kim, is an orphaned child depicted as a chameleon, able to put on any identity, but who must, as the novel unfolds, emerge to be the Briton he truly is. As Kim travels the Grand Trunk Road, moreover, he enacts the British colonial fantasy of the omniscient observer, alone able to

Plate 5.3 Rudyard Kipling stories published in cheap editions as part of the Indian Railway Library series.

know all who inhabit the land:

They met a troop of long-haired, strong-scented Sansis with baskets of lizards and other unclean food on their backs . . . moving at a quick, furtive jog-trot, and all other castes gave them ample room; for the Sansi is deep pollution. Behind them, walking wide and stiffly across the strong shadows, the memory of his leg-irons still on him, strode one newly released from the jail; his full stomach and shiny skin to prove that the Government fed its prisoners better than most honest men could feed themselves. Kim knew that walk well, and made broad jest of it as they passed. Then an Akali, a wild-eyed, wild haired Sikh devotee in the blue-checked clothes of his faith, with polished-steel quoits glistening on the cone of his tall blue turban, stalked past, returning from a visit to one of the independent Sikh States, where he had been singing the ancient glories of the Khalsa to College-trained princelings in top-boots and white-cord breeches. Kim was careful not to irritate that man; for the Akali's temper is short and his arm quick.

In Kim's India, and that of predominant British opinion, the land is peopled by the humble folk of the road, and those who work with the British to sustain the Raj. The latter are represented in the novel by two of Kim's protectors. One is Muslim, the tough horse trader of the frontier, Mahbub Ali; the other is Hindu, the educated Bengali Hurree Babu. Such English-language novels, readily available in inexpensive editions (plate 5.3), set in place, for the British and elite Indians alike, an enduring view of Indian society.

Opportunities for Indians to participate in the governing structure of empire were strongly shaped by the theories that had emerged after the 1857 revolt of an unchanging social order comprised of a mosaic of separate communities, whose 'natural leaders' spoke for them. Although by the final decades of the century some British and some Indians espoused the liberal theory of societies comprised of individuals, free to make choices and, ultimately, free to vote, the 'durbar' view of Indian governance, with 'consultation' as its primary strategy, prevailed. The princes and landed classes continued in place as a conservative bulwark of power, while new colleges were established to socialize heirs into a set of pseudo-aristocratic colonial values, from polo and tiger shooting to lavish entertainments.

Agricultural society continued to be marked by fragmentation of plots, hierarchies of tenants and, nurtured by a high and often inflexible cash revenue demand, classes of moneylenders whose advances secured high rates of return. Agricultural practices that appear from a distant perspective economically wasteful were at the time rational for the owners of land, for a secure rental income was more valuable than the uncertain returns from investing in new seeds or machinery. The tenancy laws passed in this period, furthermore, froze the pattern of smallholdings and worked on the whole to strengthen classes of rich peasants like the Bengal jotedars, who came to see their interests tied to the stability of the landed regime. Most importantly, the Punjab Land Alienation Act of 1901 prohibited the sale of agricultural property to 'non-agricultural' classes. The aim of the act was to protect debt-ridden tenants, but in fact it simultaneously strengthened landlord and Muslim interests against the urban Hindu trading and moneylending classes who had increasingly been investing in land. The Act is a reminder that the regime's theoretical commitment to *laissez-faire* and rational economics could easily be overridden by political considerations.

The Muslim leadership was cultivated as a potential bulwark of stability. British fears of an imagined threat from worldwide Muslim conspiracy in the later nineteenth century could presumably be countered by encouraging India's sturdy monotheists and former rulers. The Sikhs, too, in their case nowhere more than in the army, were encouraged to distinguish themselves from the larger society and see their interests best served by outspoken loyalty. Such loyalties could not be taken for granted. Muslims in the United Provinces, for example, were stunned by the decision in 1900 to make Hindi equal with Urdu as the language of the lower courts and administration, a decision explicitly understood by Sir Antony MacDonnell, the lieutenant governor, as a way to balance Hindus against Muslims. Urdu, with a larger admixture of Persian loan words and written in an Indo-Persian script, and Hindi, drawing more on Sanskrit loan words and written in the Sanskrit-based Devanagari script, were linguistically the same language. Although Urdu had been the lingua franca across north India since the eighteenth century and was known generally by the urban-educated, Bharatendu Harischandra of Banaras and others espoused the cause of Hindi as part of their cultural and nationalist activities. On the whole, however, Muslims, like minorities in many colonial areas, saw their interests best served by identification with the existing regime.

The Western-educated class represented an increasingly audible voice in public life. The formally educated were few in number, barely 3 per cent of the total population in 1921 (in a ratio of roughly 5 males for every 1 female), with resources continuing to be focused at the university level. The English-educated comprised less than 1 per cent of the population. For those with university education, as Naoroji's words above recalled, government employment was a major goal. With strong structural constraints operating against Indian participation in the modern business sector, government service, along with the modern professions of law, medicine, education, and journalism, were the preferred routes to employment. Still, despite their mastery of the English language, by the mid-1880s no more than a dozen Indians had succeeded in passing the examinations and entering the Indian Civil Service.

As their numbers grew, educated Indians were increasingly accommodated within the governing structure. The Municipals Council Act of 1882 had given responsibility for such areas as education, sanitation, and public health to local bodies, along with the right to levy – and be blamed for – local taxes. The Indian Councils Act of 1892 introduced the principle of limited election for legislative councils and opened up the provincial councils to discussion of the annual budget. One of the foremost early nationalists, Gopal Krishna Gokhale (1866–1915), humane and articulate professor of English literature, mathematics, and political economy, served, for example, on the Poona Municipal Council, the Bombay Legislative Council, and, finally, the Imperial Legislative Council (1902–15). There he spoke critically and creatively in the interests of good government – including the need for universal education, greater representation of Indians in government, and increased employment opportunities.

The limited public role open to educated Indians at the end of the century was a subject not only for political discussion but for literary comment. Notable were the biting Urdu couplets of the sub-judge Akbar Ilahahbadi (1846–1921) and the ironic Bengali writing of the deputy magistrate Bankim Chandra Chattopadhyay (1838–94). Their own experience of restricted professional opportunity, evident in their relatively low civil service positions, fuelled a mockery of sycophantic loyalism. Akbar, for instance, reminded the loyalist Muslims of Aligarh of the few crumbs held out to them by their rulers:

> If fifty to a hundred get good posts, what of it?
> No nation yet was ever based – on fifty to a hundred.

Like the Kalighat artist in plate 4.6, Akbar also questioned the cost of Westernized trappings to Indian social and moral life.

In 1885 some seventy English-educated Indians came together in Bombay to form the Indian National Congress. The focus of the longest-lived nationalist movement in the modern colonial world, the Congress was the model for nationalist movements elsewhere, above all in South Africa, and a force for stability in the early years of Indian independence. The catalyst for the foundation of the Congress was a retired British ICS officer, Allen Octavian Hume (1829–1912), who had spoken for nationalist interests during the furor over the Ilbert Bill. The key to the Congress's initial cohesion, however, were the shared interests and common experiences of a co-hort of Indians from across the country, many of whom had shared formative experiences in London while studying for the bar or the civil service. They were participants in the rapidly expanding communications network of their day in India: the railroads, mentioned above; the postal system, with a three- to fourfold increase in use by the end of the century; and newspapers, whose number in English approximately doubled to about 300 between 1885 and 1905, while the number of vernacular newspapers increased even more.

Many Congress members had participated earlier in more local organizations that sought to represent the interests of Indians to the government. Among these were the early Triplicane Literary Society (1868) and the later Mahajana Sabha (1894) of Madras. Surendranath Banerjea (1848–1926), a brilliant student who struggled to enter the ICS and was then dismissed on petty grounds, founded the Indian Association in Calcutta in 1876. Other comparable groups included the Allahabad People's Association (1885), the Indian Association of Lahore (1877), the Poona Sarvajanik Sabha (1867) and the Deccan Education Society (1884), the National Mohammedan Association (in Calcutta), and the Bombay Presidency Association (1885).

The organizers of the Congress made explicit efforts to draw Muslims into their meetings. Hume, for instance, invited Badr al-din Tyabji (1844–1906), a Bombay lawyer and leader of the Sunni Bohras, to preside over the Madras congress of 1887. Most Muslim leaders, however, like Sayyid Ahmad Khan, Sayyid Amir`Ali (1849–1928), the brilliant lawyer and religious thinker of Calcutta, and others, argued that Congress could not be the spokesman for the interests of the two distinct 'communities' that comprised India. Sayyid Ahmad repeated over and over that 'India is like a bride which has got two beautiful and lustrous eyes – Hindus and Mussalmans.' Representative government on the British pattern, he insisted, was ill-suited to such a land. Even Tyabji, despite his commitment to a common platform with non-Muslims in the Congress, nevertheless shared the pervasive opinion that identity rested in one's religious community.

The Congress vision, by contrast, insisted that interests of self, caste, and community be subordinated to the 'public good' and the Indian nation. In its early years, the Congress, like Sayyid Ahmad Khan, did not question the continuance of British rule. Its members largely represented the professions of law, journalism, and teaching; a small number were businessmen; some few were landowners and merchants. They wanted more Indian participation in the legislative councils, and a genuine opening of the ICS to Indians by raising the age limit for the competitive examinations and holding them simultaneously in India. They advocated less expenditure on the army, an outlay that could reach half of all Indian revenues in these years and a timely concern in the 1880s with troops deployed to Burma. The early Congress operated through petitions and addresses as a 'loyal opposition'. In its first twenty years, Congress gave little evidence of what would be its future importance. As an organization, eschewing all matters of religious controversy and social reform, it deliberately stood aside from the intense and widespread social cultural reform activities of the day.

VOLUNTARY ASSOCIATIONS, RELIGIOUS MOVEMENTS, AND TRADITIONALIST INSTITUTIONS

An extraordinary efflorescence of new associations, together with such activities as a new popular theatre and the revival of martial traditions, changed public life, as well as the everyday life of many segments of the population, during these years. These new activities must be seen against a backdrop of far-reaching social change. New markets, new communications, and new networks linked individuals to larger arenas, and brought former strangers into new settings that stimulated new styles of social interaction. Although the urban share of India's population remained fairly constant in this period, with no more than 10 per cent living in settlements larger than 5,000, individual cities, not least the three presidency capitals, grew substantially, and a town could virtually disappear or, should it, for example, fall on a new railway line, double in size. Such changes as the spread of commercial agriculture brought prosperity to some in the rural areas as well. For all, new socioreligious organizations provided routes to community, to status, and to new conceptions of self-worth.

The decennial census, begun in 1871, provided an important stimulus for the recognition of group status. Many castes, or emerging castes, as they aspired to higher status in the census listings, formed associations, typically called *sabhas*. Members would agree to a range of socially preferred behaviour, often focused on such issues as control of womenfolk (by greater seclusion or modest dress); in some cases they adopted vegetarianism or abstinence from liquor; sometimes they sought Brahman ritual services. A small but striking example of this process illustrates not only the extent of cultural change but also how relatively obscure and humble groups could take advantage of the census enumeration. In this case a group in Punjab called Mahtons sought to be recorded in the census of 1911 as high-status Rajputs based on their history and behaviour. The district census officer, on the basis of an earlier government survey, identified them as former hunters and scavengers turned agriculturalists, but noted that the Rajput Pratnik Sabha of the Punjab and Kashmir recognized them as Rajputs. If this recognition were accepted in the census, the group would then be eligible for army recruitment and a Punjab government zamindari scholarship. Such negotiations over status spread across India during these decades. 'Castes' increasingly established relations over larger areas and were more formalized in their membership and identity. To the extent that they published journals, submitted petitions, and opted for a formal organization, they were part of the widespread movement towards modern organizational forms characteristic of this period.

The 'caste system', far from unchanging, in this period took on new forms. Complementing this 'grass-roots' cultural change was the patronage of religious and cultural life provided by the princes, landlords, and business and trading classes. The role played by these classes is critical to an understanding of cultural and social life in India's colonial society. Prosperous families and individuals gained legitimacy in the eyes of both the rulers and the common people through their patronage of performances, rituals, and cultural or religious organizations. For princes and landlords, patronage, and the accompanying ritual observances, offered an opportunity to build a base of support when they were largely excluded from formal politics. The Rajas of Banaras, for example, like the Maharajas of Mysore, by their patronage of the splendid annual re-enactment of the Ramayana epic, made its symbols central to the community identity of the merchant and banking elites who contributed to its support, as well as of the specialists, performers, and viewers who participated. Princes and landlords were also key to the encouragement of art music and indigenous medicine, above all by establishing modern schools that supported, for example, both ayurveda, a medical system based in the Sanskritic tradition, and yunani tibb, the Graeco-Arabic medical tradition, the latter of which had virtually disappeared outside India by the twentieth century.

The organizations formed during these years encompassed a variety of activities. Indeed, it is difficult to categorize them in any simple way as 'religious', 'social', or 'political' in their goals. As the example of caste sabhas makes plain, a given organization might at once seek to modify practices of worship and ritual; foster changed styles of dress, diet, and sociality among its members; and call on government bodies for certain kinds of action. Whatever the focus, associations found the opportunities afforded by the inexpensive lithographic presses indispensable. A photograph from Amritsar, for example, shows Sikh booksellers marketing pamphlets and reproductions of sacred subjects to the ever-growing number of pilgrims visiting this sacred city (plate 5.4).

Many reform societies, like the Brahmo Samaj founded in Bengal a half-century earlier, adopted an ethic of individual and collective 'improvement'. In 1887, Mahadev Govind Ranade

Plate 5.4   Booksellers, Amritsar, 1908.

(1842–1901), the founder of the Poona Sarvajanik Sabha, who ultimately rose to be a judge of the Bombay High Court, founded
the National Social Conference, intended to bring together reform societies from across the country. In the south, Virasalingam
(1848–1919) founded the Rajahmundri Social Reform Association in 1887, while a Hindu Social Reform Association was established in Madras in 1892. In 1905, Ranade's younger colleague and disciple G. K. Gokhale founded the Servants of India
Society, modelled at once on the organization of the Jesuits
and of Hindu ascetics, to create a core of dedicated activists
to foster education and the uplift of girls and the depressed
classes.

By the final decades of the century, non-Brahmans in Maharashtra and Madras were beginning to press the issue of their participation in public life in the face of Brahman domination. An urban-educated member of the *mali* caste (traditionally gardeners by occupation), Jyotiba Phule (1827–90) founded the Satyashodhak Samaj (1873) to challenge both the ritual and the worldly dominance of the Brahman; support for him came primarily from the prosperous Maratha castes, backed by the Maharaja of Kolhapur. In Madras, non-Brahmans sought more educational and employment opportunities, given the fact that although Brahmans were only some 3 per cent of the Presidency's population, they comprised 70 per cent of its university graduates. As in Maharashtra, the dominant voice in the protest was that of prospering middle-caste groups, including Vellalas, Reddis, Kammas, and Nairs. Following the lead of mid-century British scholars of the Dravidian languages, these non-Brahmans, in the emerging linear narrative of India's history, identified themselves as the original 'Dravidian' inhabitants of the south, in contrast to the 'Aryan' Brahmans who had supposedly entered from the north and set themselves up as a superior ruling elite. Although focusing on different texts and symbols, these movements were similar to other movements of caste mobility in their new forms of organization, their claims on social status, and their behavioural reform.

One of the most successful socioreligious reform movements was the Arya Samaj, founded in 1875 by Swami Dayanand Saraswati (1824–83). His teaching proved most persuasive not in his native Gujarat but in the north, in the United Provinces and Punjab. The Samaj shared the larger reform agenda related to women – opposition to child marriage, support of widow remarriage, and a commitment to girls' education; it allowed foreign travel; and it favoured minimizing ascriptive status based on birth. Identifying the Vedas as the central religious text, the product of a golden age that set enduring standards of behaviour and worship, the Arya Samaj opposed both idolatry and polytheism. Defiantly Hindu, Aryas participated in public debates with members of other faiths, and, imagining that Hindus would would disappear in the face of Muslim and Christian conversion, they created new rituals to convert, or purify (by a ceremony called *shuddhi*), non-Hindus and members of lower castes. Core support came from upwardly mobile trading and professional castes (like the Khatri, Arora, and Aggarwal), who found in the reformist Arya Samaj a basis for community as well as a way to be both Hindu and 'modern' in an age of rapid change.

Radical opposition to caste, idols, and temples limited the influence of the Arya Samaj. In Bengal, many even among the Westernized class were inspired by the saintly, charismatic teaching of Shri Ramakrishna (1836–86), who did not challenge so much of conventional belief. Ramakrishna exemplified passionate devotion to God in multiple manifestations – the Divine Mother, Sita, Rama, Krishna, Muhammad, even Jesus – and inspired his followers in turn to find the divine within themselves. Ramakrishna's disciple, Narendranath Datta (1863–1902), himself a member of the Kayasth caste that had enthusiastically embraced Western education, gave up plans to study law, followed Ramakrishna, and became famous as Swami Vivekananda. He defended caste and the worship of idols, and contributed to a renewed pride in the Hindu religion by his appearance at the World Parliament of Religions at Chicago in 1893. In his subsequent preaching in America and Europe, he presented Vedantic Hinduism as a universal faith, the synthesis of all religions. Though himself a product of a Westernized colonial milieu, Vivekananda gained fame as a spokesman for the 'Spiritual East'. Inspired by the commitment to the poor of Christian missionaries, he endeavoured to evoke among Westernized Indians a sense of service to society through the social and religious activities of the Ramakrishna Mission (1897), an example that later was to inspire Gandhi.

The Ramakrishna Mission, like the reform societies, represented novel Western-inspired institutional forms, but older institutions also underwent change in this period. Learned Brahmans, backed by indigenous political authorities, had long used dharma sabhas to establish norms for moral behaviour. Now, however, although the sabhas still claimed to uphold the *sanatana* (constancy) of Sanskritic tradition, they included the new intelligentsia, were organized on British models, and more evidently accommodated change through fresh interpretations of issues related to cultural and social identity. It would therefore be incorrect to conclude that only such visibly new groups as the Brahmos and Aryas represented modern change within Hinduism. In similar fashion, alongside the better-known modernizers like Sayyid Ahmad Khan and Amir`Ali, a range of other Muslim movements, especially those associated with Deoband, the Ahl-i Sunnat wa'l-Jama`at of Maulana Ahmad Riza Khan Barelvi (1856–1918), and the Ahl-i Hadith, took up reform. All religious thinkers, even those operating in the vernacular and utilizing historic institutions, of necessity responded to the challenge of Christianity and British culture as well as to the changed social and political context of the day. Whether Hindu or Muslim, those who claimed to speak for 'tradition' did so in the context of interaction with what was 'modern'. Rather than call such thinkers 'traditional', they can best be called 'traditionalist', to signal their greater continuity with the received tradition (in terms of texts, ritual, social life, and institutions) and yet, simultaneously, their self-conscious participation in the new world around them.

Bharatendu Harischandra was an influential example of a Hindu traditionalist in northern India. He typified the refusal of those engaged with Western learning and institutions to leave authority over religious matters to traditionally educated Brahmans; and he energetically used new media, especially publications – reports, editorials and letters to the editor in his journals, literary works, and translations – to shape public opinion. In so doing, he played a major role in developing modern forms of the Hindi language. He used Vaishnava devotionalism to define a coherent Hindu religion. His initial institutional base was the Kashi Dharma Sabha, founded in the 1860s by the Maharaja of Benares in response to the more radical Hindu reformist movements. Harischandra met the contemporary Christian and Orientalist critiques of Hinduism by interpreting bhakti as devotion to a single personal god, which he traced to an unbroken tradition, and he insisted on the continued value of image worship.

Among Muslims, the Deoband movement of traditionally trained 'ulama, growing out of the academy established in that north Indian town in 1868, represented a similar strategy for reform. The Deobandi seminary (or *madrasa*) taught classical Islamic texts. But the school utilized the formal classroom pattern known from British schools, fostered Urdu as a language of prose, and forged networks of supporters through subscriptions, publications, and an annual meeting. In contrast to rationalists like Sayyid Ahmad

Khan, Deobandis cherished the sufi tradition of personal relations to holy men, devotional exercises, and belief in charisma. As Vasudha Dalmia has argued in relation to Hinduism, the traditionalist organizations and teachings were to prove the more enduring. However much they were responding to the changed conditions of their day, these reformers succeeded by drawing on symbols and language familiar from their historic traditions.

Hindu and Muslim movements also shared a focus on devotional theism and the identification of personal models for emulation and worship. Both Harischandra and Bankimchandra in Bengal celebrated Krishna, particularly the Krishna of the epics, as an ideal man committed to action. Such arguments strikingly parallel those of the Punjabi Muslim poet and philosopher, Muhammad Iqbal (1876–1938), who similarly celebrated historic models of action in contrast to an inward-looking spiritualism that romanticized 'the East' while scorning its worldly achievements. Indeed, the larger nineteenth-century Muslim focus on hadith, coupled with biographic writings like those of Shibli Nu'mani (1857–1914), similarly exalted Muhammad as object of devotion and ideal man. Although limited to a small, upwardly mobile following among Muslims, mostly in Punjab and the United Provinces, the teachings of Mirza Ghulam Ahmad (c. 1839–1908), which identified him as simultaneously Muhammad, Krishna, and Jesus, exemplify in extreme form the late nineteenth-century turn to devotion directed towards an ideal role model. Newly available lithographs, above all those pioneered by the painter Ravi Varma, influenced by Western figurative painting and photography, often rendered the gods more human, and, as such, not only objects of devotion, but of emulation (plate 5.5). The lithographs were widely reproduced, and often used (see plate 5.7 below) on advertisements and calendars.

WOMEN AND GENDER

Many movements of the later nineteenth century gave a central place to teachings related to women, seen as a particularly potent symbol of the proper moral order. The issues at stake included female literacy, the age of marriage (which particularly affected girls since they were married younger), the opportunity of widows to

Plate 5.5 *Birth of Shakuntala*, painting by Ravi Varma, incorporated in an advertising poster for baby food.

remarry, and, in the case of Muslims, the practice of polygamy. In addition, reformers often argued in favour of simpler, less extravagant observance of weddings and other life-cycle ceremonies. These concerns cut across religious groups and engaged not only Hindus but Muslims, Sikhs, Parsis, and Indian Christians as well.

This was not surprising given that the British had long made the position and treatment of women central to their criticisms of Indian society. A further similarity across religious lines was the new role of the Western-educated 'lay' population in claiming authority to address such issues, previously the sole purview of those educated in sacred texts or sustained by lineage status.

Among Muslims, the case of the Deobandis is suggestive of how a new concern for female behaviour extended beyond the Western-educated and those familiar with English. The influential volume *Bihishti Zewar*, written in Urdu by Maulana Ashraf `Ali Thanawi, a Deobandi reformer at the turn of the century, illustrates how a thinker both worked within a separate Muslim tradition and yet was shaped by the colonial context. Intended as a guide for young girls, the work provides a primer for literacy, enough detailed material on ritual and social norms to make – as it says – the female reader the equivalent 'of a middling `alim' (religious scholar), models of virtuous behaviour drawn from the lives of women of the classical age and the Prophet himself, and teachings on rigorous spiritual and moral discipline. It also includes suggestions for how widows could generate income sufficient to maintain their independence, advice on how to handle new challenges like the post office and rail travel, and detailed instructions on bookkeeping and household management. The book denounces women's folk medicine, customary celebrations, and traditional forms of female sociability. Women were meant to be literate and educated, but within precise limits; and they were meant to be primarily in their homes and under their husbands' control.

A new ideal of female domesticity, across religious lines, also took shape during the decades at the turn of the century. In that ideal, women were meant to be educated and 'respectable' according to the models of behaviour set out by government and missionary example; but, in dramatic contrast to those models, they were meant also to be upholders of their sacred religious traditions. In addition, they were conceived of as bulwarks protecting what was seen as the 'uncolonized' space of the home against an outside world dominated by colonial values. In Bengal, that woman was the *grihalakshmi*, or goddess of the home. That her proper domain was inside the home was made clear in Tagore's novel, *Ghare Baire* (The Home and the World), where a woman who overstepped that line met a tragic fate.

Far from mere imitation of European models, reform inculcated new duties within a defence of religious traditions. For women, the new domesticity offered new skills and new learning even while it provided new constraints. The 'new' women themselves soon began to play a role as writers and advocates of reform. One outspoken woman princely ruler, the Begum of Bhopal, covered from head to foot in the garment known as a *burqa*', travelled widely to encourage education of girls. Pandita Ramabai (1858–1922), rigorously educated in Sanskrit classics, travelled throughout India to advocate women's education and social reform and wrote tracts in support of her views. Widowed at age twenty-five, she travelled to England to learn English and pursue medical studies, and became a convert to a Christianity she interpreted on her own terms. In 1888, she founded a home school for widows in Bombay, followed by another in Poona. A Deccani Brahman woman, Gangabai, founded one of the most successful female institutions, the Mahakali Pathshala ('Great Kali School') in Calcutta in 1893, intended to inculcate Hindu religious and moral principles; the school had the patronage of a wealthy landlord, the Maharaja of Darbhanga. A Bengali Muslim, Begum Rokeya Sakhawat Hossain (1880–1932), set up schools for girls, denounced extreme seclusion, and wrote extensively, including a brilliant satire, *Sultana's Dream* (1905), in which the roles of men and women were reversed. In that imagined world, 'Women's intellects, untrammeled, devised such improvements as solar heat and air-machines; the population fully satisfied, there was no question of war; and men were kept in the zenana.'

The new norms of female behaviour helped draw new lines of social identity. One was that between the more and the less privileged. The opening lines of the popular Urdu novel, *Mir'atu'l-'Arus* (The Bride's Mirror) of 1869 by Deputy Nazir Ahmad (1833–1912) set the tone, as a senior woman impatiently calls the recalcitrant daughter, Akbari, to come in from the street. The girl's association with servants and the low-born is seen as a synecdoche for her general resistance to model behaviour. Akbari, like a similar daughter in a family influenced by the Brahmos or the Arya Samaj, was meant to behave differently from the lower classes. But if social and religious reform drew class lines, even more insistently did it draw lines between religious groups. Akbari was also meant to be a Muslim – as the targets of other teachings were meant to be Hindu. There is a sad irony in that movements at root so similar enhanced community separation.

The various reform movements, then, were broadly alike in offering an opportunity for individual choice. They typically emphasized a particular sacred text, and argued for the historic continuity of their interpretations. They often presented an ideal god or figure for devotion and emulation. They sought to assimilate women to what were seen as normative and scriptural instead of folk practices and beliefs. The reform movements freed followers from local, often rural customs that tied together affinity groups and bound people to specific dates and times. In so doing they ideally suited the needs of the newly mobile classes who participated in the professions, in trade, in government service, and in business. In the process, however, boundaries were drawn, between religions and between classes; and these, embedded in everyday life and sociality, existed in tension with the individualistic ideals of the nation-state. This tension is clear in the mapping of the image of the ideal woman on to the image of the community. The woman was made to represent at once language (the goddess Tamiltai in Tamilnadu; the Hindi 'Queen Nagri' in contrast to the strumpet, Begum Urdu), region (Bengal as Mother), and India itself as the Mother Goddess (Bharat Mata). Always, imagining the community entailed imagining an excluded other.

THE DECADE OF THE NINETIES: COMMUNALISM AND CALAMITIES

The boundaries between religions, especially that between Hindus and Muslims, became dramatically apparent in the last decade of the century. Even the teachings of the gentle Vivekananda mixed patriotism with a cult of manly virtue and evocations of Hindu glory. The Bengali novels of Bankim created a mythic 'history' in which brave Hindus triumphed over oppressive Muslim tyrants. Muslim writers turned to history too, both as apologetics, to counter Orientalist critiques of Muslim 'jihad' and 'perfidy', and as a way to foster community pride and self-esteem. Altaf Husain Hali's epic poem, the 'Musaddas' (1879), lamented the political decline of the

day in contrast to Muslim glories in the past; the romantic novels of 'Abdu'l-Halim Sharar (1860–1926), like the poetry of Iqbal,
celebrated Muslim rule in Sicily and Spain, when Muslims, not
Christians, ruled in southern Europe. This celebration of the past
was particularly marked in Maharashtra, where the old Maratha
chronicles offered up heroic exploits from the days of Shivaji.

Central to this endeavour was the great nationalist Bal Gangadhar
Tilak (1844–1920). A Chitpavan Brahman like Gokhale, with
whom he initially collaborated, Tilak adopted an increasingly radical position celebrating the Hindu nation and opposing colonial
rule. His famous motto was 'swaraj [self-rule] is my birthright and
I will have it.' Through processions, celebrations, and his Marathi
newspaper, *Kesari*, Tilak offered a powerful critique of the government's actions. One of the first was his challenge to the Age of
Consent Bill, proposed in 1891 to raise the age of statutory rape
from ten to twelve years. Long an issue with social reformers, the
age of consent, he argued, was not a matter for the English but for
Hindus themselves to decide.

In 1893, Tilak took up celebration of the birth of the popular
elephant-headed god, Ganesh (or Ganapati), Shiva's son. In so doing he turned what had been a congeries of annual family ceremonies
into a grand public event. The celebration included several days of
processions, music, and food, organized through subscriptions by
neighbourhood, caste, or occupation. Groups of boys, often students, drilled and provided music, not only to praise Ganesh but
also to celebrate Hindu and national glory, and to address topical
political issues. In the early years, for instance, the festival organizers urged temperance and patronage of *swadeshi* ('own country'
or locally made) goods. At the same time they called on Hindus to
protect cows and to boycott the Muharram celebrations organized
by Shi`a Muslims to commemorate the seventh-century martyrdom
of Imam Husain and his followers, in which Hindus had formerly
often participated.

Tilak sought to use events like the Ganapati festival to build a national spirit beyond the circles of the educated elites and to demonstrate to the British the unity of Hindu society (and hence the error
of the alleged government partiality for Muslims). A photograph
of the festival in one of the regional towns (plate 5.6) shows the

Plate 5.6   Procession in Ganapati festival, Dhar, western India, 1913.

assembled crowds, the armed police ready for the ever-potential violence generated by the events, and the central role of Maharashtrian
Brahmans, wearing their distinctive flat headgear, and mounted on
elephants. In 1895 Tilak inaugurated a second annual festival, this
time in honour of Shivaji, the Maratha ruler who, as we have seen
in chapter 1, defied Mughal power and, in one famous incident,
treacherously killed a Muslim noble with a concealed weapon. All
of this historical reconstruction was meant as a way of opposing
colonial rule, but, in the context of colonial institutions, with their
sociology of difference, it also exacerbated Hindu–Muslim ill-will.

The issue of cow protection moved the perceived difference of Hindu from Muslim into the realm of popular agitation. Concern for the well-being of cows, initially taken up by the Sikh Kuka (Namdhari) sect in the Punjab as early as the 1860s, spread to the Arya Samaj under Dayananda, who urged Hindus to protest 'cow slaughter' by petitioning government on the issue. In 1893 the Arya Samaj split over the linked issues of vegetarianism and cow protection. Cow protection societies, *Gaurakhshini Sabhas*, were formed during the 1880s. The cow was a powerful symbol, embodying images of maternity and fertility, and newly salient with the renewed devotion to the cowherd god Krishna. Cow protection was embraced by the upwardly mobile seeking to identify with higher-caste practices that included a repudiation of meat-eating. It also served as an opportunity for reformers to assert their credibility against 'orthodox' critics. Support, particularly on the part of the Western-educated, was often articulated by the argument that cattle slaughter contributed to the physical and moral weakness of the nation by eliminating a continuing source of dairy products. It thus reflected the larger anxiety at this time over perceived national degeneracy (like the contemporaneous issue of 'neurasthenia' and such maladies in Europe) that found expression in cults devoted to body-building. Indians were determined to demonstrate to the British that they could be strong even though they did not eat beef. The intensity of the discussion in 1892–3 owed much as well to the Age of Consent Bill and the resulting determination to protect indigenous customs from British interference. Thus the movement drew on many currents, and was not, at the outset, driven primarily by the antagonism against Muslims which fuelled its later stages.

The cow societies prepared petitions, took out processions, and even acted out dramas on the issue. Cow protectors filed suits against butchers, who were typically Muslim, and tried to intercept cattle *en route* to cattle fairs, butchers shops, or destined for sacrifice in the annual Muslim `Idu'l-Azha celebration (commemorating Abraham's sacrifice of an animal in place of his son). They also supported cattle breeding and the care of sick and aged animals. Their appeal reached far into the population, as they levied support at the level of the household for donations of grain, and even created a shadow government with courts to punish offences among

Hindus. Communal riots were triggered in 1893 by the belief that local officials were not adhering to a judicial ruling – in fact not upheld by the courts – identifying cattle as religiously protected objects. This legal controversy, with the accompanying newspaper and pamphlet debates, illustrates how far the colonial idiom of legal rights and legislative entitlements had become part of everyday language and thinking. The complex of cow-related activities became part of a shared experience that defined what was taken as the moral community of the nation. Beef was, in fact, not particularly valued as food by Muslims, and its use was associated primarily with the poor. Nor were cattle needed for sacrifice, since goats readily served that purpose. Muslims nevertheless increasingly felt compelled to insist upon the rights provided them by formal law on this issue, lest the Hindu majority also circumscribe other of their practices. The debate, though focused on the cow, engaged far larger concerns.

The 1893 Hindu–Muslim riots left more than 100 people dead in western India, the North-Western Provinces and Oudh, Bihar, and even in Rangoon, Burma. The spread of riots to such far-flung places brings home the power of the telegraph and newspapers to disseminate news that then in turn sparked further disturbances. The riots died down as it became apparent that there would be no major changes in the rules over killing animals. They left a long legacy of memories, however. The fact that many individual members of Congress supported cow protection contributed further to the view of most Muslim leaders that their interests were best served by organizations that focused exclusively on Muslim interests. For some Hindu nationalists, the behaviour of the cow activists evoked a sense of pride, for it challenged the enduring image of Hindu passivity and inaction.

Two natural calamities in the nineties produced further direct action. One was a failure of the monsoon in 1896 and again in 1899, followed by famine, particularly in the Deccan. Desperate rural people in some cases refused to pay land taxes, often explicitly justifying their actions in terms of legal rights. The second calamity was that of bubonic plague, which entered India through the port of Bombay at the end of the decade. Invasive British anti-plague measures, which, ironically, may have helped spread the plague by dispersing people, met widespread resistance. In 1897, Damodar

Chapekar along with his brother Balkrishna, who had organized a paramilitary club to march in Ganapati processions and take direct action against social reformers, assassinated Walter Rand, the Plague Commissioner, along with a second British official, as they departed from the governor's celebrations of Victoria's jubilee. Tilak, whose publications on the occasion were regarded as provocative and who almost surely concealed the identities of the perpetrators, was convicted of sedition and spent eight months in prison.

The nineties was a decade of extreme suffering, poorly handled by administrative action. Famine and plague were accompanied by what nationalists saw as wasteful military adventures, including extension of British control into easternmost Assam and Manipur in the interests of the British tea planters, and into Kalat and Chitral, producing tribal discontent and continuing military build-up, on the north-west frontier. In 1894, in a further attempt to enhance revenues, the government levied a tariff on imported cotton goods, only to be immediately required to offset this measure of protection by a countervailing excise of an equivalent 5 per cent placed on indigenous goods. This excise was a dramatic symbol of the imperial government's concern for the interests of British manufacturers at the cost of Indian industry. Despite the provisions of the new Famine Code and the ability to move grain via rail, many peasants, increasingly dependent on cash and imported food, faced desperate conditions. The toll of depression, famine, and plague was evident in the absolute decline in population in the 1890s in contrast to the steady growth evident earlier in the century.

LORD CURZON AND THE PARTITION OF BENGAL

George Nathaniel Curzon arrived in India in 1899, convinced that efficient administration by benevolent autocratic rulers best served the country. He worked incessantly, and he was eloquent, effective, overbearing, and arrogant. He stabilized the troubled north-west by the use of tribal levies, creating a separate province of the North-West Frontier Province (renaming the North-Western Provinces and Oudh as the United Provinces to avoid confusion). He initiated a mission into Tibet (which culminated in its recognition as an autonomous region within China). Within India, he fought to streamline a bloated bureaucracy. He established a separate police service, attempted to rationalize land assessments, created a department of commerce and industry, supported agricultural research, and established the Archeological Survey of India to study and protect historic monuments. He especially cherished the Taj Mahal, which he embellished with an ornate light fixture over the central tomb. Curzon's style was clear in his appointment of a commission to study the problems of university education: not a single Indian was included. The 1904 Universities Act, which appeared to enhance government control over higher education, was resented and criticized by Gokhale and others of the educated elite. The public outcry should have been a clear sign that administrative efficiency alone would not, as Curzon imagined, keep the masses content and the politically active chastened. All this was to become even more clear in the partition of Bengal, announced in 1905.

Bengal had long been regarded as too large a province to govern efficiently. Curzon therefore united the eastern regions of Bengal with Assam, forming a new province of some 31 million, leaving almost 50 million to a second province in the west that included half of Bengal with Bihar and Orissa. Even with this reorganization each province was still larger than many major nations. Splitting the province in this fashion, however, made Muslims the majority community in eastern Bengal, while non-Bengalis (Biharis and Oriyas) formed the majority in the west. To the English-educated Bengali middle class this was a vivisection of their beloved homeland and a blatant attempt to reduce their power. To oppose the partition they organized a campaign of swadeshi, encouraging use of local products and a boycott of British imports. The movement was led by Surendranath Banerjea and other moderates, but small groups committed to terrorist activity also began to mobilize under its banner. Participation in the movement made clear, as the historian Sumit Sarkar has argued, that political leadership in Bengal was provided by the male Hindu bhadralok and rentier classes. The movement itself thus reinforced, inasmuch as the peasant class was primarily Muslim, the evolving, and divisive, religious identities of 'Hindu' and 'Muslim'.

Much nationalist rhetoric in the preceding decades had made 'Bengal' a focus for loyalty, as in the celebrated novel *Anandamath*, where Bankim imagined the land as the divine Mother, whose freedom from Muslim oppression would be secured by the militancy of her sons. The song 'Bande Mataram', set to music by the celebrated literary figure Rabindranath Tagore (1861–1941), became the informal anthem of the nationalist movement after 1905:

Mother, I bow to thee!
Rich with thy hurrying streams,
Bright with thy orchard gleams,
Cool with thy winds of delight,
Dark fields waving, Mother of might,
Mother free...
Who hath said thou art weak in thy lands,
When the swords flash out in twice seventy million hands...
To thee I call, Mother and Lord!...
Thou art wisdom, thou art law,
Thou our heart, our soul, our breath,
Thou the love divine, the awe
In our hearts that conquers death...
Every image made divine
In our temples is but thine.
Thou are Durga, Lady and Queen,
With her hands that strike and her swords of sheen,
Thou are Lakshmi lotus-throned...
Mother sweet, I bow to thee
Mother great and free!

Those associated with the terrorist secret societies imagined Bengal less as a beneficent mother and more as the goddess of power and destruction, Shiva's consort, Kali, to whom they dedicated their weapons. The lithographed advertisement for Kali Cigarettes (plate 5.7) links an item of new middle-class consumption to swadeshi and to an image of the power the national struggle could unleash. In this vision the cigarette, not just a 'good smoke', is political and Hindu.

Nationalists across the country took up Bengal's cause, appalled at British arrogance, contempt for public opinion, and what appeared as blatant tactics of divide and rule. Calcutta came alive with rallies, bonfires of foreign goods, petitions, newspapers, and posters. Agitation particularly spread to the Punjab and to Bombay and Poona. The Ganapati festivals in western India were revived in 1905 and, increasingly anti-British, were largely suppressed by

Plate 5.7 'Kali Trampling her Consort, Siva', 1908. Chromolithograph
calendar for Kali Cigarettes of Bowbazar Street, Calcutta.

about 1910. Curzon had regarded Congress as a spent force;
instead, in what proved to be his last significant action, he gave
it a cause that supplied it with new strength and new tactics of
mobilizing public support.

In 1905 Curzon resigned, not over the Bengal imbroglio, but rather as the loser in a power struggle with his hand-picked commander-in-chief, Lord Kitchener. In the same year, with the Liberal electoral triumph in Britain, John Morley was appointed Secretary of State for India. An admirer of Gokhale and an architect of Irish home rule, Morley was determined to win back the loyalty of India's political moderates by a large measure of reform. Curzon's successor Lord Minto, a Whig left in place by the new cabinet, by contrast preferred advisory councils, including the princes at all levels, as the major component of reform, a telling indication of his commitment to a continued 'durbar' style of governance. Meanwhile, against a backdrop of increased agitation, Minto turned to a heavy-handed repression. Arrests were made on the grounds of sedition; emergency orders suspended public meetings; the press was curtailed; marchers were attacked. The triumph of Japan over Russia in 1905 fired the imagination of protesters as the first-ever Asian military victory over a European power. But the harsh reality in India was evident in ever more curbs on civil liberties.

Gopal Krishna Gokhale, a 'Moderate' who had been elected Congress president in 1906, continued to press for Morley's promised constitutional reforms with the support of the Congress majority. But a strong voice within Congress, the 'Extremists' led by Tilak, now called for more radical action. This tension between Moderates and Extremists provoked a split in the Congress in 1907. That same year Tilak, charged with sedition, was sentenced to six years in prison, and transported to Mandalay. During the subsequent decade the Congress was dominated by the Moderates. Among Tilak's close colleagues was Aurobindo Ghosh (1872–1950), a Bengali educated in England. Devoted to Ramakrishna and Vivekananda, and inspired by the novels of Bankim, Ghosh reclaimed his alienated Bengali roots and joined the partition struggle. But after a period in jail for suspected terrorism, in 1910 he withdrew to the French territory of Pondicherry for a life of spiritual devotion. There his fervor and his vision of a religious nationalism drew a large following to him.

Meanwhile, the Bengal partition and the proposed reforms stimulated a Muslim reaction. Muslim leaders had not originally supported the partition. But faced with the rhetoric of 'Bande Mataram', with its implication that Bengal was a Hindu land, and the riotous behaviour of the Hindu crowds, Muslims turned to the new province as a way to secure a place for themselves in eastern India. British officials at the same time eagerly exploited the possibilities of a separate Muslim interest as a counterweight to the Hindu domination of the old Bengal. The small Muslim elite in East Bengal, led by Nawab `Ali Chowdhry of Dacca (1863–1929), saw in the new province the hope of increased education, increased opportunities for employment, and, free of the domination of Calcutta, an increased economic and political voice generally. The Bengali Muslim community increasingly drew closer in outlook to the Muslims of the upper provinces, who had come to see themselves as disadvantaged in education, employment, and political voice.

With the intervention of the English principal of the Aligarh College, a group of some thirty-five Muslims, led by the Bombay-based Isma`ili leader, the Aga Khan (1877–1957), secured an audience with Minto in the autumn of 1906. They urged the viceroy in the proposed constitutional reforms to grant Muslims a representation that would reflect not only their numerical strength, but also their political importance. They argued that Muslims 'are a distinct community with additional interests...which are not shared by other communities and these...have not been adequately represented'. In Minto, these arguments, first honed by Sayyid Ahmad Khan, found a receptive audience. 'I am firmly convinced,' the viceroy replied, 'as I believe you to be, that any electoral representation in India would be doomed to mischievous failure which aimed at granting a personal enfranchisement regardless of the beliefs and traditions of the communities composing the population of this continent.' Imperial and upper-class Muslim interests here converged in the assumption that India consisted of discrete communities, each of whom deserved representation as a community.

The Indian Councils Act of 1909, known as the Morley–Minto Reforms, did not empower the legislature to control the executive, still firmly in British hands, nor did it overturn the consultative 'durbar' model of government. It did, however, create non-official Indian majorities in the provincial legislatures (though not at the centre), and the principle of election was established at all levels. These elections were primarily indirect. Various public bodies (municipal and district boards, chambers of commerce, universities, landholders, and special constituencies like tea and jute planters) chose the members of the provincial assemblies, while the provincial legislatures elected the members of the central legislative council. Members of these legislative bodies were now empowered to ask supplementary questions and table resolutions. There was, thus, a modest enlargement of the councils, and an expansion of their powers. One portentous innovation was the inauguration, for the first time in the provincial and central legislative bodies, of separate electorates in which only Muslims could vote, and reserved seats in the councils for Muslims. This provision implied that only a Muslim could represent Muslims, or protect Muslim interests – a presumption that would shape political life in India for decades to come. In December 1906 in Dacca the All-India Moslem League was formed. At the time this organization included only a handful of landed and aristocratic elites, but it took as its objective advancing the interests of all Muslims.

In 1911 the new viceroy Lord Hardinge orchestrated the extraordinary spectacle of the imperial durbar at Delhi. On this occasion the newly crowned King-Emperor George V and his Queen presented themselves to their Indian subjects, the only visit ever paid by a ruling British monarch to India during the Raj. The extravagant pageantry, with vast camps and an amphitheatre created for the event, could not have posed a more dramatic counterpoint to Indian cries for increased self-rule. The image was that of the viceroy as Mughal emperor; and the orchestration of precedence, gift exchange, the central role accorded to the princes, and the royal appearance at the Mughal Red Fort, were all intended to convey what the British imagined to be an appropriate style of governing India. The king-emperor announced three 'boons'. First was the well-kept secret decision to shift the capital from Calcutta to Delhi. This site was considered more centrally located as well as more convenient to the summer capital at Simla, but the British saw in the change as well a way to associate themselves, and also their loyal Muslim subjects, with a remembered Mughal glory. It was also, of course, a move away from the centre of political activism in Calcutta. The planning of the new capital, known as New Delhi, located south of the old Mughal city, was entrusted to the architects Sir Edwin Lutyens and Sir Herbert

Baker. Their imperial vision of a *beaux-arts* capital focused on a vast Viceroy's Palace would, as it happened, be realized hardly more than a decade before it was handed over to an independent democracy.

The second 'boon' was the revocation of the partition of Bengal, or more precisely, the redefinition of the province. Assam, Bihar, and Orissa were given separate status as provinces in their own right; the two halves of Bengal, east and west, were reunited. Finally, as the third boon, Bengal was raised to the status of a governor's province, comparable to Madras and Bombay, an act appropriate to its size and importance. The Congress, weakened by the 1907 split and satisfied with the new reforms, abandoned agitation. The Muslim leaders, betrayed by the revocation of partition, were increasingly uncertain of their ground. The illusion of stability produced by the spectacle of the durbar would soon give way to new issues, new leaders, and new alliances.

WORLD WAR ONE, NEW GOALS, NEW ALLIANCES

In the decade following the imperial durbar, Indian political life was shaped above all by events on the international scene. Muslim opinion, stunned in 1912 by the reversal of the Bengal partition, was further alienated by Britain's unwillingness to defend the Ottoman Empire against Russia and against uprisings in Greece and the Balkans. From the end of the nineteenth century, Muslims had debated the position of the Ottoman sultan as *khalifa* of all Muslims. Support of the khalifa, like the concept of an 'Islamic world' generally, had less to do with existing institutions than with the quest for an ideal higher than Western racialism and imperialism. Loyalist spokesmen, whether Sayyid Ahmad Khan or religious leaders like Mirza Ghulam Ahmad and Maulana Ahmad Riza Khan, denied that the sultan had any worldwide spiritual authority. The cause of the Ottomans and the khalifa was instead initially taken up by a number of younger, Western-educated Muslims, among them Muhammad 'Ali (1878–1931) writing in the *Comrade*, Zafar 'Ali Khan in his *Zamindar* in Punjab, and Abu'l Kalam Azad (1887–1958), who had earlier been a member of a terrorist group in Calcutta, in his *Al-Hilal*. They were soon joined, among others, by a group of influential Lucknow 'ulama. A medical mission went out to aid Turkish troops in the Balkan war of 1912, and an organization was formed to support protection of the pilgrimage places in the Hejaz. The call for 'pan-Islam' went hand in hand with a move away from the loyalism of the older generation to a commitment to seek an alliance with Congress. In 1912 Muhammad 'Ali's group dominated the Muslim League session in Lucknow, passing a resolution calling for self-government. British profanation of a mosque in Kanpur in the following year led to a riot in which twenty-three were killed and dozens arrested. This incident was both a reminder of the tenuousness of the sorely frayed relations of Muslims with the government, and a demonstration of the extent to which a local affray could engage a national Muslim interest, uniting for the first time conservative loyalists with the younger radical group.

In August 1914, Britain declared war with Germany for herself and for the entire empire, including India. All parties, with perhaps surprising alacrity, proclaimed their commitment to the British cause. Even when hostilities were extended to Ottoman Turkey that November, the Muslim League extended its support. The war years, however, saw a heightening of expectations that India would now win the self-determination the Allies claimed to be fighting for. To this end, new alliances formed among moderates and radicals, Congress and the League.

India made extraordinary sacrifices for the war effort. Well over a million Indians were recruited into the army, serving in France and especially in the Middle East, with a heavy cost of lives on all fronts. The contribution of Indian revenues was also substantial, with demand going up approximately 10 to 15 per cent in each year from 1916 to 1918. External markets were disrupted. In 1918 the monsoon failed with resultant food scarcity. The price of food grains almost doubled; the price of imported goods almost tripled. The war years were a boon for some of India's key indigenous industries, particularly cotton textiles and iron and steel. But for the population as a whole, this was a period of acute distress, intensified by the spread in 1918 of the worldwide influenza pandemic.

Despite the virtual withdrawal from India of British troops, there were no terrorist activities as dramatic as those before the war, as for example the 1912 bomb attack on the viceroy Lord Hardinge as he opened the new imperial capital at Delhi. Abroad, most notable were events on the west coast of America. There, with a base of about 15,000, mostly Punjabi, immigrants, Sikh activists in the Ghadr ('Revolution') Movement sought to provoke an uprising within India. Early in the war, many Ghadr members returned to India, hoping to join conspirators in Bengal, but most were interned and the plan collapsed. The British also feared pan-Islamic conspiracy in these years. A leading Deobandi, Maulana Mahmud al-Hasan (1851–1920) tried to establish links with Turks in the Hijaz, but was handed over to the British and interned in Malta from 1917 until 1920. Another Deobandi, Maulana `Ubaidu'llah Sindhi (1872–1944), similarly apprehended, had gone to Afghanistan to work with Germans and Turks in the hope of fomenting unrest on the frontier. Muhammad `Ali and his brother Shaukat `Ali were interned from the time Turkey entered the war until its conclusion. The British responded to these presumed internal threats by extreme repressive measures, above all the Defence of India Act, March 1915, which abrogated a wide range of civil rights.

In 1915, Tilak, newly returned from Mandalay, re-entered the Indian National Congress, in part because of what seemed a new spirit of moderation on his side and in part as a result of the death in that year of both Gokhale and his Moderate colleague, Pherozeshah Mehta (1845–1915). Indian politics were further revitalized by the activities of newly formed Home Rule Leagues, whose name, goals, and style were inspired by Irish nationalist agitation. The initiative came from an Englishwoman, Annie Besant (1847–1933), who had come to India as a convert to theosophy and soon became head of the Theosophical Society, based in Adyar, Madras. A religious movement, founded by the Russian Madame Blavatsky, theosophy preached a mixture of social reform, cultivation of occult practices, and celebration of ancient Hindu wisdom that predated Western civilization. The movement had considerable appeal among Western-educated Indians (including for a time Gokhale), as well as among a sprinkling of Europeans both in India and Europe. Using her theosophical followers as a core group of supporters, Besant worked through Madras and Bombay newspapers to stimulate interest in the Home Rule League's militant politics. Tilak initiated a second league, mostly based in western India. Both established discussion groups and reading rooms, disseminated not only periodicals but posters and picture cards as well, organized lecture tours, and utilized dramas and songs to spread their message. The result was an expansion in the geographic base and, to some extent, the social diversity of those committed to self-rule. Besant was interned in 1917 and by the end of the war had developed a more quietist politics.

In both 1915 and 1916 the Congress and Muslim League met jointly, first in Bombay and then in Lucknow. In Lucknow the two resolved, in what was subsequently known as the 'Lucknow Pact', to demand elected majorities on all councils, a wider franchise, and separate electorates for Muslims, with, in addition, what was called 'weightage' in the minority provinces. This last provision worked to favour Muslims in places like the United Provinces, where they were 14 per cent of the population but were to secure 50 per cent of the seats, while disadvantaging, for example, Bengali and Punjabi Muslims whose small majorities in each province were reduced to an exact 50 per cent of the seats in Punjab and only 40 per cent in Bengal. Muhammad `Ali Jinnah (1876–1948), who was to be the key Muslim political leader by the time of independence, participated in these negotiations. A Bombay barrister who had been strongly influenced by both Naoroji and Gohkale in London and was elected to the Legislative Council in 1910, he had also joined the Muslim League after its change to more activist leadership before the war.

In 1917, confronted with this alliance of India's major political parties, Edwin Montagu, the Liberal Secretary of State for India, announced the British Government's intention to move towards 'self-governing' institutions and ultimately 'responsible government' in India. During the last years of the war, however, two portents of change altered the way the new order was to take shape. In 1915, Mohandas Karamchand Gandhi (1868–1948) returned to his native India from South Africa, where for twenty years he had defended the interests of the Indian population. By 1917–18 he had begun using the techniques of passive resistance he had devised in South Africa to confront indigo planters in Champaran (Bihar), mill owners in Ahmedabad, and government officials in the interests of non-payment of revenue in Kheda (also in Gujarat). Meanwhile, following the armistice in 1918, a wide range of Muslim opinion watched in anger and dismay as the victors moved to dismember Ottoman lands and deliver key areas, including the Arab holy places, to European puppet rulers. In 1919 the All-India Khilafat Committee was formed. In the harsh repression that followed the war, Gandhi, other Congress leaders, and the Khilafatists would come together in a shared moral vision that saw British perfidy in policies that denied Indians their rightful rule, exploited the poor, and created a new domain of European imperialism in the Muslim lands of the Middle East.

In one of his most celebrated poems the Punjabi philospher and litterateur Muhammad Iqbal expressed a vision of India's plight that linked it to oppression and exploitation around the world, not only among the colonized but in Europe as well. Iqbal put into the voice of the mythical Islamic prophet Khizr a denunciation of the categories that intoxicated rulers and ruled alike – including community (*qaum*), race (*nasl*), and colour (*rang*) – as 'imaginary gods' that distracted humans from their real needs and fostered the fundamentally corrupt interests of capitalist imperialism:

> Go! give my message to the working man
> This is not just Khizr's message but the message of Creation.
> The cunning capitalist has sucked you dry!
> For ages you've had dreams – not compensation...
> The Assassins have drugged you with hashish
> And you, unwitting dotard, think it delectation.
> *Race, People, Church, Kingship, Civilization, Colour* –
> 'Imperialism' has used these as sedation!
> The ignorant have perished for imaginary gods;
> In stupefaction spent their very animation.
> *Arise! Into the world's assembly a new way comes.*
> In East and West, your era has begun.

To escape from the entangling imperialist net, Iqbal drew, like Tagore, on the symbols of 'Asia' or the 'East', or, more often in his case, on 'Islam', to sing a vision of a just and humane society without divisions. In India, as elsewhere, however, it would be the 'imaginary gods' that prevailed.

6

The crisis of the colonial order: reform, disillusionment, division, 1919–1939

The year 1919 was a watershed in the modern history of India. Nothing was the same afterwards. By its end the Montagu–Chelmsford reforms, in prospect since the previous year, were enacted. While the reforms withheld *swaraj*, the 'self-rule' increasingly demanded by nationalists, they foreshadowed a period when Indians would determine their own fate. The year, however, also brought the repressive Rowlatt bills and the catastrophe of the Amritsar massacre. For many, if not most, Indians the reforms had become a poisoned chalice. They chose instead a novel course of political action, that of 'non-violent non-cooperation', and a new leader, Mohandas K. Gandhi, only recently returned from twenty years in South Africa. Gandhi would endure as a lasting symbol of moral leadership for the entire world community.

REFORM AND REPRESSION

In August 1917 Edwin Montagu announced that the objective of British rule in India would be the 'gradual development of self-governing institutions with a view to the progressive realization of responsible government in India as an integral part of the British Empire'. This declaration decisively repudiated the old 'durbar' model of Indian politics. India would instead follow the path already chalked out by the white-settler dominions of Canada, Australia, and New Zealand. Inevitably, too, it meant that, rather than disdaining the educated as an unrepresentative minority, the

British would repose in them the confidence due future leaders of India. These men were, Montagu averred, in a telling comment on the declaration, 'intellectually our children', who had 'imbibed ideas which we ourselves have set before them'. Britain, however, retained the right to set the pace of reform, which was to be slow and measured, a boon, as the British saw it, to be conferred upon the Indians as they qualified for its benefits.

For the first step in this progress towards self-government, the British devised an ingenious constitutional device called dyarchy, which split the functions of government into two. Although the central government, situated in the spacious garden city of New Delhi, now under construction, remained wholly under British control, in the provinces some areas, among them agriculture and education, along with responsibility for raising the necessary taxes, were transferred to Indian ministers responsible to local legislatures. The electorate for these new provincial legislative bodies was expanded so that it now comprised about one-tenth of the adult male population. British governors retained crucial 'reserved' subjects, such as law and order, under their own control.

The reforms might well have been accepted, even by the Congress, had their enactment not been accompanied by a panic-stricken recourse to coercion on the part of the British in India. The spectre of a revival of revolutionary terrorism, together with the uncertainties of postwar economic dislocation, impelled the government in early 1919 to continue many of the powers of detention and trial without jury that had been in force during the wartime emergency. Known from the name of their author as the Rowlatt Acts, these measures aroused an intense hostility among Indians, to whom they appeared as a bitter reward for their wartime sacrifices. In response, Indians adopted new measures of protest, most notably that of a nation-wide *hartal*, or work stoppage, linked to marches in major cities. So effective were these protests, which sometimes spilled over into violence, that the government in some areas introduced martial law. In the Punjab city of Amritsar, the general commanding the local garrison, Reginald Dyer, took it upon himself on 13 April 1919 to disperse by force an illegal, though peaceable, crowd gathered in the enclosed Jallianwalla Bagh. Drawing up his Gurkha troops at the entrance, he fired until some 370 trapped protestors lay dead and over 1,000 wounded.

This terrible massacre, the worst in the history of the British Raj, was an isolated incident, yet it became a symbol of colonial injustice, remembered in speech, song, and drama. Plate 6.1 shows the title page of a Hindi play written shortly after the event. It depicts 'Martial Law' as a policeman above the female figure of 'Punjab' praying for help, the law book of colonial promise set aside, while 'Satyagraha', representing Gandhi, looks on in despair. For many among the British, the massacre confirmed widely held assumptions about how Indians ought to be governed. Dyer, for one, was not repentant. The firing was justified, he later said, for its 'moral effect' in the Punjab. Indians, like children, when naughty needed to be severely punished. They were not capable of governing themselves. Opposition to the established order could lead only to anarchy. Although the Government of India forced Dyer to resign his commission, and Montagu staunchly opposed this recourse to violence, Dyer's reception on his return to England, where he was received like a conquering hero and awarded a purse of £30,000, undercut the effects of the censure. Throughout the years leading up to independence the process of reform had always to contend with the heavy weight of 'diehard' English opposition. At its centre stood the popular figure of the Conservative leader Winston Churchill, who resigned from the government rather than support the subsequent 1935 reform measure.

THE ADVENT OF GANDHI

The massacre, together with the government's failure wholly to repudiate it – Gandhi described the investigative report as 'thinly disguised whitewash' – precipitated a wrenching loss of faith in Britain's good intentions. As Gandhi wrote in 1920, 'I can no longer retain affection for a Government so evilly manned as it is nowadays.' Until 1919 a minor figure on the Indian stage, Gandhi took upon himself the task of devising a way out of this impasse. In so doing he emerged not only as a principal architect of India's independence, but as one of the most original and influential thinkers of the twentieth century.

राष्ट्रीय सा॰ जुल्मीडायर

या

जलियां वाला बाग़

लेखक व प्रकाशक—

मनोहर लाल शुक्ल

Plate 6.1   Title page of *Rashtriya Sangit Julmi Daayar –
Jallianwalla Bagh*, in Hindi, by Manohar Lal Shukla,
Kanpur, 1922.

Born in 1869 into a trading family in princely Saurashtra, on the remote western coast of Gujarat, Gandhi grew up awkward, shy, and yet ambitious. Leaving a young wife behind, and defying attempts to outcaste him, Gandhi at the age of eighteen sailed to England to study for the bar. Upon his return, he found himself unable to compete as a barrister in the crowded legal world of Bombay, and so he set forth once again, this time to South Africa, in 1893. There, as the only Indian lawyer, he soon grew wealthy defending the local Indian business community; but, moved by his experience of racial prejudice in this white-settler dominated colony, he went on to organize Indian opinion against the colonial, and then after 1910 the Afrikaner, rulers of South Africa. Gandhi's South African experience proved crucial to his subsequent leadership of India's freedom struggle. Above all, in South Africa, a colonial society where a small Indian community was ranged against whites and blacks, an identity as 'Indian' inevitably took precedence over those of region, religion, and caste that mattered so much at home. Often, from Gandhi's time up to the present, whether for political figures or for writers like V. S. Naipaul and Salman Rushdie, the experience of living abroad has provided insights into the complexity and coherence of their homeland.

Gandhi's distinctive social and political outlook was the product too of his upbringing in Gujarat, in an environment so different from that which shaped the cosmopolitan elite of the great presidency capitals. In the small isolated towns of its princely states, English education was a rarity, while Gandhi's family had close ties with Jainism, a religion with many followers in Gujarat. Together with his *bania*, or trader, caste affiliation, these ties encouraged belief in a non-violent form of Hinduism, for both Jainism and the life of commerce recoiled from violence and the taking of life. As a youth, Gandhi struggled to shake off this heritage and reconstruct himself in keeping with British ideals of masculinity. The British ruled India, so common opinion had it, because they were tough, manly, meat-eating. Therefore the way to oust them was to surpass them at their own game. In pursuit of this objective, Gandhi became friends with a young Muslim Sheikh Mehtab (for some of these qualities were presumed to adhere to Muslims), and with him ventured out to the local brothel, and undertook secretive experiments in meat-eating.

Even though none of this was wholly satisfying, and Gandhi swore off meat to appease his mother's anxieties, he continued to pursue this strategy during his early days in England. He dressed in the style of the late Victorian dandy, took up dancing and the violin only to abandon them, and finally found solace, and a public platform, in vegetarianism. His association with English vegetarians introduced Gandhi to a strand of Western thought that, while usually submerged in the dominant discourse of Victorian masculinity, had nevertheless a powerful appeal for him. Above all, from reading Tolstoy and Ruskin, with their commitment to pacifism and an ethical life, Gandhi began to formulate his own critique of the materialist West. At the same time he found a way of coming to terms with his own heritage. Repudiating the association of 'feminine' qualities with weakness, he began to construct a 'new courage' in which nonviolence, and passive resistance, were transformed into strength. He would be strong, he proclaimed, as a woman was strong.

During his twenty years in South Africa, from 1893 until 1914, Gandhi put together his new vision of society. At its heart was a fierce criticism of what he saw as a Western obsession with material goods, and the culture of competition necessary to secure them. Not only the purchase of English goods but industrial development itself had to be avoided. Machinery, as he wrote, 'is the chief symbol of modern civilization; it represents a great sin'. In its place, he put forth the ideal of a simple life based in a society, like that of his imagined traditional Indian village, in which each member unselfishly looked after the others. True independence, as he envisioned it in *Hind Swaraj* (1909), was not a simple matter of Indians replacing Britons in the seat of government. It involved a wholesale transformation of society from the bottom up, as all individuals came to realize their true spiritual worth. The ideal form of the state, for Gandhi, would be a loosely linked grouping of nearly self-sufficient village republics. Harkening back to the ancient past, Gandhi described his ideal society by evoking the mythic kingdom of Lord Ram:

In my opinion swaraj and Ramarajya are one and the same thing . . . We call a state Ramarajya when both the ruler and his subjects are straightforward, when both are pure in heart, when both are inclined towards self-sacrifice, when both exercise restraint and self-control while enjoying worldly pleasures, and, when the relationship between the two is as good as that between a father and son.

As Gandhi sought a moral, not simply a political, transformation of human society, he could not accept the view, common in many nationalist movements, that the end – of freedom – justified whatever means might be necessary to bring it about. Not only must the leader himself eschew violence, but his followers must also be disciplined to accept without retaliation whatever blows might fall upon them. Similarly, the transformative love that Gandhi held out as the basis of a new India must encompass not only all Indians, from the wealthy zamindar to the despised untouchable, but the British as well. No one, whether Muslim, Hindu, or Christian, was inherently unworthy.

Gandhi in time abandoned 'passive resistance' as a description of his strategy in favour of the more active *satyagraha*, or truth-force. For Gandhi, the pursuit of satyagraha involved a range of behaviours that together would create an India, both of individuals and as a nation, capable of self-rule. Above all it involved settling disputes by seeking truths shared with an opponent whom one must always respect, even love. Gandhi's search for truth by its very nature involved a disciplining of the passions and an avoidance of violence. A vegetarian diet, as he saw it, avoided violence to animals as well as the consumption of food, such as meat, that inflamed the passions. Gandhi further advocated *brahmacharya*, or sexual abstinence. He himself after many years of married life abandoned sexual relations with his wife, and, on occasion, to a storm of controversy, took young women into his bed to 'test' his mastery of sexual desire. The disciplining of the acquisitive passions was to be accomplished by simplicity of dress and the promotion of hand-spun fabrics (*khadi*). Every nationalist was expected to spend a certain number of hours each day at the spinning wheel.

The appealing figure of the loin-cloth-clad 'mahatma' (see plate 6.2) must not be allowed to obscure aspects of his philosophy that opened Gandhi up to charges of self-righteousness and condescension. He was prepared to love his opponents, but only on his terms, and his attitude towards large segments of society – Muslims,

Plate 6.2   Gandhi at his writing table.

women, and untouchables among them – was defined by an inability or unwillingness to accept the legitimacy of grievances which did not accord with his conception of a proper moral order. Above all, Gandhi never advocated a wholesale repudiation of the Hindu caste system, nor of the patriarchal family structure. Much as he sought to ease caste rigidities and improve the status of untouchables, for instance, he spoke always with the patronizing assurance of the upper-caste Hindu. Gandhi's fasts too, in his view a form of self-cleansing or self-suffering to atone for errors, though non-violent could be harshly coercive.

Gandhi never claimed to speak for Hinduism, and he did not seek an avowedly Hindu India. Indeed the non-violence that he preached has never been a core value of the Hindu tradition. Unlike latter-day Hindu nationalists, Gandhi sought an India built on a coalition of religious communities, not one of Hindu dominance. Nevertheless, Gandhi's entire manner, dress, and vocabulary were suffused with Hinduism. Religion, in his view, formed the binding glue of the nation. Even as he reached out to other communities, this 'mahatma' inevitably embodied a deeply Hindu sensibility. As the years went by he shrewdly turned it to political advantage. The costs, however, were substantial.

Gandhi's personality alone cannot explain his ascent to the leadership of the Indian national movement. In a largely pre-literate society much of his appeal lay in the visual symbolism he projected, travelling the country like the ordinary peasant, in third-class railway carriages, wearing the loin cloth of the Hindu holyman (*sannyasin*). At every station stop on his travels he would emerge to speak at a mass rally. These images were then amplified by news reports and photographs and the new medium of the movie newsreel. Gandhi offered India's political elite, moreover, a compelling strategy of political action. While a few moderates still clung to constitutionalist protest, the failure of such a strategy, after the Amritsar massacre, was only too obvious. So too had the populist politics of the 'street' outlived their usefulness. From the time of the 1892 cow protection campaign onwards, eruptions of popular sentiment testified to an enduring, and deeply felt, animosity towards British colonialism in India. While these movements had some successes to their credit, most notably the revocation of the partition of Bengal, neither the plotting of secret societies nor riotous mobs in the streets offered much prospect of an independent India. Furthermore, as a moralist who sought class harmony, Gandhi offered the educated elite a critical reassurance. The Congress leadership were not Marxists, and they dared not put their own dominance at risk by stirring up class animosities. With Gandhi they had a leader who could at once appeal effectively to those outside the narrow constituency of the educated, and yet contain any potential threat to their own predominance in society.

THE POWER OF GANDHI'S NAME: SUPPORTERS AND OPPONENTS

Although Gandhi by 1919 had found a responsive audience for a new political practice – as crowds turned out in their thousands to shout 'Mahatma Gandhi ki jai' (Long live the Mahatma) – his appeal was never uniform across India, and many, while following him, made of him the 'mahatma' they wanted. To understand Gandhian nationalism, therefore, it is necessary at the outset to take account of who supported him, and why, as well as who did not. Gandhi's most committed followers, not surprisingly, were those closest to him in background and sentiment. In the province of Gujarat, his home region, Gandhi set up his ashram, near its capital city of Ahmedabad; and in its rural reaches, he organized his successful experiments in disciplined peasant agitation. What was sometimes referred to as a vani–vakil–pattidar alliance, that brought together traders and professionals with the well-off landowning peasants of the pattidar caste, formed an unwavering core of support for Gandhi's social and moral, as well as his political, activism. Even the wealthiest Gujarati traders and industrialists, whom one might imagine would oppose his hand-spinning utopia, committed their time and money to Gandhi's activities. They shared, after all, common caste and regional values, and, insofar as Gandhi encouraged swadeshi production, they saw profit for their manufacturing enterprises.

Outside Gujarat, Gandhian nationalism flourished most strongly through the middle Gangetic valley, especially in the provinces of Bihar and UP. In this populous heartland of 'Hindustan', Gandhi found devoted lieutenants, men such as Govind Ballabh Pant and Motilal Nehru (1861–1931), together with Nehru's son Jawaharlal (1889–1964), who ultimately became Gandhi's chosen successor. In this region too, as in Gujarat, Gandhi drew to himself the professional elite, the trading community, and the more substantial peasantry. But the commitment to Gandhi's programme among these men was often of a different sort from that of their counterparts in Gujarat. Men like the Nehrus, committed to a modern India that could hold its own with the industrialized West, found little to attract them either in Gandhi's utopian pastoralism or in his moralizing asceticism. The young Jawaharlal Nehru even saw in socialist Russia a model of economic development. As he put it in an address to the Congress in 1936:

I see no way of ending the poverty, the vast unemployment, the degradation and the subjection of the Indian people except through socialism. That involves vast and revolutionary changes in our political and social structure... the ending of private property, except in a restricted sense, and the replacement of the present profit system by a higher ideal of cooperative service... If the future is full of hope it is largely because of Soviet Russia and what it has done.

Yet Jawaharlal had to acknowledge that Gandhi was 'a man of commanding personality who inspired devotion in India's millions', that because of him the people of India, throwing off their fear of the British, had 'straightened their backs and raised their heads'. In part simply because Gandhi offered Indian nationalism a prospect of success in place of the deadends of an ineffectual constitutionalism and a self-destructive terrorism, but also because they could take pride in the way this 'mahatma' embodied the 'authentic' spirit of a resurgent India, the Nehrus, father and son, and many like them, threw themselves into the non-cooperation movement. The price was often high, for Gandhi demanded the return of titles and government honours, the abandonment of often lucrative legal practices, and lengthy periods in jail. Yet the sacrifices were gladly made, for, as Jawaharlal Nehru wrote in his autobiography, we had a 'feeling of satisfaction at doing effective political work which was changing the face of India before our eyes', and even, he admitted, 'an agreeable sense of moral superiority over our opponents'.

In Bihar and UP the cry of 'Mahatma Gandhi ki jai' radiated outwards to the foothills of the Himalayas and down to the oppressed tenantry of the region's great landlords. Yet in these remote areas, as it circulated among an impoverished peasantry, Gandhi's message took on unexpected shapes. Gandhi, and his volunteer workers in the localities, had devised what they saw as an appropriate role for these peasant masses. They were meant to come out in their thousands and to receive *darshan*, in which the devotee enters the presence of the divine and secures his blessing, in this case that of the 'mahatma'. They were not, however, to act on their own without instructions, nor were they on any account to challenge the gaping distinctions of class that structured their lives. But it was not easy so to constrain peasant action or peasant belief. From the very beginning of Gandhi's leadership of the national movement, as Shahid Amin has forcefully argued, the peasantry made of this 'great-souled mahatma' the possessor of occult powers, a man able magically to right wrongs and to transform the exploitative power relationships of rural society. His boons even took the form of the regeneration of trees and wells:

In mohalla Humayunpur...two dead trees which had fallen in the garden of Babu Yugal Kishore, vakil, have planted themselves back! Many believe that this is due to the grace of Mahatmaji. This [is] because the person who cut the trees said that if the spiritual power of Mahatmaji was genuine the trees would stand up on their own! Thousands gather at this site every day and *batashas* (a kind of sweetmeat), money and ornaments are offered by men and women alike.

In effect Gandhi, as someone who could remove afflictions, was fitted into the pantheon of Hindu deities; and swaraj took on the shape of the coming end of time, in which taxes and oppression of all kinds would vanish. To hurry on this millennial order the peasants of UP had no hesitation, in Gandhi's name, in looting bazaars and attacking landlords. Eventually, in February 1922, in an incident which caused a horror-striken Gandhi to call off the entire non-cooperation movement, a peasant mob in Chauri Chaura, Gorakhpur district, locked twenty-two Indian policemen in the local police station and then set fire to the building, killing everyone inside.

In some areas, and among some groups, Gandhi found very little, or at best a reluctant, support for non-cooperation. In the princely states, as well as in the thinly settled hills of central India, Gandhi's message foundered, for the Congress volunteers, frequently urban students, had no way of gaining access. The princes, sustained in power by the British since 1858, were determined to keep their states walled off from nationalism, while railways and newspapers rarely penetrated the jungle-clad districts of the interior. The lowest elements of the social order too, artisans and the landless, preoccupied with desperate struggles for existence, remained outside. Some, indeed, especially among the untouchables, as we shall see, disdaining Gandhi's attempt to act on their behalf, preferred to organize separately under leaders who addressed their own concerns.

Perhaps unsurprisingly, the most intense opposition to Gandhi, and his new style of political activity, came from those who saw their own pre-eminence threatened by this upstart Gujarati with his novel ideas of non-cooperation. Gandhi's most reluctant converts were those who had led the Congress before 1920, especially the educated elites of Calcutta, Bombay, and Madras. The Bengal bhadralok, for instance, committed to constitutional methods, enjoyed substantial benefits from their participation in the law courts and legislative councils, and did not relish giving them up; nor did they care to unleash mass movements whose outcomes they could not control.

C. R. Das (1870–1925), at the head of the Bengal Congress, joined Gandhi only at the last minute, at the special Congress session of September 1920, when he found he could not defeat the non-cooperation programme. In similar fashion, Tilak's supporters in Maharashtra dragged their feet until Tilak's death in 1920 opened the way to younger, and more militant, political activists. Others disliked what the poet Rabindranath Tagore called Gandhi's focus on one 'narrow' field alone at the expense of a wider cosmopolitan sympathy. 'To one and all', Tagore wrote, 'he simply says: Spin and weave, spin and weave.' Of ultimately great significance, M. A. Jinnah, whose political skills had been honed in cooperation with Gokhale, and who was committed to constitutionalism, resigned from the Congress, and turned to the Muslim League, rather than support what he saw as an unseemly mass movement.

Often, too, the adherence of one group provoked local rivals to join opposition parties, or remain quiescent. In the Bombay city hartal of 1919, for instance, the lead taken by the Gujarati business classes kept the Maratha industrial workers at home. As one contemporary observer wrote, 'The Marathas rarely forget that they are Marathas, and that he [Gandhi] is a Gujarati; amongst them his vogue has been fitful and wavering.' In Punjab and Madras, provincial caste and class antagonisms restricted Gandhi's base of support throughout the 1920s. In both provinces, the major supporters of the Congress were urban traders and professionals. In Punjab the predominance of this class in the Congress encouraged the majority rural population, both Hindu and Muslim, landlord and tenant, to organize their own competing Unionist Party under landlord leadership. Sustained by the benefits agriculturists had secured under the 1901 land alienation act, their cross-class electoral alliances further cemented by tribal ties, rural Punjabis, defiantly participating in the reformed political system, kept the Unionists in power until the mid-1940s. In the Tamil areas of the south, where the Brahman community had long championed the nationalist cause, and dominated Annie Besant's Home Rule League, suspicious non-Brahmans saw no point in exchanging British for Brahman dominance. They were antagonized as well by Gandhi's preaching of Hindi as a national language. Hence well-to-do non-Brahman landlords organized the Justice Party, which, in office throughout the 1920s, worked with the British to secure a larger share of government and university places for their community. Confronted with this lack of enthusiasm throughout much of India, Gandhi secured Congress approval of non-cooperation only by forming an alliance with the Muslim supporters of the Ottoman khilafat. Without their votes, the non-cooperation motion at the September 1920 Congress would have gone down to defeat. Yet the Khilafatists were unlike Gandhi's other supporters in that they were organized separately under their own leaders. The Congress–Muslim alliance, a product, as we have seen, of the 1916 Lucknow Pact, had gained strength as the war drew to a close. With the defeat of Turkey, complemented by the punitive 1920 Treaty of Sevres, increasing numbers of India's Muslims began to fear for the independence of the Ottoman sultan, whose position as khalifa (caliph) of Islam provided, so they believed, an ordering point that sustained the law and faith of Muslims everywhere. The issue stimulated the first mass mobilization of Muslims, employing meetings, oratory, and protest marches. In so doing, the Khilafat agitation, with its distinctive organization and symbolic repertoire, helped define the emerging identity of 'Indian Muslims'.

British support of harsh sanctions against Turkey in the postwar settlement drove large numbers of Muslims, from conservative Deobandis to Western-educated Aligarh graduates, ever closer to Gandhi, for whom the British treatment of Turkey deserved condemnation alongside that meted out to India. At no time, however, did more than a handful of these Muslims join the Congress Party as individuals. The All-India Khilafat Committee, though it coordinated its activities closely with Gandhi, always remained a separate body; and its vision of India's future, as elaborated by the 'ulama of the Jamiyyat ul-ulama-i Hind, was no less utopian than that of Gandhi himself. The proposals put forward by the Jamiyyat imagined an India composed of two separate communities – of Hindus and Muslims – each with its own laws, courts, and educational system. Despite its anti-colonial stance, the Jamiyyat paid little heed to Congress's call for a sovereign government with authority over citizens who shared common goals and aspirations. Instead, India's Muslims, though scattered all over the country and divided among themselves by language and customs, would live, so far as possible, in a kind of self-imposed isolation, rather like Gandhi's imagined village communities, together yet apart from their fellows.

The Congress–Khilafat alliance has often been evoked by nationalist Indians, in the years since 1947, in a kind of nostalgic reverie, as an era of amity that anticipated a road not taken – to an unpartitioned independent India. To be sure, these years, from 1916 to 1922, were a period of communal harmony never again to be recovered. But the distinctions between communities were not broken down. Neither Gandhi nor the Khilafat leaders ever envisaged an India in which religious communities were not the primary players. Indeed, the organization of parallel, yet separate, processions and meetings by the Congress and by the Khilafatists only intensified, and so institutionalized, this distinction between communities. Even the khilafat flag itself, by juxtaposing Hindu and Muslim emblems, visibly manifested communal difference. Hence, it is not surprising that the union between Hindu and Muslim collapsed once the single thread that linked them had been cut. In 1924 the new secular Turkish regime of Attaturk itself abolished the khilafat. Bereft of this shared grievance, their separate political ambitions heightened by the promise of power held out under Montagu–Chelmsford reforms, Hindu and Muslim leaders turned instead increasingly to mobilizing followers by the use of each religion's distinctive symbols. The result was an explosive era of rioting and recrimination.

THE COURSE OF NON-COOPERATION

For the British, Gandhi's turn to non-cooperation posed a seemingly intractable dilemma. Over the years the British had devised ever more effective strategies for dealing with nationalists. The moderates among them could be conciliated, or ignored; the revolutionary terrorists could be clapped in jail and kept there for years on end. But Gandhi's non-cooperation was a baffling novelty, and the British did not initially know how to respond. The Conservatives at home, along with the military in India, argued for outright repression by force. But the Indian Government, loath to face more Amritsar massacres, and anxious to get some support for the new dyarchy constitution, especially among the large bodies of opinion not enamoured of Gandhi, did not want to risk policies that would antagonize still more of the Indian people. Furthermore, they realized that to club and jail vast numbers of peaceable demonstrators would make the government, if not the British as a whole, look like bullies in the eyes of the world, and even to themselves. Indeed, Gandhi had contrived his style of agitation in part with this objective in mind – by claiming the moral high ground for himself, he wanted to appeal to the British conscience, and so to make them feel they were violating their own principles if they moved forcibly against him. The government could not, however, openly embrace Gandhi, or accept his political demands. The Raj still mattered to most Englishmen, in part because by the 1920s the Indian market loomed ever larger as a crucial vent for British exports. By and large, too, apart from a few Christian liberals like C. F. Andrews, the British did not trust Gandhi. Churchill's derisive dismissal of Gandhi as 'a half-naked fakir' resonated with much British opinion. Although viceroys were occasionally tempted, as we shall see, to come to terms with Gandhi, they were always restrained by the strength of imperialist and conservative sentiment.

Hence the British were driven towards a delicate and complex policy of manoeuvre. As they saw it, they had to treat Gandhi gently enough so that he did not become a martyr in Indian eyes. Yet at the same time they had to act sufficiently forcefully to make visible to all that they, not Gandhi, sat in the driver's seat. In practice, this often meant that, rather than placing him under arrest at once, the British would stalk and watch Gandhi, giving him, as it were, an ample supply of rope. During the 1920–22 non-cooperation movement, this policy of restraint paid large dividends. As he ran his campaign, Gandhi was left undisturbed until the Chauri Chaura killings; then, with Indian opinion turning against non-cooperation, and Gandhi having himself called it off, the British felt the time had come when they could safely place him under arrest. Gandhi's subsequent trial for sedition, far from provoking an uprising, only signalled the end of this first movement. By tactical flexibility, using the skills they honed during this first encounter with Gandhi, the British were able to keep nationalism from reaching a crescendo that might overwhelm them. They adroitly waited out eras of excitement, took advantage of periods of quiescence, and so kept control of the process of the devolution of power. But manoeuvre alone could not halt or reverse the continuous draining away of the authority of the Raj.

With the ending of the first Gandhian non-cooperation campaign, British relations with the Congress fell into a pattern that, while it could not be called amicable, still built upon a set of shared assumptions that shaped the growth of Indian nationalism during the quarter-century from 1922 to 1947. First among these was the British conviction that Gandhi could be relied upon not to raise up a violent revolution. Many among the British, in the early years after 1919, were convinced Gandhi was riding a whirlwind he could not control. The aftermath of Chauri Chaura reassured them that, if not a friend of the Raj, Gandhi was still committed to a course of non-violent action. This made credible the policy of watching and waiting, of mild restraint rather than a ready recourse to force. On Gandhi's side, the British repudiation, after Amritsar, of rule by military might gave hope that perhaps an appeal to British moral values might work, that British consciences might be pricked, and so encouraged Gandhi to stay within the bounds of non-violence. Violent revolution was not only morally wrong, it was unnecessary.

To be sure, under extreme provocation the Congress could, most notably as we shall see in 1942, wink at violence; while the British, when faced with widespread civil disobedience, did sometimes crack down with a brutal harshness marked by lathi charges and mass arrests. Still, a surprising amount of reasonableness, if not of actual goodwill, did pervade dealings between the British and the Congress. Oddly perhaps, this manifested itself most visibly in jail, where Congress leaders were accorded a special A-class accommodation that allowed them books, visitors, and food not permitted ordinary prisoners. Gandhi's 1922 sedition trial set the tone. After describing how the events of 1919 had led him to 'preach disaffection' towards the Raj, Gandhi went on to 'invite and cheerfully to submit to the highest penalty that can be inflicted upon me'. The judge, on his part, said that the charges carried a prison term of six years, but he added that if the government later saw fit to reduce the sentence, 'no one would be better pleased than I'. Gandhi also used the trial to articulate in dramatic fashion central elements of his political style. Refusing to be placed in the powerless and humiliating position of the usual defendant, Gandhi defiantly pleaded guilty and even took upon himself responsibility for the acts of others. In the process he at once embraced, yet repudiated as incompatible with colonialism, British notions of 'justice'. At the same time, by bringing suffering upon himself, he enhanced his saintly role as one who sacrifices for the good of all.

As the collapse of non-cooperation after Chauri Chaura makes clear, the movement towards independence was not to be marked by a steady unrelenting pressure sustained year after year. To the contrary, Congress activities during the 1920s and 1930s, and into the 1940s, went through a series of ups and downs in both intensity and focus. One can identify, perhaps, three major cycles. Each began with a blundering act of provocation on the part of the British. This would be followed by an escalation of excitement, culminating in a programme of civil disobedience under Gandhi's leadership. The British would respond with a judicious combination of concessions and arrests. Increasingly demoralized, their enthusiasm spent, the nationalist cadres would then slowly lapse into inactivity. The result would be a prolonged period of quiescence. During these years Gandhi would retire from politics, and throw himself instead into what he called his 'constructive' work, above all the promotion of hand-spinning and improvement of the condition of the untouchables. Meanwhile, the more politically engaged members of the Congress, drawn by the lure of the reformed legislatures, which offered ever wider opportunities for wielding power within the system, would abandon non-cooperation in favour of an active participation in the British Indian political order. This style of political activity would continue until yet another provocative incident triggered yet another outburst of nationalist enthusiasm.

After 1922, as active non-cooperation moved into a quiescent phase, a number of prominent Congress politicians, among them C. R. Das and Motilal Nehru, anxious to re-enter the fray, formed the Swarajist Party, and successfully contested elections for the reformed assemblies. Simultaneously, with Gandhi's encouragement, the khadi movement, through the All-India Spinners Association, took on organizational form. For Gandhian nationalists, khadi's significance extended far beyond its role as a signifier of swadeshi production, or even its assertion of the value of artisanal handwork. Use of this coarse, simple, usually white, cloth, by eradicating distinctions of region, along with those of caste, class and religion, defined the wearer as a member of a universal Indian nation. Rejecting the British view of India as a land of separate communities whose varied clothing styles visually announced their unfitness for self-rule, khadi constructed an India that was united, disciplined, and cohesive.

Khadi further opened up new opportunities for India's women. Whereas before nationalist rhetoric had defined women as the guardians of an inner 'spiritual' India, now, by spinning and by wearing khadi, India's women participated actively in the creation of the nation. This was not an easy or uncomplicated transformation. Many elite women were loath to give up the shimmering silk saris that defined their high status in favour of the rough white cloth previously associated with prostitutes, widows, and the impoverished. Some, not only women but men like Nehru as well, sought a compromise by the use of high-count or textured fabrics. Still, khadi mattered, for, as Gandhi wrote, this cloth 'binds all brothers and sisters of India into one, which purifies and ennobles their soul and will lift them to freedom from the present life of poverty and bondage'. The visual power of khadi is readily apparent in the contrasting apparel of the Congress in 1919 (plate 6.3), when Western dress was still dominant, and a meeting of Congress workers in 1924 (plate 6.4) when simple khadi, with the Gandhi *topi* (cap), predominated.

AGRARIAN AND INDUSTRIAL UPHEAVALS

Alongside the rise of the Gandhian Congress, the immediate postwar years also witnessed the emergence of class-based protest movements. These drew sustenance from the economic dislocation of the last years of the war. During the short period from 1917 to 1920 price levels rose by nearly 50 per cent, with those of the coarse food grains that constituted the staple of the poor rising further than those of higher-quality crops. Combined with the effects of a poor monsoon and the influenza pandemic in 1918, the hardship of these years fuelled a variety of protests. Most prominent were the *kisan sabha* (peasant society) movements of 1920–22 in the UP and Bihar. Under the leadership of the charismatic Baba Ramchandra,

Plate 6.3   Delegates to the 1919 Congress session in Amritsar.

Plate 6.4   Congress Workers in south India, 1924. Jawaharlal Nehru
(with sash) in front row centre.

this movement, which secured its greatest appeal in the landlord-
dominated districts of southern and eastern Oudh, sought to put
peasant, not nationalist, interests at the top of the agenda. Coun-
selling tenants to withhold unjust rents, made more onerous by the
high food prices, Ramchandra inspired a number of riotous demonstrations on landlord properties. Rioters also sometimes attacked
bazaars and merchant property in an effort to secure fixed prices
for basic commodities. The residents of the Himalayan foothills expressed their grievances by breaking into reserved forests and setting them on fire. Little, however, came of these peasant protests.
The British pushed through, over landlord opposition, legislation
that capped rental increases and secured occupancy tenants from
eviction. But the act did not fundamentally alter the bases of rural
power. Indeed, this challenge to their power only served to propel
the landlords into the political arena, where their so-called National
Agriculturists Party took office under the dyarchy constitution in
the UP.

The Congress offered but little more support to these peasant
movements than did the British. Young Jawaharlal Nehru, who had

never set foot in a village before in his life, returned in 1920 from a season of 'wanderings among the kisans' to express sympathy with their plight. Subsequently, inspired by socialist ideals, as we have seen above, he argued that a more equitable distribution of wealth was essential to full independence. But, drawn away by the nationalist struggle, and frequently in jail, Nehru had no occasion to offer leadership to the countryside. Gandhi, for his part, was positively hostile to any class-based agitation. He was prepared to countenance rural struggle only when it was directed against the British, as in the early Champaran satyagraha against British planters who forced peasants to grow indigo on unfavourable terms, and in his tightly organized 'no tax campaigns', in which landowning Pattidari peasants in selected areas of his home province of Gujarat, above all in Bardoli in 1928, refused payment of the government's land revenue demand. Inspired by the vision of a society organized apart from capitalist self-interest, he appealled to India's wealthy landlords and industrialists to act as trustees for the less privileged. Such a notion of class harmony of course advanced the political interests of the Congress; when class was not pitted against class, all could work together on behalf of the anti-colonial struggle. Such counsels were, furthermore, not uncongenial to the groups which made up the bulk of the Congress's supporters. Neither the well-to-do Marwari industrialist nor the peasant proprietor who tilled his land with the help of low-caste bonded labourers had much enthusiasm for class warfare or a property redistribution of which he was likely to be the loser. As we shall see, neither during their 1937–9 ministries, nor indeed after 1947, did the Congress enact far-reaching agrarian reform legislation.

The years of unrest following the First World War also saw an unprecedented wave of strikes among factory labour, accompanied by the formation of India's first trade unions. Through the All-India Trade Union Congress, the Congress endeavoured to control, and subordinate to its own nationalist purposes, the burgeoning labour movement. But the middle-class Congress leadership was unable to restrain the militancy of those on the shop floor. Labour organizing thus provided an opening for India's fledgling Communists. Inspired by the success of the 1917 Bolshevik revolution in Russia, the committed revolutionary M. N. Roy (1887–1954), living in exile first in Mexico and then in the new Soviet Union, established the Communist Party of India in 1920. By the middle years of the 1920s, though the party itself was proscribed and Roy remained in exile, Communist organizers had set up unions and organized strikes in India's textile, jute, and steel mills, and in its railway workshops. In 1928, when Bombay textile workers stayed out on strike for over six months to protest wage cuts, workers' mill committees came together to form the Communist-led Girni Kamgar Union, which at its height had some 60,000 members.

Such successes were, however, short-lived. Government repression was fierce. A 'conspiracy' trial, held in 1929, ended with the jailing of all the major Communist leaders for over four years. Lacking support from Gandhi and the Congress, and often regarded with suspicion even by the workers themselves, for many of its leaders were high-caste men who had never engaged in manual labour, the Indian Communist Party had great difficulty consolidating its position. Unlike their Chinese colleagues under Mao during these years, they were never able to penetrate the countryside. They succeeded only in areas where they drew support from discontented kisan leaders such as Swami Sahajanand in Bihar. Abrupt changes in the Communist Party 'line' laid down in Moscow further left the Indian Communists adrift and ineffectual.

NON-COOPERATION: ROUND TWO, 1927–1934

In 1927, anticipating by two years the statutory revision of the Montagu–Chelmsford reforms, the British Government appointed a commission, under the Liberal Sir John Simon, to recommend a further reform of India's constitution. Instead of the expected gratitude, however, the British reaped only animosity, for the commissioners were all members of the British Parliament. Across an extraordinarily wide spectrum of Indian opinion, from Congress and the Muslim League to Hindu nationalists and moderate Liberals, this all-British commission carried with it the implication that Indians were incapable of deciding their own fate, that they were still children who needed all-knowing parents to legislate for them. This blunder set in motion the second great cycle of Gandhian non-cooperation, which lasted, with a brief truce in 1931, from 1930 to 1934.

Confronted with this unexpected hostility, the viceroy Lord Irwin (1927–31), supported by a Labour government newly come to power in Britain, issued a declaration that the natural outcome of India's constitutional progress would be 'Dominion' status. Much the same had been said by Montagu in 1917, and there was still no timetable for independence. Nevertheless, as the white-settler dominions, such as Canada and Australia, had recently secured full control of both their internal and external affairs, Irwin's declaration implied that Britain had relinquished any hope of retaining lasting authority over an Indian dominion. As Indian distrust of the Simon Commission showed no signs of abating, with plans for another non-cooperation movement underway, the Ramsey MacDonald government was driven, in 1930, to yet another concession. Leaving the forlorn Simon to twist in the wind, the British convened a series of round table conferences in London, to which all elements of Indian political opinion were invited, and from which it was hoped that an agreed scheme for constitutional reform could emerge. In this expectation, MacDonald was to be mistaken.

During 1928, as the machinery was being geared up for non-cooperation, Indian nationalists scrambled to produce some common front that they could present to their rulers. The most notable of these documents, the so-called Nehru Report, named for its author Motilal Nehru, was not only unacceptable to the British, with its demand for immediate home rule, but widened the gulf already emerging between the Congress and much Muslim opinion. Repudiating the 1916 Congress commitment to separate communal electorates, the Nehru Report laid out a scheme for a federal India much like that which emerged after 1947, with a strong centre possessing all residual powers and no reservation of seats in the central legislature for the Muslim community. Far from assuaging Muslim fears, the Nehru Report only reignited suspicion of a 'Hindu Raj', and united most Muslim political leaders, apart from a small group of 'Nationalist Muslims', in opposition to the Congress. Jinnah, for instance, had been prepared to give up separate electorates if he could secure reservation of one-third of the legislative seats and assignment of residual powers to the provinces. This distrust was never subsequently to be overcome. The way forward, however, as the Muslim leaders wrangled among themselves, was for a long time unclear. They never sought to institute Islamically based policies, but rather to protect the interests of India's Muslims. Their disagreements turned upon the most effective constitutional strategy, among those being debated on all sides, to secure that end. As the sometime Khilafat leader Muhammed ʿAli wrote in 1930, 'I belong to two circles of equal size but which are not concentric. One is India and the other is the Muslim world... We belong to these circles, and we can leave neither.'

The second non-cooperation, or civil disobedience, movement had many elements in common with the first. But it also included several unique features. Most startling was Gandhi's decision to inaugurate the movement in March 1930 by a 240-mile march from his ashram to the sea, followed by an illicit manufacture of salt by boiling sea water. As the salt tax was not a major source of government revenue, many within the Congress looked on in dismay, while the British, puzzled, stood by watching. But the salt march was a stroke of genius. Gandhi's frail figure, striding forward staff-in-hand to confront British imperialism over access to a basic commodity, fast became the focus of sympathetic attention not only throughout India but around the world, above all in the United States where the salt march first brought Gandhi to public notice. The powerful visual imagery of the march was further enhanced by its ranks of khadi-clad demonstrators, including for the first time marching women. Although the government arrested Gandhi soon after the march, the damage had been done. More disciplined in its organization, if less apocalyptic in its expectations than its predecessor a decade before, the civil disobedience movement spread rapidly throughout India. Its appeal was further enhanced by the Great Depression. As prices fell, farmers caught in a vice between declining returns for their crops and inflexible land taxes readily turned to civil disobedience, while traders found hartals much less onerous in a slump than if times had been prosperous.

This second campaign caught up a number of groups who had not previously participated. Women for the first time came out on to the streets; protests against forest regulations took place in central India; on the North-West Frontier, despite the region's reputation for violence, a movement among Muslim Pathans led by Abdul Ghaffer Khan, who became known as the 'Frontier Gandhi', allied itself with Gandhi. Apart from the Frontier, however, in contrast to 1920, most Muslims stayed studiously, and ominously, aloof. Most significant perhaps were the inroads that Gandhi now began to make into south India. During the 1920s south India had remained aloof from nationalism. But by 1930, with non-Brahmans securing ever more places in the government and universities, the Justice Party had fulfilled much of its mission. At the same time, Tamil poets and intellectuals, utilizing Tamil symbols, including the construction of the god Shiva as Dravidian in origin and the deification of the Tamil language as a goddess deserving reverence in place of Sanskrit, as Sumathi Ramaswami has shown, had helped create an increasingly self-confident south Indian culture. Neither nationalism nor Gandhi were any longer so threatening. Furthermore, the Congress leadership worked energetically to build bridges to the larger south Indian populace. One element of the Congress programme that struck an especially resonant chord among upwardly mobile peasant groups was its advocacy of prohibition, for in the south tapping palm trees and drinking the fermented juice marked out low-caste status. By the mid-1930s, pushing aside the inept Justice Party, the Congress had become the dominant political organization in south India. Nevertheless, Dravidian sentiment remained powerful. During these years it took the form of the militant 'Self-Respect' movement under the leadership of E. V. Ramaswami Naicker (1880–1974).

Confronted with its growing popular appeal, the British began to fear an ebbing away of their authority into the hands of the Congress. Most alarming perhaps, especially to Conservatives at home such as Churchill, was the spectacle in March 1931 of Gandhi marching up the steps of the recently completed Viceroy's House in New Delhi, there to parley, seemingly on equal terms, with Lord Irwin. No less devout than Gandhi himself, and moved by a similar sense of moral purpose, Irwin was determined to reach out to his antagonist. The resulting Gandhi–Irwin pact, which brought a temporary halt to civil disobedience and enabled Gandhi himself to attend the second round table conference, secured little for the British, and, denounced by Nehru and others as a 'sell-out', even less of immediate advantage for the Congress. Still, these events announced that the Congress had gained an unprecedented legitimacy as the representative of an embryonic Indian nation. In consequence, when the Gandhi–Irwin pact collapsed in early 1932, with Gandhi's return empty-handed from London, the new viceroy Lord Willingdon (1931–6), anxious to reassure Britain's supporters in India that the Raj was still in control, cracked down on the Congress with exceptional severity. Some 40,000 Indians were arrested within three months, and many, including Gandhi himself, languished in jail for up to two years.

NEW OPPORTUNITIES, AND NEW CONFLICTS

With the Congress out of action, the British moved forwards on their own to restructure the government of India. Most significant was the endeavour to bring India's princes into the political system. Walled off from each other until the creation of the Chamber of Princes in 1920, with only the loosest supervision from the British residents posted at their courts, the princes stood forth as the ideal representatives of the 'feudal' India the British had created to assure their predominance. As the Congress movement gathered strength, the princes, jolted into an awareness of their own vulnerability, proposed that British and princely India be joined into a single federal state. Such a scheme had advantages not only for princes, who would now be built into the new India at the outset, but for others as well. The Muslims saw in federation a way of securing conservative allies against the Congress, while for the British a federal state provided a heaven-sent opportunity to blunt the power of the Congress juggernaut. Most British Conservatives had never been reconciled to the prospect of an independent India. After 1931, with a Conservative-dominated national government in power in London, they determined to devise ways of holding on to India, or, as the Indian secretary Samuel Hoare put it, of giving 'a semblance of responsible government' to Indians while keeping 'for ourselves the threads that really direct the system of government'. This meant that Congress politicians should be diverted to and then kept bottled up in the provinces, while the central government, with power shared among Muslims, princes, and other groups such as Sikhs and untouchables, would be in the hands of those who could be relied upon to secure Britain's interests.

In pursuit of this objective, the 1932 Communal Award sought to give special treatment, including separate electorates, to a variety of so-called 'minorities'. These included above all the untouchables, who had begun to organize themselves under B. R. Ambedkar (1891–1956), in opposition to Gandhi. Unwilling to see untouchables split off from the larger Hindu community, and imagining himself as the guardian of these downtrodden people, whom he called *harijans* (children of god), Gandhi, while still in jail, embarked on a momentous 'fast to the death' to secure the abrogation of this award. As Gandhi grew weaker, a compromise was reached in which separate electorates restricted to untouchable voters were replaced by seats reserved for untouchables in the various Indian legislatures. Although this brought the immediate crisis to an end, and, combined with promises of equal access to wells, roads, temples, and other public places, portended the inclusion of untouchables as equal members into the Indian state, significant improvement was to be a matter of decades. Even at the present time, untouchables, now known as *dalits*, can hardly be said to be fully free of the stigma of their depressed status.

The Communal Award was followed by the Government of India Act of 1935. Meant to set in place a framework for the Conservative vision of India, it made provision for a federal centre and, doing away with dyarchy, substantially extended provincial autonomy, with ministers responsible to their local legislatures now in charge of all branches of the government. This act was to have far-reaching consequences, though not, for the most part, those intended by its Conservative authors. The federal centre was to come into existence when one-half of the major princes acceded to its terms. By 1935, however, the princes were rapidly getting cold feet. Fearful of the loss of sovereignty entailed by federation, and content to sit back and watch the politicians of British India fight among themselves, they started bargaining for better terms, and so in the end torpedoed the whole scheme. The British, on their part, were reluctant to push these men too hard, for the princes had powerful friends among the 'diehard' Conservatives in Parliament, and the officials in New Delhi were in any case not unwilling to see the centre remain in British hands for a few more years. The appearance, in the later 1930s, within a number of states, of popular movements for the reform of princely autocracy, some supported by local Congressmen, reinforced the princes' waning enthusiasm for federation. The princes were, however, to pay a heavy price for this short-sighted behaviour. For, when their British patrons went home, they found themselves left behind, like beached whales, with few friends and no institutional base in the new political order.

In the provinces the new act energized politics. The electorate had been vastly extended, so that some 30 million Indians – one-sixth of the adult population, including some women – now had the vote. Released from an increasingly sterile confrontation, the Congress leaders, as a decade before in the mid-1920s, looked forward eagerly to a resumption of electoral activity. They were, however, in a much stronger position than before. The prestige of the Congress, with Gandhi at its head, had reached unparalleled heights as a result of the civil disobedience campaign, while volunteer workers had spread its message throughout the country. All that was required was to turn this enhanced stature, as India's pre-eminent nationalist organization, into votes. With the elections under the 1935 Act, Congress began the process of transforming itself from a mass movement into a political party. In a stunning triumph, winning 758 of some 1,500 seats in the various provincial legislatures, the Congress in 1937 formed governments in seven provinces, including Madras, Bombay, the Central Provinces, Bihar, and UP.

In office the Congress did few of the things it had said it would do. It did not subvert the 1935 Act, but rather cooperated amicably with the British provincial governors, and enforced law and order much as its predecessors had done. An organization of commercial and professional elites and substantial peasants, it did not, apart from measures to relieve indebtedness, enact extensive agrarian reforms. The Congress was also caught up in an enduring tension between its India-wide structure, with a High Command dictating policy, and the increasing importance of the provinces, where local leaders pursued their own interests supported by their own followers. Nevertheless, the long-term effects of the Congress ministries were immense. One was simply the training Congress politicians, used only to agitation and opposition, received in the practice of government. By the time war broke out in 1939, capable and experienced, they were well prepared take up the reins and themselves rule India, as they were to do only a few years later.

Unfortunately, however, the Congress governments were wholly unsuccessful in winning over their Muslim compatriots. Much of this was the product of unintended slights, together with an insensitivity to deeply felt anxieties. In the UP, for instance, as the new government was being formed, the Congress disdained overtures from the Muslim League for a coalition. They arrogantly told its provincial leader Chaudhuri Khaliquzzaman that the League's members could participate in the new government only by dissolving the League and accepting the discipline of the Congress Party. The Congress, with an absolute majority of legislative seats, had no need of League support. They seemed not to notice, or care, however, that, while they had won the bulk of the open seats in the UP legislature, the Muslim League had won twenty-nine of those reserved for Muslims, and the Congress none at all. In addition, men like Nehru, with his socialist idealism, mistrusted the League's leaders as representatives of 'feudal' landlord interests. Whatever its motives, this high-handed treatment did not reassure Muslim opinion.

Enraged by this humiliation at the hands of the Congress, the Muslim League redoubled its efforts to gain a mass following. This was not to be an easy task. Throughout India, in the 1937 elections, the League had received under 5 per cent of the total Muslim vote, and had emerged as the predominant party in none of the Muslim majority provinces. In the Punjab and Bengal, regional parties took office. Although the leaders of these parties were themselves Muslims, as were the bulk of their followers, and they undertook to support Jinnah on all-India Muslim issues, neither party was formed along communal lines. In Bengal, Fazl al-Haq's Krishak Praja Party, which led various coalition governments after 1937, was dedicated to the uplift of the East Bengal tenantry; while in the Punjab Sikander Hayat's Unionist Party, which had long had Hindu members, always represented itself as the defender of all Punjab's agricultural classes.

Elsewhere, in the provinces with substantial Muslim minorities, Congress and the League each jockeyed for position during the later 1930s. In an attempt to reach over the heads of the Muslim politicians, Congress embarked on a 'mass contact' campaign, which only further antagonized Muslim leaders and facilitated their efforts to enroll new members in the League. Muslim leaders, on their part, complained of favouritism towards Hindus, and propagation of Hindu symbols such as the cow and the Hindi language, by the Congress governments. Such allegations had little substance at the level of policy, for the Congress leadership tried scrupulously to be fair, but the flood of new recruits into the party, many from villages, others seeking jobs and power, inevitably enhanced its Hindu character. By 1939, fearful of a Congress takeover of the centre, many Muslims began to cast about for new ways of securing their interests. Among them was the novel idea that India's Muslims comprised a nation entitled to a separate state of their own. Others remained committed to a united India. Maulana Azad, as Congress president in 1940, phrased this position most forcefully:

I am proud of being an Indian. I am part of the indivisible unity that is Indian nationality . . . Islam has now as great a claim on the soil of India as Hinduism. If Hinduism has been the religion of the people here for several thousands of years, Islam has also been their religion for a thousand years. Just as a Hindu can say with pride that he is an Indian and follows Hinduism, so also can we say with equal pride that we are Indians and follow Islam.

INDUSTRY AND THE ECONOMY

The interwar years were marked not only by dramatic political upheavals, but by a grinding economic decline which fuelled much of the nationalist frustration. Many of the crises which hammered India, among them the influenza pandemic of 1918 and the Great Depression of the 1930s, had their origins elsewhere. They had nevertheless a devastating impact. After a period of relative stability in the mid-1920s, the Depression touched off a precipitous fall in prices. As a result, the value of the crops grown by India's peasantry fell by one-half, while the country's overseas markets for agricultural produce dried up. To make matters worse the prices of food and raw materials fell further than those of imported manufactured goods. The squeeze was made even more intolerable by the fact that the agriculturalists' costs, especially their land taxes and their accumulated indebtedness, fixed in cash, remained unchanged; hence their effective burden was doubled.

Within India, a vicious combination of population growth and soil exhaustion combined to worsen the larger impact of the slump. Until the 1920s, India's population had been kept in check by a high death rate, the product of famine, poverty, and disease. Modest improvements in public health, with the almost complete disappearance of major famines for fifty years after 1910, set in motion a slow but accelerating growth in population. During the interwar years this increase amounted on average to over 1 per cent per annum. Unfortunately, population growth was not matched by a corresponding increase in food production. To be sure, commercial cropping expanded, as did the area under irrigation. But this was largely confined to the Punjab, which during these years, the beneficiary of a vast network of perennial canals fed by Himalayan rivers, took up the role it has retained to the present, of South Asia's bread-basket. Elsewhere, especially in India's rice-growing regions, ever more intensive cultivation kept production at best up to previous levels. As a result, India saw an overall decline in the per capita output of food grains. In Bengal, the decline amounted to almost 40 per cent over the period from 1911 to 1941, a shortfall made good only by imports of rice from Burma.

Industry, though still only a tiny fraction of the larger Indian economy, fared substantially better than agriculture. During these years, even though it remained under British rule, India began the process of disengaging its economy from its long colonial subservience to Britain's. The process was most visible in India's pre-eminent manufacturing industry, that of cotton textiles. Textile imports, which had crested at 2,400 million yards of cloth in 1913, fell off dramatically in subsequent years. By the late 1930s Indian mills had secured up to two-thirds of the domestic market for piece-goods. At the same time industry began to spread outside its established centres in western India, while several communities long active in trade, among them Marwaris and Chettiars, for the first time began investing in manufacturing. The ideals of swadeshi were recruited to encourage consumer purchases in a growing urban middle-class market. The advertisement in plate 6.5 shows how one textile firm sought to identify its products with India itself.

Responding to the increasing importance of India's manufacturing industry, and anxious to secure the support of the country's

Plate 6.5   Advertisement for E. D. Sassoon & Co. 'EDSU' fabrics, with
sari-clad women plotted onto the map of India.

industrialists in the struggle with Gandhian nationalism, the colonial government, over howls of protest from Britain, abandoned its long-standing solicitude for the interests of British industry. From the mid-1920s a measure of 'discriminating protection' was granted to such major industries as iron and steel, textiles, sugar, paper, and matches. The effects of these measures were, however, inhibited by the government's fiscal constraints. Especially during the economic crisis of the 1930s, hamstrung by a commitment to deflationary finance, which India shared with Britain, the government stood by helplessly. Nevertheless, the new industrial and tariff policy set in motion a process that over time freed India's economy from European dominance, yet walled it off from the world. Reinforced by nationalist sentiment, this inward-looking pattern of growth persisted until the 1980s.

The interwar years, when Congress and the British remained locked in wary combat, set precedents, and established institutions, that endured for decades to come. Above all, this extended period of struggle created in the Indian National Congress a disciplined nationalist movement, with a tested leadership at the centre and devoted workers throughout India's myriad villages. Unparalleled among the other 'new nations' that emerged from the upheavals of mid-century, this organizational structure, with its ability to turn out people in their thousands, whether to demonstrate in the streets or to vote at the polls, insured the Congress dominance of the Indian political system until the 1970s. Indeed, for many years, as the only nationwide body apart from the government, the Congress visibly represented the 'imagined community' of the nation. Although the dramatic confrontations with the British on such occasions as the salt march stirred the public imagination, more important in the long run was the slow widening of the circle of the public. Increasingly, from the dyarchy legislatures on through the ministries of 1937–9, Indians secured spaces in which they could take some responsibility for running their country. Not least in importance was the institutionalization of elections as the appropriate device for popular participation in politics. By the time of independence, democratic ways had become so deeply rooted in India that their repudiation was unthinkable. In the end, one might argue, the ritual 'dance' of the Congress and the Raj over so many years enforced compromise and taught each the limits of the possible in ways that facilitated not just a smooth transfer of power but a lasting commitment to a liberal society.

Yet, at the same time, this new politics widened fissures in society that had previously been of little importance, and might well have faded away had self-government been secured in the 1920s. Instead, descriptive categories – Muslim, non-Brahman, agriculturalist – deployed by the British for their own purposes, now became the focus of intense competition. As more and more people gained access to power, but found the centre shut off, these local tensions of caste and community acquired a new political salience, and fluid boundaries hardened into engrained practice. The act of voting itself, by forcing people as individuals to make conscious choices, accelerated this process. As the Congress strove to unite all Indians under its own tent, other allegiances, especially at the newly empowered level of the province, found receptive soil as well. Nation and community, Gandhian universalism and intensely felt parochialisms, emerged together strengthened from the schooling of the interwar decades. They were to make the 1940s a period of triumph – and of tragedy.

7

The 1940s: triumph and tragedy

On 3 September 1939, on the outbreak of the Second World War, the viceroy Lord Linlithgow declared India, alongside Britain itself, at war with Hitler's Germany. Two months laters, in protest against this unilateral act, which appeared to Indians as a reassertion of high-handed British imperialism, the Congress ministries in the provinces resigned. In March of 1940, taking advantage of what they saw as a fortuitous 'deliverance' from Congress rule, the Muslim League, at its annual meeting in Lahore, enacted the Pakistan Resolution. The stage was set for the crises that were to dominate the decade of the 1940s – the war, the Congress's final movement of non-cooperation, the rise of Muslim nationalism, and then, finally, in 1947 independence, with the partition of the subcontinent into two states.

The unilateral declaration of war, a provocative act of the sort that had so often characterized British policy in India, was a tactical blunder. So too, however, was the resignation of the Congress ministries, which set in motion a protracted series of negotiations and acts of civil disobedience that were to culminate in the climactic August 'rising' of 1942. During the later 1930s Britain and India had been drifting slowly towards an amicable parting of the ways. Britain's stake in India had been declining as economic nationalism took hold around the world, while on the political front, after 1937, Congress politicians had demonstrated an ability to govern that augured well for an independent India. The coming of the war, with the resignation of the Congress ministries, changed everything.

Now, suddenly, with its back to the wall, fighting first Hitler, and then from December 1941 the Japanese as well, the British desperately needed the resources, in men and matériel, as well as the secure bases that India supplied. The Indian Army was increased in size tenfold to fight in the Middle East and South-East Asia, as well as to protect the homeland as the Japanese in 1942 advanced on Assam. As the British endeavoured to feed, cloth, and arm this immense force, they consumed their investments in India; by the end of the war, no longer Britain's debtor, India had piled up sterling balances in London of over 1,000 million pounds.

FROM NEGOTIATION TO THE AUGUST 'RISING'

As the Congress and the British warily circled each other during the years from 1939 to 1942, each sought to secure a decisive advantage for themselves from the wartime crisis. Yet the impasse that emerged by the summer of 1942 was an outcome of no one's choosing. By contrast with 1914, at the outbreak of the First World War, the Congress did not in 1939 offer unquestioning support of the war effort. Feeling that their assistance on that occasion had been taken for granted, and that they had been shabbily treated at war's end, the Congress was determined this time to exact from the British a substantial price for their wartime cooperation. At the same time, however, the character of the war – as a struggle against fascism – gave it an appeal, especially to liberal internationalists like Jawaharlal Nehru, who had toured Europe in the 1930s. To be sure, some in the Congress stood apart. Gandhi's commitment to non-violence disabled him from participation, while a few, above all Subhas Chandra Bose (1897–1945), as we will see, sought India's freedom by alliance with the fascist powers. But Nehru's views predominated in the Working Committee, with the result that Congress's consistent negotiating position was that India ought to participate in this worldwide struggle for freedom, but that it could do so meaningfully only if it were itself free. As Britain's military situation became ever more desperate, from the fall of France in 1940 on through the fall of Singapore and Burma to the Japanese in early 1942, the Congress leaders invested ever more urgency in their negotiations. But the fundamental insistence on a substantial immediate transfer of power was never abandoned.

On their part, and with a similarly increasing sense of urgency, the British sought Congress support for the war effort. Each crisis on the battlefield produced better terms. By the time of the flying visit of Sir Stafford Cripps to Delhi in April 1942, the British were willing to offer India independence, by the convening of a constituent assembly, at the end of the war, but with the important proviso that no unwilling portion of the country should be forced to join the new state. During the war, to facilitate collaboration, Indians were to be given more seats on the viceroy's executive council. Britain was willing to go so far – much further than it had ever gone before – in part to accommodate rising anti-colonialist sentiment around the world. Above all, Britain's indispensable ally, the United States under President Franklin Roosevelt, insisted that it was not fighting the war in order to preserve the British Empire; hence the American representative in Delhi, Louis Johnson, sought always to push the Indian Government towards concilation.

The Cripps mission was nevertheless doomed. Its proposals did not, as the Congress demanded, transform the viceroy's council into a cabinet responsible to an Indian legislature, or even transfer the defence ministry to Indian hands. A leftist member of the Labour Party and a friend of Nehru, Cripps did his best to contrive an agreement. But the level of suspicion was simply too high, and too many influential figures did not want the negotiations to succeed. By 1942 the ardent imperialist Winston Churchill had become head of a wartime coalition government, and he insisted that he had not become the king's chief minister 'to preside over the liquidation of the British Empire'. Gandhi too, anticipating a possible British defeat in the war, disdained the Cripps offer as a 'postdated cheque on a failing bank'. There was to be no going back on the promise of postwar independence enunciated in the Cripps offer, but in the eyes of a beleagured Britain the control of India during the war was essential for victory.

Confronted with the collapse of these negotiations, the Congress grew desperate. In the summer of 1942 they determined upon a massive act of defiance, known as the 'Quit India' movement. Unlike the earlier Gandhian campaigns of 1920–2 and 1930–2, that of August

1942 was not a disciplined movement of civil disobedience. Rather, from the start, in part because the Congress leadership were peremptorily jailed, the movement erupted into uncoordinated violence, as low-level leaders, students, and other activists took matters into their own hands. Within days this August 'rising' had become the gravest threat to British rule in India since the revolt of 1857. The mystique of Gandhian non-violence has often obscured the unique character of this upheaval. Indeed, Gandhi's role in this movement has itself been the subject of controversy. In jail, unable to communicate with his followers, he could not offer it leadership. Yet earlier, depicting India as a young woman attacked by a soldier, he had argued that she ought to fight back with teeth and nails rather than submit to rape. Violence was preferable to cowardice.

The rising gained its initial support in the city of Bombay, where factory workers took the lead with strikes and attacks on the police, but its centre soon shifted to the countryside, especially eastern UP, Bihar, and westernmost Bengal. Here, in an uncanny replay of 1857, which had also found much support in these eastern Gangetic districts, the 'Quit India' movement took the shape of a peasant rebellion. Militant students, fanning out from Benares and Patna, joined with small and middle peasants, who had earlier been recruited by radical kisan sabha organizations not associated with the Congress. Together they launched a massive attack on government property and the communications network of the Raj. Hundreds of railway stations and a vast mileage of track were destroyed, while telegraph lines were pulled down, poles and all, by villagers, at times aided by elephants. In Bihar, where the kisan sabha movement was strongest, some 170 police stations, post offices, and other government buildings were destroyed, and the province was effectively cut off from the rest of the country. Several district administrations collapsed in UP, and a 'national' government was set up in Midnapur (Bengal).

Despite the passions it unleashed, the 'Quit India' movement did not drive the British from India. To the contrary, it was ruthlessly suppressed. Taking advantage of the vast number of troops in the country on account of the war, and sustained by a belief that the war justified stringent reprisals against domestic rebels, the British mobilized some fifty battalions, and crushed the uprising, apart from a few pockets of guerilla resistance in isolated areas, within little more than six weeks. All Congress leaders were kept in detention for nearly three years, until the end of the war. Nevertheless, in part perhaps it was the last mass movement of the colonial era – for independence came five years later without further non-cooperation – 'Quit India' took on for many, as they looked back in later years, a mythic stature as a remembered moment of idealism and sacrifice. The movement even threw up heroic figures, such as the socialist Jayaprakash Narayan (1902–79), who established a 'provisional government' on the Nepal border. Many in the professional and commercial elite, too, quietly sympathized with the movement. On the other side, there existed police and lower civil servants who years later recounted how, when the British had fled, they had themselves kept open communications, or held isolated police posts against riotous mobs, in Azamgarh or Faizabad. The satisfactions of duty discharged in a time of crisis complemented the proud recollections of the 'freedom fighter of 1942'.

JINNAH AND THE PAKISTAN IDEA

The renewed disaffection of the Congress, from the initial resignation of its ministries through the subsequent abortive negotiations to the final upheaval of 'Quit India', forced the British to look elsewhere for support for the war, and even opened up an opportunity, some thought, to regain the political initiative, and so arrange a transfer of power to groups more accommodating than the Congress. Most prominent among these beneficiaries was the Muslim League. In 1940, when the League adopted Pakistan as its goal for the political evolution of their community, the idea had been in existence for only a decade. The notion that India's Muslims were an embryonic nation which deserved some kind of autonomous political entity found its first expression in the writings of the poet Muhammad Iqbal, but took the shape of a state called 'Pakistan' only among a group of Cambridge Muslim students in 1933. This notion was for a long time not practical politics, for Muslim interests seemed sufficiently well protected by regional parties in the Muslim-majority areas of the north-west and east that would inevitably comprise a 'Pakistan', while minority Muslims in other regions would gain nothing from a state that excluded them. By 1940, however, Muslim anxiety over their fate in an India fast approaching independence impelled the League to proclaim that in any constitutional plan 'the areas in which the Muslims are numerically in a majority should be grouped to constitute "independent states" in which the constituent units should be autonomous and sovereign'. As Jinnah put it in his presidential address to the League that year:

Mussalmans [Muslims] are not a minority as it is commonly known and understood... Mussulmans are a nation according to any definition of a nation, and they must have their homelands, their territory, and their state. We wish to live in peace and harmony with our neighbours as a free and independent people. We wish our people to develop to the fullest our spiritual, cultural, economic, social, and political life in a way that we think best and in consonance with our own ideals and according to the genius of our people.

Appearances to the contrary, nothing at this point was certain, much less inevitable. Above all, it is important to avoid reading back into the 1940 Resolution the Pakistan state that emerged in 1947. Although the course of Muslim politics during those seven years has been the subject of much contention, until 1946 no one, neither Jinnah, the provincial Muslim leaders, nor the British, envisaged, much less desired, the partition that ultimately took place. Many Muslims, indeed, opposed any partition at all. During the early 1940s Sikander Hayat's Unionist Party had the Punjab, the keystone of any Pakistan, securely under its control, and they saw no benefit in such a state. Others, including many of the ulama, especially those of Deoband, allied with the Congress, sought to promote individual morality among Muslims, and saw no need for a separate state. Until the very end, too, the borders of a Pakistan remained uncertain, and even whether it ought to comprise one state or two. Jinnah himself, as Ayesha Jalal has argued in her revisionist account *The Sole Spokesman*, initially envisaged 'Pakistan' not as a separate state, but as a useful bargaining card, or chip, to play in a postwar settlement. In this sense, the 1940 Resolution continued the decades-long strategy, central to the colonial idiom of government by 'community', in which Muslims sought to secure a better position for themselves by such means as separate electorates, reservation of seats, or Muslim majority provinces. Nevertheless, its simplicity gave the Pakistan idea a compelling attraction for fearful Muslims;

and the British, in their anxiety to secure Muslim support during the war, helped it along by such acts as the provision in the Cripps proposals that allowed provinces to 'opt out' of any independent India.

WAR AND FAMINE

Meanwhile, events in war-torn India were rushing towards a crisis, as the Japanese penetrated the jungles of Assam. Most devastating in its impact was the great Bengal famine of 1943, in which some 2 million people may have perished. As in the case of Bengal's only previous major famine, that of 1770, at the outset of British rule, that of 1943 was a product of administrative failure. Precipitated by the stoppage of rice imports from Japanese-occupied Burma, the food shortage was allowed to worsen into a crisis by the government's decision to divert grain from the countryside to the city in order to make available ample food supplies for the military and the restive population of Calcutta. After these wartime images of suffering and death, the enduring image of 'sonar Bangla' (golden Bengal) as a land of plenty, could never be recovered.

On the battle front, in addition to the Japanese and the British, two Indian armies confronted each other. Together their existence announced the breakdown of the old colonial tradition of loyalty, together with the idea that there existed distinct 'martial races' alone fit for war. Desperate to enlarge their military force, which reached a size of over 2 million men by 1945, the British abandoned the recruiting strategy that had shaped the Indian Army since the 1860s. Soldiers were recruited from throughout the country, and Indian officers for the first time found themselves propelled, by the exigencies of war, to positions of command. By 1945 India thus possessed an army, 'national' in all except its topmost ranks, prepared to lead the country into independence. Loyalty to the British could, however, no longer be taken for granted. After the fall of Singapore, the Japanese formed many of the Indian soldiers captured during that campaign into a force, known as the Indian National Army, under the command of Subhas Chandra Bose. A leftist who had broken with Gandhi when denied the Congress presidency he had won in 1939, Bose embraced fascism, and fled India, first to Hitler's Germany, then, on a German submarine, to Japanese-occuped Singapore. The force that he put together, largely from among prisoners-of-war, but including a novel women's detachment named after the 'mutiny' heroine the Rani of Jhansi, saw action against the British in Burma, but accomplished little on the battlefield. Its existence nevertheless evoked a sense of pride in India even among those who repudiated its fascist ties. A British move, in late 1945 after the war, to try three selected INA officers – one Hindu, one Muslim, and one Sikh – for disloyalty provoked widespread demonstrations, and secured the reputation of the INA as fighters for India's freedom. Bose himself died in an airplane crash trying to reach Tokyo in the last months of the war. His romantic saga, and its tragic end, with his defiant nationalism, has gained Bose an enduring popularity, especially in his native Bengal.

FROM THE SIMLA CONFERENCE TO THE CABINET MISSION

As the war drew to a close, the British reopened negotiations on India's future. In June 1945 the viceroy Lord Wavell brought together, in the summer capital of Simla, Gandhi, Jinnah, and the Congress leadership, only now released from jail. Plate 7.1 shows Nehru and Jinnah during a break in the negotiations. Wavell sought to resolve the political deadlock by setting up an executive council wholly Indian (apart from himself and the commander-in-chief) to run an interim government. Though the council would comprise equal numbers of 'Caste Hindus' and Muslims, thus embracing a key Muslim demand, the negotiations collapsed when Jinnah insisted upon the right of the Muslim League to nominate all its Muslim members. Asserting a claim to be 'sole spokesman' for India's Muslims, Jinnah preferred no political advance at all to any acknowledgement of the right of the Congress, or the Punjab Unionists, to represent Muslim opinion. That the British let Jinnah wreck the Simla conference, rather than proceed without him, was testimony to the leverage the League had secured by its wartime collaboration with the imperial government.

In the months that followed, Britain increasingly lost both the power and the will to control events in India. In July 1945 a Labour ministry under Clement Attlee replaced Churchill's Conservative

Plate 7.1   Jawaharlal Nehru (left) and M. A. Jinnah (right)
walking in the garden during the Simla conference, June 1945.

government. Although Labour had never been as hostile to empire
as is sometimes claimed, still Attlee's victory gave the cause of Indian
independence, and the Congress in particular, a sympathetic audience. More importantly, though victorious in the war, Britain had
suffered immensely in the struggle. It simply did not possess the
manpower or the economic resources required to coerce a restive

India. For the British public, the jobs and housing promised by the new socialist government took precedence over a costly reassertion of the Raj. In India itself, a naval mutiny in Bombay in 1946 underscored the fact that the allegiance of the subordinate services could no longer be relied upon. Further, the elite Indian Civil Service, the 'steel frame' of the Raj, had by 1945 become over one-half Indian, and these men, though still loyal, had begun to look ahead to service under a national government. By 1946, all that Britain could hope to do, as men like Wavell realized, was to arrange a transfer of power to those whom 'the Indian people have chosen for themselves'. This was not be an easy or straightforward task.

The opening round in the 'endgame' of the Raj took place with the elections held during the winter of 1945/46. These, by sweeping the board of minor players, reduced the political scene to the Congress and the Muslim League, now as never before pitted directly against each other. For the Congress the outcome, never in doubt, was in large part a replay of 1937, with the party's reputation now enhanced by recollection of its role in the August 1942 movement. The Congress won 90 per cent of the votes cast for the central legislature in open (non-Muslim) constituencies, and formed governments in eight provinces. The Muslim League, on its part, won all 30 reserved Muslim seats in the central legislature, and 442 of the 500 Muslim seats in the provincial assemblies. In striking contrast to its dismal showing in 1937, the League had now made good on Jinnah's claim that the League, and the League alone, represented India's Muslims. This was a dramatic electoral transformation, yet what the vote meant for those who had given the League their ballots was not immediately obvious.

Cold, aloof, an elegant figure in Western dress (see plate 7.1), Jinnah did not, in any obvious way, embody the idea of a charismatic leader. Indeed, from Wavell at the Simla conference up to the historians of the present day, many have found Jinnah's presumed arrogance, with his unwillingness to engage in the give and take of negotiation, infuriating, if not repellent. Yet the force of his personality could be compelling. The young Begam Ikramullah, at first reluctant to meet Jinnah, because he was, she had heard, 'very rude and snubs everybody', came away from a visit marvelling that 'to listen to him and not be convinced was not possible'. He was, she

said, 'so thoroughly, so single-mindedly, so intensely convinced of
the truth of his point of view that you could not help but be convinced also'. Such personal appeals, on behalf of a Pakistan kept
purposely ambiguous, not surprisingly achieved their greatest success among the educated Muslim community, products of institutions such as Aligarh University, where the modern ideal of Muslim
nationalism had been born.

To reach the large rural population, especially in the Muslim-
majority provinces, was a more difficult matter. Unlike the elite,
whose political consciousness had been shaped by fear for their
place in a Congress-run India, Punjabi and Bengali Muslims were
protected by their majority position in provinces possessing a large
measure of autonomy. Yet the support of these provinces was essential if a Pakistan of any sort was to come into being, and so Jinnah
set out to win their allegiance for the Muslim League. In Bengal,
Fazl-ul-Haq's Krishak Praja Party, never commanding a majority in
the legislature by itself, had always depended upon coalition partners. After 1940, with both Congress and the League in opposition,
its support base slowly dwindled away, until in 1943, in the crisis
of the famine, Fazl-ul-Haq's ministry gave way to a Muslim League
government under Khwaja Nazimuddin. In the Punjab, the Unionist
Party, resting upon ties of kin and clan that linked landlord and peasant across religious community, was much more resistant to appeals
on the basis of Muslim solidarity. Although the Unionist chief minister Sikander Hayat Khan had agreed to follow Jinnah on all-India
questions, his successor Khizr Hayat Khan in 1944 defiantly broke
with Jinnah, and so set the stage for a head-to-head confrontation
in this most critical of Muslim provinces.

Jinnah's strategy, as he sought to undermine the Unionists, was
twofold. On the one hand, he sought to take advantage of factional
rivalries among the loosely knit groups of landlords that made up
the Unionist Party; and, on the other, he endeavoured to appeal over
the heads of these clan leaders directly to the peasant voter. In so doing he turned for help to the *pirs* (spiritual guides) of the sufi shrines
scattered about the countryside. With the legitimacy these pirs conferred on his campaign, deploying groups of student activists who
came out from the cities, Jinnah rallied the rural voters of the Punjab
with the cry of 'Islam in Danger!' It should not be imagined that

Jinnah secured his victory solely by the manipulation of elites, like a puppet master, or by bamboozling a credulous peasantry. Though Indians after 1947 often wished to think so, Jinnah did not create Pakistan from nothing by craft and artifice. To the contrary, the vision of 'Pakistan' that was presented to Punjabi and other Muslims resonated with an enduring, and deeply felt, religious loyalty. Previously, private belief had had little to do with public identity; a 'Muslim' was someone defined, by the arithmetic of colonialism, as a member of an 'objectively' fixed Muslim community. Appeals based on religion itself, in fact, were rigidly excluded from the electoral process. Under the pressure of the 1946 election campaign, with its explosive communal rhetoric, all this was changed. Now, as Muslim League activists toured the countryside, personal commitment to Islam became fused with an assertion of Muslim community solidarity. Voting became a ritual act of incorporation in the body of Islam. As one election agent reported, 'wherever I went, everyone kept saying, bhai (brother), if we did not vote for the League we would have become kafir (an infidel)'.

As a result, for the average Muslim voter, Pakistan came to mean two things at once. It was, as a modern nation-state for India's Muslim peoples, the logical culmination of the long process of colonial Muslim politics. At the same time, however, as a symbol of Muslim identity, Pakistan transcended the ordinary structures of the state. As such it evoked an ideal Islamic political order, in which the realization of an Islamic life would be fused with the state's ritual authority. This Pakistan would not be simply an arena in which politicians, even if Muslims, pursued their everyday disputes. During the bloody upheavals of 1946 and 1947, Pakistan underwent a transformation from visionary ideal to territorial state. Yet it could not, after independence, shake off the legacy of its origin as a 'pure' land at once of Muslims and of a confessional Islam.

Unable to secure agreement on anything from India's two antagonistic political parties, the British authorized a high-level Cabinet mission, sent to India in March 1946, to devise a plan of its own. Its proposal for an independent India involved a complex, three-tiered federation, whose central feature was the creation of groups of provinces. Two of these groups would comprise the Muslim majority provinces of east and west; a third would include the Hindu majority regions of the centre and south. These groups, given responsibility for most of the functions of government, would be subordinated to a Union government controlling defence, foreign affairs, and communications. By this scheme, the British hoped they could at once preserve the united India desired by the Congress, and by themselves, and at the same time, through the groups, secure the essence of Jinnah's demand for a 'Pakistan'. This proposal came tantalizingly close to giving Jinnah what he most wanted – which was not so much an independent state, but a 'large' Pakistan of provinces. At all costs Jinnah wished to avoid what he called in 1944 a 'maimed, mutilated, and moth-eaten' Pakistan in which all non-Muslim majority districts, regions comprising some 40 per cent of Bengal and Punjab, would be shorn from the new state. By bringing entire provinces, especially the key provinces of Punjab in the west and Bengal in the east, into his Pakistan, Jinnah could conciliate their provincial Muslim leaders, fearful of the disorder and loss of power for themselves if their provinces were split into two. In addition, the large Hindu populations of Bengal and the Punjab would insure fair treatment for the substantial Muslim populations inevitably left behind in the Hindu-majority provinces.

Above all, Jinnah wanted parity for his Pakistan with Hindu India. This, he felt, could best be secured by a set of grouped provinces. Repudiating the liberal democratic idea of India as a country where majorities ruled, Jinnah argued that, as Muslim India comprised a 'nation' as much as Hindu India did, it was entitled to equal representation in any central government institutions. The liberal electoral logic that saw Muslims as a minority community, whose members were free to choose whom they wished to represent them, had to give way, in this view, to the assertion that Muslims and non-Muslims were members of two fixed and distinct political entities, each entitled to its own self-governing institutions. Indeed, as an expression of this dichotomy, Jinnah would have preferred only two groups – a Pakistan and a Hindustan – instead of the Cabinet mission's three. Nevertheless, the Muslim League accepted the Cabinet mission's proposals.

The ball was now in the Congress's court. Although the grouping scheme preserved a united India, the Congress leadership, above all Jawaharlal Nehru, now slated to be Gandhi's successor, increasingly came to the conclusion that, under the Cabinet mission proposals, the centre would be too weak to achieve the goals of the Congress, which envisioned itself as the successor to the Raj. Looking ahead to the future, the Congress, especially its socialist wing headed by Nehru, wanted a central government that could direct and plan for an India, free of colonialism, that might eradicate its people's poverty and grow into an industrial power. India's business community also supported the idea of a strong central government. Indeed, in 1944 a group of leading industralists had already formulated, in the Bombay Plan, a scheme for the rapid development of basic industries under the leadership of the state. In a provocative speech on 10 July 1946, Nehru repudiated the notion of compulsory grouping of provinces, the key to Jinnah's Pakistan. Provinces, he said, must be free to join any group, or none. With this speech Nehru effectively torpedoed the Cabinet mission scheme, and with it, any hope for a united India. Better a wholly independent Pakistan, so the Congress reluctantly concluded, than a state hobbled by too strong provinces and by the communal and landlord interests the League was seen to represent.

MASSACRE AND PARTITION

Backed into a corner, denied his Pakistan of 'groups', Jinnah grew desperate. He had now of necessity to accept the 'moth-eaten' Pakistan he had previously spurned. To get it, to enforce upon the Congress that he could not simply be pushed aside in the final settlement, Jinnah turned to 'direct action', and so precipitated the horrors of riot and massacre that were to disfigure the coming of independence. In the Great Calcutta Killing, from the 16th to the 20th of August 1946, as mobs roamed the streets of the city, some 4,000 people of both communities were killed, with thousands more wounded or made homeless (see plate 7.2). The killing of some 7,000 Muslims in Bihar, and a lesser number of Hindus in the Bengal district of Noakhali, promptly followed. It is unlikely that Jinnah actively sought such carnage, but passions on both sides had become so enflamed that, except when Gandhi himself was physically present, as for a time in Noakhali, exhortations to non-violence fell on deaf ears.

Plate 7.2 Rioters in Calcutta, August 1946.

The struggle for control of the Punjab followed in 1947. There, despite his victory among the province's Muslim electorate, Jinnah was enraged to find installed in office, under Khizr Hayat, a ministry comprising the remnants of his Unionists, now reduced to ten seats in the legislature, allied with the Congress and the Akali Sikhs. In March, by a campaign of civil disobedience, he brought down that government. The riots that ensued opened the way to what was to be the greatest holocaust of all – that in the Punjab. The contest in the Punjab, however, did not simply pit Hindu against Muslim. Critical to its outcome were the province's Sikhs. Clustered in its central districts, around Lahore and their holy city of Amritsar, the Sikhs comprised a substantial minority of the province's populace, some 13 per cent, but they were nowhere a majority. Hence any partition was anathama to them. They feared inclusion in a Pakistan, at the mercy of Muslims whom they distrusted. Even more, perhaps, they feared a partition of the Punjab itself, along a line that set apart Hindu from Muslim majority districts, for that would leave their small community powerless, split between the two new states. But, once a united India had been abandoned, no other way of demarcating the boundary could in fairness be adopted than one which ran along the line separating Hindu and Muslim majority districts.

As northern and eastern India sank into chaos, British prime minister Attlee announced the appointment in February 1947 of the dashing young Lord Mountbatten as the last viceroy. Mountbatten brought with him instructions to transfer power by June 1948, a date soon moved up to 15 August 1947. The Conservatives at home bitterly denounced this 'scuttle'; but, given Britain's own economic plight, which had grown worse in the immediate postwar years, there seemed to be no alternative to a rapid transfer to successor governments who alone might be able to impose order. Hence, under immense time pressure, the clock steadily ticking away, Mountbatten and his staff had to make a host of momentous decisions – above all, whether power was to be handed over to two, three, or more successor states; and where the boundary line between them was to be drawn. There remained, in addition, the fate of the princely states, linked only to the Crown, with no recognized place in the Indian constitutional order.

By the time Mountbatten took office, a united India was out of the question. But it was by no means certain that there would be only two successor states. Initially, in the Plan Balkan, Mountbatten had proposed transferring power to the various provinces, who could join India, Pakistan, or remain independent. Shown this plan beforehand, Nehru, determined to avert a true 'Balkanization' of India into small states, got Mountbatten to agree to hand over power directly, on the basis of the 1935 Act, to two Dominions, who would remain in the Commonwealth in order to smooth the transition. At this point two other options vanished. One was a united independent Bengal, a scheme floated by Bengali Muslim leaders reluctant to be subordinated to the far-away Punjab. But, as Joya Chatterjee has argued, the local Congress preferred the province's partition – which they had so bitterly opposed in 1905 – so that they might reclaim control of at least its western half. In Bengal, as at the centre, much of the responsibility for partition lay with those who ostensibly opposed it. The other lost opportunity was that of an independent Muslim state in the east, envisaged in the 1940 Pakistan resolution itself. By 1947, however, Jinnah's commitment to the 'two nation' theory had turned him against such an outcome, while the Boundary Commission's award of Calcutta to India, by depriving eastern Bengal of the major outlet for processing and shipment of its exports,

Plate 7.3   Nehru addressing the nation from the Red Fort,
Delhi, on Independence Day 1947.

made it appear economically unviable on its own. Some twenty-five
years later, in 1971, eastern Bengal, aggrieved at its treatment within
Pakistan, was to make good its claim to independence as the state
of Bangladesh.

At midnight on 15 August 1947, in a dramatic gesture that stirred
feelings of pride throughout the land, Jawaharlal Nehru, as the
country's first prime minister, stood up in the parliament chamber
and announced that India had claimed its freedom. With eloquent
words he told the assembly that

> Long years ago, we made a tryst with destiny, and now the time comes
> when we shall redeem our pledge, not wholly or in full measure, but very
> substantially. At the stroke of the midnight hour, when the world sleeps,
> India will wake to life and freedom.

In subsequent years, up to the present, the central image of India's
Independence Day celebration has been an address to the nation
by the prime minister from the walls of Shah Jahan's historic Red
Fort. Plate 7.3 shows Nehru on the ramparts of the fort, beneath
the Indian flag, with Delhi's historic Jama Masjid in the distance.

Independence was, however, to be disfigured by the ugly horrors of riot and massacre, above all in the Punjab. The initial attacks, in March, had been directed against Hindus and Sikhs in Muslim West Punjab. As independence neared, the violence spread throughout the province, and caught up all communities, especially the Sikhs, who saw their community, with its lands and shrines, sliced in two by the Boundary Award announced on 16 August. The escalation of violence in the Punjab has usually been attributed to a mindless frenzy in which, overnight, otherwise contented villagers embarked on the murder and rape of those who had been their friends. This story has been told in such fictional accounts as the short stories of Saadat Hasan Manto and Khushwant Singh's gripping novel *Train to Pakistan*. Yet the massacres were not wholly without direction, and new details about their horrors have recently come to light.

A highly militarized society, long the recruiting ground for the Indian Army, with one-third of its eligible males having served in the war, the Punjab in 1947 contained vast numbers of demobilized soldiers. Many of these were Sikhs, who, as those who had lost the most from partition, took advantage of their military training and knowledge of modern weaponry, to organize and direct attacks, in methodical and systematic fashion, on villages, trains, and refugee columns. Ex-INA and ex-Indian Army men together, they formed into mobile bands called *jathas*, marked out targets, and then carried out raids, often at the rate of three or four a night, on Muslim-majority villages in East Punjab. Such raids were by no means confined to Sikhs. Frequently, especially when Muslims attacked Hindu villages, men forced their women to jump into wells to preserve their purity unsullied, and then fought to the end themselves. Trains carrying refugees across the border were especially tempting targets for all sides (see plate 7.4). These trains would be ambushed or derailed, and the hapless passengers murdered as they sat in their compartments or after being tossed out on to the tracks. Frequently, trains would arrive at their destinations carrying on board hundreds of dead bodies. The arrival of each such train would in turn provoke a cry for vengeance from the aggrieved community. These trains, all too similar to those that carried Jews to their death in Germany a few years before, left permanent scars on the memories of the two new nations.

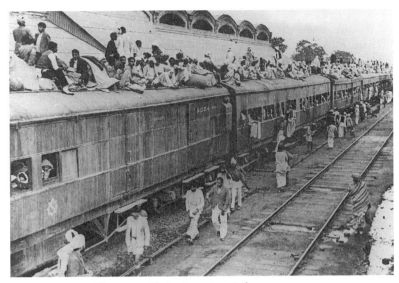

Plate 7.4   Train Carrying Refugees, 1947.

The loss of life was immense, with estimates ranging from several hundred thousand up to a million. But, even for those who survived, fear generated a widespread perception that one could be safe only among the members of one's own community; and this in turn helped consolidate loyalties towards the state, whether India or Pakistan, in which one might find a secure haven. This was especially important for Pakistan, where the succour it offered to Muslims gave that state for the first time a visible territorial reality. Fear too drove forward a mass migration unparalleled in the history of South Asia. Within a period of some three or four months in late 1947 a number of Hindus and Sikhs estimated at some 5 million moved from West Punjab into India, while 5.5 million Muslims travelled in the opposite direction. The outcome, akin to what today is called 'ethnic cleansing', produced an Indian Punjab 60 per cent Hindu and 35 per cent Sikh, while the Pakistan Punjab became almost wholly Muslim. A similar, though less extensive, migration took place between east and west Bengal, though murderous attacks on fleeing refugees, with the attendant loss of life, were much less extensive in the eastern region. Even those who did not move, if of the wrong community, often found themselves treated as though they were the enemy. In Delhi itself, the city's Muslims, cowering in an old fort, were for several months after partition regarded with intense suspicion and hostility. Overall, partition uprooted some 12.5 million of undivided India's people.

Although scrambling to establish themselves in office, the new governments on both sides of the border were able with surprising speed to contain the violence. In most areas, they brought it under control before the end of 1947. This success testifies to the resilience of the structures of the colonial state on which the two successor states had established themselves. British officials remained in place only on the Pakistan side, for that state had the difficult task of setting up a central government from scratch. Nevertheless, both states, possessing disciplined armies and civil servants, moved quickly to organize refugee resettlement and, more generally, to recapture authority and legitimacy for themselves. Although for a time weakened, the state in South Asia never collapsed. This resiliency further enabled the new governments to suppress other challenges that emerged during the turbulence of transition. Among these were peasant-based movements, often led by Communists, that threatened the dominance of the conservative elites, in Congress and Muslim League alike, who controlled the new governments. Most notable were the Tebhaga movement in Bengal, of sharecroppers and tribals demanding a fairer distribution of the crop, and the massive Telengana uprising in princely Hyderabad, which caught up thousands of poor peasants in a guerrilla struggle against the Nizam's government and was put down only by the Indian Army.

DEFINING THE NATION: PRINCES, KASHMIR, ABDUCTED WOMEN

The Telengana movement was part of a large and extremely tangled question – that of the fate of the hundreds of princely states scattered across the subcontinent. As the princes under the Raj possessed ties only to the British, the coming of independence left them wholly on their own. Mountbatten, insisting that they could expect no assistance from Britain, counselled the princes to make the best terms they could with the new regimes. The new governments too, anxious to avoid a further Balkanization of India, determined to bring about their integration. Understandably reluctant to see their states abruptly disappear from the map, the princes pleaded for time and for better terms. But such cries were unavailing, for the isolated princes had very little bargaining leverage over the powerful Indian Government. To ease the blow of integration, the States minister Vallabhbhai Patel (1875–1950), and his aide V. P. Menon, proceeded in stages, first asking for simple accession to the Indian Union, and only afterwards for complete administrative merger; and they offered lush privy purses to the princes themselves. A combination of threats and intimidation – at times involving peremptory orders to hand over power within a fixed time, often set in hours, or face the consequences, frequently portrayed as a popular uprising – secured the accession of all the princes but a few by the date of independence. Merger and consolidation of these erstwhile princely states, some into neighbouring provinces, others grouped together as provinces themselves, followed in 1948.

Of the hold-outs, one was the Nizam of Hyderabad. Ruler of a large and populous state, the nizam, a Muslim, opted for independence, which he sought to enforce by an irregular army recruited from among the Muslim aristocracy of the state. But the dream was in vain. His state was surrounded on all sides by Indian territory; the bulk of his subjects were Hindus; and his irregular force was unable to subjugate even the Telengana rebels. In September 1948 the Indian Army marched in to end the Nizam's two centuries' long dynasty, and with it the only site for patronage of Islamic culture and learning in the Deccan. The other major hold-out was the Hindu Maharaja of Kashmir. Set apart from the Indian plains, surrounded by high mountains, Kashmir was the only major state that shared a boundary with both India and Pakistan. Its ruler could thus appropriately join either. Uncertain what course to take, the maharaja vacillated until an invasion by Pakistani army irregulars forced his hand. He then, in October 1947, acceded to India. Thus began a saga of conflict between India and Pakistan which has lasted to the present day, and in which the people of Kashmir, often reduced to the status of pawns, have suffered immeasurably.

Kashmir mattered not so much because it possessed rich mineral or other resources, though it was the original home of the Nehru family, but because for both sides it raised issues central to their self-definition as nations. For Pakistan, the critical fact was Kashmir's overwhelmingly Muslim population. The decision of the Kashmir maharaja to join India flew in the face of the logic by which British India had been partitioned. Pakistan's existence was premised upon its status as a Muslim homeland. Even though millions of Muslims had had to be left behind scattered across India, Kashmir, as a Muslim majority state, in the Pakistani view rightly belonged to it. Indeed, had Kashmir been an ordinary Indian province it would almost certainly have been part of Pakistan from the start. A Hindu maharaja ought not, Pakistanis argued, have been allowed wilfully to defy the interests of his Muslim subjects. To right this presumed wrong, Pakistan fought three wars with India in twenty-five years. In the first of these wars, in 1948, they secured a portion of western Kashmir, together with the northern regions of Gilgit and Baltistan; but they were never able to gain possession of the rich valley centred on Srinagar which forms the heart of the state.

From the Indian perspective other issues were at stake. Nehru, and with him the Congress, although obliged to accept the creation of Pakistan, had never accepted the 'two nation' theory. India was not, in this view, a 'Hindustan', or land of Hindus. Conceiving of Pakistan as simply a portion of India which had seceded, Nehru always regarded his state as the rightful successor to its British predecessor. He refused, for instance, to change the name of the state; and he encouraged Lord Mountbatten to stay on for a year as its titular governor-general. Pakistan, by contrast, rejected Mountbatten's offer to remain as its Governor-General as well. In the view of the Congress, India was not only successor to the Raj, but also a secular state, in which Muslims, with all other minorities, stood, in principle, on equal footing with their Hindu fellow citizens. Millions of Muslims, remaining behind after partition by choice or necessity, already lived within India. The addition of the residents of Kashmir would only further testify to the inclusive nature of the new state. Inasmuch as the Kashmir maharaja's accession was, by the terms of the partition agreements, perfectly legal, Nehru saw no reason to undo it. Indeed, to the contrary, he felt he had acted appropriately in responding to the maharaja's call for assistance in repelling the Pakistani raiders as they advanced on Srinagar.

Such considerations did not, however, end the dispute. Seeking international support, Pakistan took the Kashmir issue to the fledgling United Nations. The UN brokered, in 1948, a ceasefire along the line of control, which it then policed by sending to Kashmir a contingent of observers. This UN observer force has remained in Kashmir to the present. At the time of the maharaja's accession, Nehru had agreed to hold a plebiscite among its people to decide Kashmir's subsequent status. This referendum has never taken place. In India's view, Pakistan's refusal to withdraw its 'raiders' from the province voided the conditions under which India's agreement to a plebiscite had been secured. As evidence of India's perfidy, this refusal to poll Kashmir's people has fuelled Pakistani anger ever since. If they were asked, however, it has for some years been assumed that the majority of Kashmir's people would prefer independence, as a Himalayan state comparable to Nepal or Bhutan, to union with either of the two South Asian powers.

Kashmir did not provide the only issue around which issues of national identity were being defined in the early years of independence. Powerful emotions were also aroused by the abduction, during the partition riots, of women who, rather than being murdered in attacks on villages or refugee columns, were carried off as trophies by their abductors. As one Indian official wrote of an attack on refugees in Gujranwala, 'After the massacre was over, the girls were distributed like sweets.' Frequently sold or abandoned after being raped, these women were also sometimes forcibly married to their abductors. Estimates of such abductions range from 40 to 50,000; due in part to the activities of the organized Sikh jathas, perhaps twice as many Muslim as Hindu and Sikh women were taken. Soon after the restoration of order, in late 1947, the two governments both set to work locating abducted women so that they could be returned to the nation to which they were 'properly' meant to belong. The effort put into the task testifies, not only to the horror with which these abductions were greeted, but to the power of the communal logic by which, in practice, the two new states defined themselves. Muslim women were meant to be in Pakistan; Hindu and Sikh in India. A proper moral order demanded the restoration of these women, if not to their own families, at least to their national 'homes'.

For Hindu Indians, especially, used to conceiving of the nation in gendered terms, as a land in which women represented the purity of the 'mother', such abductions evoked a powerful sense of outrage. The issue even generated heated debate in the Constituent Assembly.

Such logic, as in the case of the Kashmiris, took little account of the wishes and desires of the women themselves. While many returned women were welcomed by their families, some men did not want to take back women who had been 'defiled'. Sometimes women, filled with shame and guilt at their fate, were reluctant to return to an uncertain reception. Many had settled in their new homes, with children and husbands, and had no desire to uproot themselves yet again. Yet others had lost all their relatives. As one woman told her 'rescuer', 'I have lost my husband and have now gone in for another. You want me to go to India where I have got nobody.' For the Indian and Pakistani governments, however, none of this mattered. Not until 1954 was forcible repatriation abandoned as official policy.

THE HINDU RIGHT AND THE ASSASSINATION OF GANDHI

On 30 January 1948 Mahatma Gandhi was murdered by a Hindu zealot as he was leading a prayer meeting in New Delhi. Jawaharlal Nehru spoke for a grief-striken nation when he told India in a radio broadcast, 'The light has gone out of our lives and there is darkness everywhere.' Despite the deep sense of loss the Mahatma's death, at age seventy-eight, produced in India, Gandhi had become increasingly marginal to the Indian political scene ever since the end of the war. He had let his chosen heir Nehru, first in the interim government of 1946–7, and then as prime minister of independent India, take the initiative in the questions of policy and administration that accompanied the transfer of power. Deeply grieved by the prospect of partition, Gandhi stood aloof from the negotiations that brought it about. Indeed, to avert such an outcome he put forward the radical suggestion that Jinnah be installed as prime minister of a united India; the only response was a deafening silence. Later, Gandhi argued that the Congress, its mission accomplished with the creation of an independent India, ought to dissolve itself. Again, there was no response. Just before his death Gandhi did, however, make one last decisive intervention in the Indian political process. By a combination of prayer and fasting he forced a contrite ministry to hand over to Pakistan its share of the cash assets of undivided India, some 40 million pounds sterling, which had so far been retained in defiance of the partition agreements.

Gandhi's assassination brought into public view a Hindu nationalism that had, during the Congress-led anti-colonial struggle, rarely been visible. It did not, however, spring suddenly into existence with the desperate act of Gandhi's assailant Nathuram Godse. Rather, as we have seen in chapter 5, an avowedly Hindu nationalism can be traced back to the cow protection movement of the later nineteenth century. In 1915 it took institutional shape with the founding of the Hindu Mahasabha. A loose alliance of Hindu enthusiasts, largely in the UP and Punjab, the Mahasabha worked on behalf of cow protection and the Hindi language, together with educational and social welfare activities among Hindus more generally. Its goals, and even its membership, were often not distinct from those of the Congress itself, for men like Pandit Madan Mohan Malaviya were active in both. The Mahasabha was perhaps most visibly set off from the Congress by its propagation of Sanskritized Hindi written in Devanagari script. Gandhi, by contrast, anxious to create a language that would bring people together, advocated the use of the shared north Indian vernacular, called Hindustani, written in both Nagri and Indo-Persian script.

Most outspoken among the early proponents of what he named as 'Hindutva', or 'Hinduness', was V. D. Savarkar (1883–1966). An English-educated Chitpavan Brahman, like Tilak and Gokhale, Savarkar as a youth participated in revolutionary politics; on release from an extended stay in jail he took up leadership of the Mahasabha. In his 1923 treatise on 'Hindutva', he celebrated the greatness and the unity of the Hindu people:

The ideal conditions... under which a nation can attain perfect solidarity and cohesion would, other things being equal, be found in the case of those people who inhabit the land they adore, the land of whose forefathers is also the land of their Gods and Angels, of Seers and Prophets; the scenes of whose history are also the scenes of their mythology. The

Hindus are about the only people who are blessed with these ideal conditions that are at the same time incentive to national solidarity, cohesion, and greatness.

Hindu nationalism took on a more militant shape with the founding of the Rashtriya Swayamsevak Sangh, or RSS, in 1925. An organization largely of upper-caste Maharashtrians, the RSS organized itself, in opposition to the Gandhian Congress, as a disciplined cadre-based party. It did not contest elections, nor seek a mass base, but rather formed its members into uniformed paramilitary cells. Although Gandhi himself, as the 'Mahatma', was often seen by Indians in Hindu terms, he insisted that an independent India must welcome the members of all communities. The RSS, by contrast, put forth a vision of India as a land of, and for, Hindus. Proponents of a mystical nationalism, with racial overtones that evoked sympathetic parallels with German fascism, the RSS was stridently anti-Muslim. It opposed, above all, the conciliation of Muslims involved in the partition, which its supporters decried as the 'vivisection' of the motherland. As independence neared, the RSS drew support from among students, refugees, and the urban lower middle classes, fearful of the violence and turmoil around them. For such people protection of the Hindu 'mother' could easily be made to require the removal of the figure who most visibly personified the weak effeminate India they so abhorred – Mohandas Gandhi. In the aftermath of the assassination, for Godse was an RSS supporter and follower of Savarkar, not surprisingly Hindu nationalism fell into deep disfavour. The RSS itself was for some years outlawed, and revulsion against such violence inhibited the formation of other parties devoted to advocacy of an avowedly Hindu India. Only in the late 1970s did the Hindu right begin to reorganize; only in the 1990s, over forty years after his death, was it finally able to cast off the stigma of Gandhi's assassination.

By 1950 India had survived an extraordinary decade, perhaps unlike any the country had gone through before – one that witnessed the triumph of independence, accompanied by the tragedies of war, partition, and unparalleled civil violence. Much, nevertheless, had withstood the traumas of that decade and so continued little altered. The Congress Party, as the embodiment of Indian nationalism, had emerged strengthened and ready for the electoral contests that were to follow. It had even negotiated without strife a change in leadership, its first in twenty-five years, as Gandhi handed over direction to Nehru. Above all, the structures of the state, with its disciplined civil service and military, survived intact, transferred with but little disruption from the hands of the British into those of the two successor governments. The inauguration of a new constitution, on 26 January 1950, signified for India the coming of a new era – of nation-building and economic development.

8

Congress Raj: democracy and development, 1950–1989

Hammered out during intense debates in a constituent assembly which sat from 1947 to 1949, India's constitution established a set of principles and institutions that have governed the country's political life up to the present. Under it, as Nehru sought to create a 'modern' free India, the country decisively repudiated much of its colonial heritage. Although remaining a member of the Commonwealth, India was proclaimed a republic, thus ending its allegiance to the British Crown, when the constitution was inaugurated. That date, 26 January, known as Republic Day, with a massive parade in New Delhi, has remained a major focus for India's celebration of its nationhood. Rejecting the imperial vice-regal style of government associated with the Raj, the new India nevertheless sought inspiration in domestic British political practice. The constitution put in place a Westminster style of government, with a parliament comprising two houses, and a prime minister selected by the majority party in the lower house, called the Lok Sabha or House of the People. Nehru took up the position of prime minister, while the president, installed in the old vice-regal palace, acted, like the sovereign in Britain, as titular head of state. The old colonial separate electorates, with their divisive tendencies, were in similar fashion abolished in favour of single member constituencies, modelled on those in Britain itself, open to all.

Elements of the old colonial style of governance nevertheless persisted under the new order. Some 200 articles of the Government of India Act of 1935, for instance, were incorporated into the new

constitution. The federal structure, in which power was shared between the centre and the former provinces, now become states,
remained intact. So too, oddly perhaps, did the provision of the
1935 act which awarded the provincial governor, and president,
imperial-style power to set aside elected ministries in times of emergency. These powers were often employed in independent India to
intimidate recalcitrant state governments, and, in one exceptional
instance, to facilitate a period of authoritarian 'emergency' rule
throughout the country. In addition, the administrative structure of
the Indian Civil Service, renamed the Indian Administrative Service,
remained in place. This 'steel frame', its British members replaced by
Indians trained in the same spirit of impartial governance, was seen,
in the tumultuous years after independence, as a necessary bulwark
of stability for the new government. One American idea incorporated in the new constitution was that of a Supreme Court with
powers of judicial review of legislation. At no time, significantly,
did the constituent assembly ever consider instituting a Gandhian-
styled non-party government, with a weak centre and power
diffused among self-governing villages. The new India was not to be
modelled on a vision of its ancient past.

All were agreed that the new India must be a democratic land,
with universal suffrage and freedom of press and speech. Troubled,
however, by the persisting discrimination against 'untouchables' and
other disadvantaged groups, the Congress Party took steps to insure that these groups had a voice in the new constitutional order.
One was the appointment of the distinguished 'untouchable' leader
Dr B. R. Ambedkar to chair the drafting committee for the constitution. Since their tense stand-off over the Communal Award in 1932,
Ambedkar, a graduate of Columbia University in New York, had
never been reconciled with Gandhi. Calling Hinduism a 'veritable
chamber of horrors', he had argued that all Gandhism had done
was to 'smoothen its surface and give it the appearance of decency
and respectability'. Before his death in 1956, Ambedkar converted
to Buddhism. The new constitution itself outlawed untouchability,
but of greater importance over the long term was the reservation of
seats in the legislatures for the former untouchables, and with them
the depressed forest tribes. These groups were listed on a special
schedule in the constitution, and so became known as 'Scheduled

Castes and Tribes'. The members of these castes stood for election in regular constituencies where they alone were allowed to be candidates. In this way the state avoided the use of colonial-style separate electorates, but secured 'untouchable' inclusion in the legislature. Their presence offered visible evidence of the state's concern for the welfare of their communities. As time went on, as we shall see, these reservations grew to include preferential access to educational institutions and the administrative services, while the existence of such benefits for the 'scheduled' castes inspired other 'backward' classes to demand similar treatment.

The Congress Party under Nehru's leadership was committed as well to the principles of secularism and socialism. Despite the predominance of Hindus among its membership, the Congress had always proclaimed itself a secular organization, and Nehru was determined that India should be a secular state. In the 1940s and 1950s, especially in the wake of partition and Gandhi's assassination, this principle encountered little overt opposition. Nehru took care to disassociate the state both from religion and from the Congress itself, by, for instance, such measures as installing the lion capital of the Buddhist ruler Asoka as the central device on the country's flag and coinage (see plate 8.4 below) instead of adopting a Hindu icon or even the Gandhian spinning wheel which adorned the Congress's Party flag. By contrast with its American variant, which sought to impose a 'wall' between church and state, Indian secularism sought to engage with, and so sustain, all of India's various religions. This form of secularism, with its communally based schools and codes of law, was hard to put into practice. Furthermore, the policy encouraged a persisting allegiance to 'community' at odds with the individualism of a democratic polity. The constitution further enshrined among its directive principles, not only the fundamental right of private property, but a commitment to economic justice, defined as distributing the material resources of the country in such a way as to promote the common good and an equitable sharing of wealth. How far, and in what ways, this socialist ideal took shape will form a central theme of this chapter.

India's first general elections under universal suffrage took place in the winter of 1951/2. To hold a free election on such a massive scale, with an electorate of 200 million, was unprecedented in the entire

Plate 8.1   Vijayalakshmi Pandit addressing village election rally,
Phulpur, Allahabad, 1964.

world. Its successful completion, the first of many such elections that
were to take place during the subsequent fifty years, was a testimony,
in large part, to the political training Indians had received during
the later decades of the Raj, most notably in the elections of 1937
and 1946. By the time of independence the principle that voting, not
violence or a military *coup d'etat*, was the way to bring governments
into office had become accepted among all classes of Indians. By
his unwavering commitment to the democratic process during his
tenure as prime minister, Nehru engrained this principle deeply into
Indian political behaviour. Plate 8.1 shows how even an eminent
person like Nehru's sister Vijayalakshmi Pandit, campaigning here
in 1964, had to secure support from the remotest villages in order
to win election to Parliament.

    The 1951/2 election swept the Congress Party into power at na-
tional and state levels alike. In the new Lok Sabha the party won
364 of the 489 seats. This electoral victory, capitalizing as it did
upon the appeal of the Congress as the party that had brought independence to India, and wrapping itself in the saintly legacy of the
martyred Mahatma Gandhi, was hardly surprising. Support for the

Congress was, however, by no means universal. Indeed, of the votes cast, the Congress secured only some 45 per cent. The remainder was split amongst an array of opposition parties, rightist, leftist, and regional, pushed to the margins by Congress's domination of the political centre. This disjuncture between the Congress Party's limited popular appeal, and its domination of the legislature, was to be a feature of Indian politics for decades to come.

The first two decades of India's independence can aptly be characterized as the age of Nehru. Several elements together shaped the political life of the country through the 1950s and into the 1960s. These include a politics of brokerage, a commitment to economic development, and a struggle to contain fissiparous linguistic regionalism. All were knitted together by Nehru's commanding presence. Forced for the first years of his rule to share power with the imperious Sardar Vallabhbhai Patel, after Patel's death in 1950 Nehru successfully turned back the sole remaining challenge to his authority, that of Purushottam Das Tandon at the head of the Congress Working Committee. From then on until his death in 1964, Nehru was unchallenged master of the Indian scene. Operating from a position of unquestioned strength, but never ruthless or vindictive, Nehru impressed his will upon the administrative services, the military, and the legislature. Admired, even idolized as 'Panditji', his signature rose pinned to his *shervani* (jacket), Nehru represented the newly independent India to itself, as well as to the world at large.

Nehru's vision of the new India took perhaps its most visible shape on the plains of the Punjab, with the construction of Chandigarh. As India had lost the province's old capital, Lahore, to Pakistan, some new site was urgently required. For Nehru this had to be a wholly new city, one 'symbolic of the freedom of India, unfettered by the traditions of the past . . . an expression of the nation's faith in the future'. Hence none of the existing architectural styles, such as Indo-Saracenic, tainted by colonialism, would be appropriate, nor would the archaic 'Hindu' being employed by the state government of Orissa in its new capital in Bhubaneshwar. Instead, Nehru turned to the internationally renowned French architect LeCorbusier, who designed for him a starkly modernist city, its civic buildings shaped by sweeping lines and bold colours (see plate 8.2). The whole was set within a rigidly demarcated plan of 'sectors', in which everything

Plate 8.2   Detail of architecture, Chandigarh.

from roadways and parks to residences for different classes of civil servants, each clustered by rank, was laid out in painstaking detail. While admired for the boldness of its conception, Chandigarh has frequently been subjected to criticism for its disregard of Indian

Plate 8.3   Scene from the film *Pukar*, 1939.

conditions and India's architectural heritage. Too sprawling, too forbidding in its monumentality, the city appeared remote from the realities of Indian life. But that was precisely Nehru's intention – to use LeCorbusier's internationalist modernism as the vehicle for the creation of an India fit for the second half of the twentieth century.

Some of the same Nehruvian idealism can be seen in the Indian cinema of the 1950s. Popular and accessible, the products of the huge Bombay studios, soon to be known as 'Bollywood', commercial films have always captured the mood of their times in India. In addition to the usual tales of escapist romance (for an early instance see plate 8.3), the films of the Nehru era made explicit the ideals of nationalism, with the stars portraying the 'modern' Indian who placed 'nation' before 'self'. Film music was increasingly in the air, disseminated first on radio and then as cassette tapes. 'Shree 420' playfully celebrated both nationalism and the appeal of imported consumer goods:

> Mere juutee hain japaanii
> Yeh patluun inglistaanii

> Sar peh laal topii ruusii
> Phir bhii dil hai hindustanii
> On my feet shoes from Japan
> But from England come my pants
> On my head, a red Russian hat
> My heart's INDIAN for all that!

A paradigmatic film of the Nehru era was *Mughal-e-Azam* (1960), an historical parable which made the emperor Akbar into an idealized Nehru, ruling a land where Hindu and Muslim coexisted happily and personal desires were willingly sacrificed for the good of the nation. Lest the point be missed, the film opened and closed with an outline map of pre-partition India rising from the horizon intoning 'I am India.' *Mother India* (1957) gave the iconic role of representing the nation to a woman who, for the sake of the greater good, herself killed her bandit son. Optimistic in tone, these films celebrate an India in which righteousness triumphs, and the country's liberal institutions mould patriotic citizens for a free land.

THE NEW POLITICAL ORDER

The political system in the 1950s relied for its effective functioning upon a collaboration that brought together Nehru's leadership with the local connections of a range of party 'bosses'. Though Nehru's tireless campaigning and his stature as Gandhi's chosen heir gave the Congress its electoral successes, its authority could only be exercised through the party's organization. By his initial mobilization of the masses for non-cooperation in the 1920s, Gandhi had moulded the Congress into a powerful organization that reached deep into India's villages; from the time of the 1937 elections onwards the party had been slowly transformed from an agitational into a vote-getting body. In the 1950s Nehru sat atop this organization, but he did not control the levers by which it functioned. He was, to be sure, indispensable. Whenever he threatened to resign, cries of 'Panditji, do not desert us' rang through the halls of Parliament. But in his cabinet, apart from his prickly defence minister V. K. Krishna Menon, Nehru was surrounded by conservative organization men, such as Govind Balabh Pant, S. K. Patil, and Morarji Desai, whose power was embedded in their control of state- and district-level party organizations. In similar fashion, the state chief ministers, though linked to the centre through participation in the Congress Working Committee, were largely autonomous in the exercise of power in their states. Together, these men made the Congress system work. In essence, the party bosses dispensed jobs and development funds to the lower-level Congress workers in the districts; and they, in turn, brokered these funds to the controllers of the crucial 'vote banks' in the villages, usually leaders of rich peasant castes who could bring their fellows to the polls to vote for Congress. In a manner reminiscent of American Chicago-style 'machine' politics, patronage was exchanged for votes in each locality, with the whole integrated at the top through the Congress organization.

But a populist politics was by no means non-existent in the India of the 1950s. No sooner had the new constitution been inaugurated than Nehru had to contend with a tumultous movement for the reorganization of India's provinces. The origins of the problem lay deep in India's colonial past. As the British formed their provinces, and separated the hundreds of India's princely states from them, they took account only of their own administrative convenience and the political needs of the moment. As a result some language groups, most notably Oriya and Telegu speakers, were split among two or even three provinces, while others were incorporated into large multilinguistic provinces such as Madras and Bombay. The integration of the princely states after 1947 made matters worse by adding to the mix yet more arbitrarily defined units, a few of which were large free-standing states such as Mysore and Hyderabad, while others were small principalities hurriedly cobbled together into such unwieldy administrative structures as Madhya Bharat in central India.

In 1920, as part of his restructuring of the Congress, Gandhi had set up provincial Congress committees along linguistic lines. In this way, so he reasoned, by approaching each in its own language, the Congress could become more responsive to the needs of India's various peoples. When it became possible, after independence, to translate these language-based provinces into the administrative structure of the Indian state, however, Nehru dug in his heels. Against the ominous backdrop of partition and the 'Plan Balkan', which envisaged the break-up of India, Nehru was determined to do nothing that would encourage separatism of any sort. Throughout his tenure of office, maintaining the unity of India was always Nehru's upmost priority. Yet he could not, as a democratic ruler, ignore the increasing clamour for linguistic states that began in the south and then spread to the west and north of the country. The Telegu-speaking Andhras had long chafed under the domination of the better-educated Tamil speakers in the multilingual Madras Presidency, and they had sought a state of their own even before independence. Confronted with Nehru's obstinate opposition, the Andhra leader Potti Sriramalu began a fast to the death in October 1952. In December Sriramalu died; three days later the government agreed to establish an Andhra state.

Once begun, the process of reorganization could not be stopped. A States Reorganization Commission was set up, and its report, implemented in 1956, brought into existence a comprehensively reordered India, divided into fourteen states on the basis of language. The state of Kerala was established for Malayalam speakers; the old Mysore, now Karnataka, accommodated Kannada speakers; Madras, later renamed Tamilnadu, was made a home for Tamil speakers; and so on. The populous Hindi-speaking states of UP, renamed Uttar Pradesh, and Bihar, with the already unilingual West Bengal, remained unaffected. In addition six small Union territories governed directly from Delhi were created. States reorganization encouraged a new regional linguistic politics, yet at the same time, by peaceably accommodating an intensely felt popular sentiment, the move helped stem separatist enthusiasm. Indeed, throughout much of India, Congress, like the Indian nation itself, emerged stronger for having successfully met, in democratic fashion, this challenge to its authority. This accommodation of linguistic diversity can be seen even on Indian currency notes. In plate 8.4, although English and Hindi predominate, the words 'ten rupees' are printed in all fourteen official languages of India.

The Nehru government sought to exempt from this reorganization two of the old provinces, those of Bombay and Punjab. Although the old Bombay Presidency contained two clearly demarcated linguistic regions, of Gujarati speakers in the north and Marathi speakers in the south, its metropolitan centre, the city of Bombay, contained a mixed population, with Gujaratis dominant in its trade and industry and a majority Marathi-speaking working class. The endeavour

Plate 8.4   Facsimile reproduction of Indian 10 rupee currency note.

to retain the old structure was, however, doomed from the outset. Spurred by the changes elsewhere, two new political parties at once sprang into existence to demand a separate Maharashtrian state. Accompanied by a series of deadly riots in Bombay city, the separation of Gujarat from Maharashtra finally took place in 1960, with Bombay, later renamed Mumbai, remaining the capital of the latter.

The Punjab posed a much more intractable problem. While combining, in the remnant province left to India after 1947, both Punjabi and Hindi speakers, the state was also home to a religious community, that of the Sikhs. The Sikhs dominated the Punjabi-speaking portion of the state, and, through their Akali Dal, organized a campaign for a Punjabi-speaking state. Inevitably, this gave to the claim for such a state the appearance of a demand for a Sikh homeland. After the bruising experience of partition, Nehru was unalterably opposed to the creation of any state based upon religious conviction. Eventually, after Nehru's death, a reorganization did take place, ostensibly upon linguistic, not religious grounds, with the carving out, in 1966, of a Punjabi-speaking Punjab state; the remaining Hindi-speaking areas were given statehood of their own as Haryana and Himachal Pradesh. The place of the Sikhs in the Indian Union, however, remained unresolved, and came back to haunt the government afresh in the 1980s.

Nehru solved one further territorial problem by force of arms. Britain's departure from India had left untouched the tiny colonial enclaves of France and Portugal. France was persuaded to hand over peaceably its territory, centred upon the town of Pondicherry. Portugal, whose control over Goa went back 450 years, resisted stubbornly. Eventually, in 1959, an exasperated Nehru marched the army into the territory, easily defeated the Portuguese garrison, and incorporated Goa, with its dependencies of Diu and Daman in Gujarat, into the Indian Union. These former colonies remain to the present separate states with their own distinctive characters.

THE NEW ECONOMIC ORDER

Even before independence, India's leaders had determined that the economic backwardness which had characterised so much of the country's colonial experience must be broken. As we have seen, the Congress in the years before independence strove to mute class difference in favour of anti-colonial protest. As independence drew near, however, it became ever more difficult to contain those who wanted radical social change. As a result the Congress leadership, first under Gandhi and then under Nehru, had to fend off demands from the left for a socialist revolution, in which the propertied elites would be displaced in favour of a state dominated by workers and peasants. The Marxist-oriented Congress Socialist Party, formed in 1934, endeavoured throughout the subsequent decade to push the Congress to the left. For much of this time they were joined by the radical activists of the Communist Party of India (CPI), linked to the Soviet-dominated Communist International. Although the CPI, already weakened by fierce repression, brought discredit upon itself by supporting, at the request of the Soviet Union, the Second World War, nevertheless the party remained attractive to many intellectuals, and found followers among the poor peasants of the countryside. At the time of independence, Communists emerged to take leading roles in the Telengana uprising in Hyderabad, as well as encouraging militant peasant movements in Bengal and Kerala.

Nehru's commitment to socialism had always been ambivalent. Though drawn by his training and convictions to the Congress Socialist group, he was never one of them. With Gandhi, he abhorred violence, and he sought always to make the Congress a unifying, not a divisive, force in India's political life. Still, his belief in the urgent necessity of a more equitable social order led Nehru as prime minister to support ever more wide-ranging measures on behalf of agrarian reform and state control of India's economy. Initially put forward as a policy objective in 1947, by 1955 the Congress had formally committed itself to the principle that 'planning should take place with a view to the establishment of a socialistic pattern of society where the principal means of production are under social ownership or control'.

The first measure to be taken up was zamindari abolition. Incorporated in the Congress Party platform in 1946, it took legislative shape in the early 1950s. Although the provisions of these acts varied from state to state, they generally set land ceilings, and vested the proprietary rights of the large estate holders in the state governments. By the end of the decade, the great barons of the Indian countryside, many of whose properties went back to the earliest days of colonial rule, were no more. Yet the extent of the transformation can easily be exaggerated. Despite protests from India's socialists, the landlords were guaranteed compensation for all property taken. Further, under the constitution land reform as a subject was allocated to the states, not the centre, with the result that the well-to-do peasant castes who dominated the state Congress parties saw to it that ceilings were set high enough so that they would not be adversely affected. In addition, the abolition legislation was itself riddled with loopholes. By adroit measures, such as division of their estates among family members before ceiling legislation came into effect, or placing land in groves or under personal cultivation, which exempted it from confiscation, many landlords were able to preserve substantial properties, and with them a footing in the new political order. Landless peasants gained little from zamindari abolition, while the cultivating tenants, to gain full title to their land, had to make payments to the government over a series of years.

The precedent set by zamindari abolition was followed up in subsequent measures of agrarian reform. Ambitious plans, announcing fundamental transformations of rural society, ended up producing modest measures of change. One scheme that went nowhere was cooperative farming. Inspired by the example of Mao's China, and convinced that only holdings larger than petty peasant plots offered hope of a more productive agriculture, Nehru pushed through the

Congress in 1959 a resolution that called for pooling land for 'cooperative joint farming'. As this scheme frontally challenged the power of the dominant landed castes, who would have had to share land with their poorer neighbours, it never took shape on the ground. More successful, because congruent with the interests of the well-to-do village elites, were the linked projects of Community Development (1952) and Panchayati Raj (1959). The former broke the country into development blocks, and made available in each block trained village-level workers, who could advise farmers on the use of improved seeds, fertilizers, and the like. The latter created institutions of self-government, named for the traditional councils of five ('panch') elders, at the local level. Upon each block, and even more on village *panchayats* (councils), fell the tasks of devising development plans and allocating government funds among the projects each local community preferred. Behind the scheme lay a vision of India's villagers, no longer passive recipients of government aid, working together in democratic fashion for the benefit of all. Despite this well-intentioned rhetoric, however, the dominant landed castes, by securing their own election to the panchayats, effectively captured these new institutions. As a result they directed scarce development funds to their own farms, and strengthened their position as entrenched intermediaries between the village and the larger political system. The rural development schemes of the Nehru years achieved results insofar as they encouraged prospering peasant landowners to shake off the agricultural inefficiencies of the colonial era. They made no contribution towards reducing income inequalities or poverty among India's millions of poor and landless villagers. Gandhian schemes, such as the *bhoodan* movement of Vinoba Bhave, which sought gifts of land for the landless, though they attracted much publicity, fared little better in securing a more equitable distribution of arable land.

Central to Nehru's conception of the new India was a planned economy. Towards this end he established in 1950 a planning commission, which formulated sequential five-year plans for India's development. The first, for the period 1951–6, focused upon agriculture; the second, for 1956–61, on industry. At the heart of the planning enterprise lay a commitment to creating a substantially enlarged industrial base. Heavy industry, such as iron and steel, was to

Plate 8.5   Durgapur steel mill, West Bengal, built with British aid.

be given preference over the production of consumer goods; import substitution was to secure a greater economic self-sufficiency for the country, with the result that India's isolation from the world capitalist system, growing since the Depression of the 1930s, became ever more pronounced; and the public sector was to be favoured over private enterprise in the allocation of investment funds. The 'commanding heights of the economy', above all such critical activities as railways, airlines, and energy production, were to be under exclusive government control. Other government industrial undertakings, such as the Durgapur steel mill built with British aid shown in plate 8.5, complemented those that remained under private ownership.

This decade of planned development successfully broke the trap of economic stagnation which had marked the last decades of the colonial era. Agricultural production grew by 25 per cent during the first plan, and a further 20 per cent in the second. Industrial output grew by an average of some 7 per cent a year into the early 1960s. Overall, India's national income rose by some 4 per cent a year over the course of the first two plans. Although a population growth of

2 per cent dissipated much of this gain, there still remained a per capita increase in income of nearly 2 per cent. These modest successes, however, came at a substantial cost. The focus on industry diverted funds that could have been used to raise agricultural output to showpiece projects, and left the country with an array of inefficient 'white elephants' that continued for decades to soak up scarce funds. The insistence on self-sufficiency drove up consumer prices, and saddled the country with goods such as the Hindustan Ambassador car, whose design remained unchanged for forty years. Although India's capitalists were tightly regulated, they commanded the domestic market without fear of competition. Nehru's socialism, unlike Mao's, never sought to encompass the entire economy. Often little more than a tangle of permits, licences, and credits, it never brought under its control the vast world inhabited by the petty trader and moneylender. Beneath the 'smallish socialized sector' there existed what US Ambassador J. K. Galbraith once called 'the world's greatest example of functioning anarchy'.

With economic development went a commitment to removing the barriers that had held back India's women. Women secured full voting rights under the constitution, and had no hesitation in exercising them. Legislative enactments in the Nehru era, several of them part of a revised code of Hindu law, gave Hindu women the right to sue for divorce, to inherit property on equal terms with males, and to adopt children. In 1961 dowry was outlawed. In practice, however, given women's lack of resources and the pervasive constraints under which they still laboured, especially in the countryside, these laws were little more than statements of good intention. The 1975 government report 'Toward Equality' revealed the widespread discrimination faced by girl children and women, and energized a newly invigorated Indian women's movement.

WAR, FAMINE, AND POLITICAL TURMOIL

As the 1950s drew to a close an aging Nehru had to confront crises he had never anticipated. Food production stagnated, and then began to decline. At the same time an unexpected conflict with China left India's foreign policy in ruins. From the outset Nehru had committed India to non-alignment in the Cold War, and, motivated in part by Gandhian idealism, he sought to project India, along with supposedly like-minded states such as Mao's China and Sukarno's Indonesia, as a mediator between the two superpowers. This Sino-Indian friendship, memorably captured in the phrase 'Hindi-Chini-bhai-bhai' (Indians and Chinese are brothers), fell to pieces following the Chinese takeover of Tibet. In 1959 the Tibetan religious leader the Dalai Lama, with thousands of other refugees, fled to India, where he received asylum and remains in exile to the present. Three years later, in 1962, after Nehru had sought unsuccessfully to push the Chinese out of the contested Aksai Chin region north of Kashmir, which the British had claimed for India but never occupied, the Chinese in reprisal invaded India. In a stunning show of force they marched unhindered into the plains of Assam. Although the Chinese withdrew unilaterally across the eastern Himalayas, they never abandoned the Aksai Chin plateau. This humiliating defeat was followed by a Chinese turn towards Pakistan, and it drove India for a time closer to the United States. It precipitated as well a massive diversion of funds from development to the military, which, neglected, had remained unchanged from the colonial era. His socialist policies under broad attack, Nehru died in May 1964. The moderate Lal Bahadur Shastri (1904–66) succeeded to the post of prime minister.

During 1965 India staggered under a further series of crises. One arose over the issue of language. The constituent assembly had determined that Hindi in the Devanagari script should be the official language of the new India. Tainted by its association with Pakistan, Urdu fast faded from use in favour of a Sanskritized version of Hindi promoted by enthusiasts on All-India Radio and in the schools. To ease the transition from English to Hindi, the constitution provided for a fifteen-year phasing out period during which the language of the colonial master would continue to be used. Hindi, however, was the mother tongue of fewer than half the people of India, and these were concentrated in the northern portion of the country. The non-Hindi speakers in the south and east had no wish to see their languages relegated to subordinate status, and themselves disadvantaged in the competition for scarce government jobs. Many among the Indian elites wished as well to retain English as a 'window on the world'.

Hence the end of the fifteen-year transition period, in 1965, was accompanied by a massive outburst of anti-Hindi sentiment. The centre of this agitation was Tamilnadu. Passionate believers in the beauty and purity of their own 'mother tongue', Tamilians fought against the newcomer from the north by such desperate acts as self-immolation. In the end, a compromise retained English as an associate language, used largely for interregional communication. While the continued use of English has given educated Indians unparalleled access to the largely English-speaking global economy, it also perpetuated, alongside the enduring divisions of caste and religion, a divide between those, no more than 5 per cent of the population, whose knowledge of English places them in the elite, and those who must live within the narrower confines of the vernacular languages. As in the earlier case of linguistic states, so too with the anti-Hindi agitation, the central government's ability to accommodate language-based regionalism in the south testified to the strength of India's democracy. Subsequent regional movements, in the far north-east and north, as we will see, were to put India's unity to a more severe test.

The year 1965 also saw the continuing tension with Pakistan boil over into outright warfare. Aggrieved by India's refusal to conduct a plebiscite in Kashmir, Pakistan first probed its southern border with India, in the Rann of Kutch, and then in September sent guerilla raiders, followed by regular army troops, into Kashmir itself. India responded by sending tanks across the Punjab plains to the outskirts of Lahore. A ceasefire after three weeks of fighting, confirmed by a settlement in January 1966 brokered by the Soviet Union in a meeting in Tashkent between Shastri and the Pakistani general Ayub Khan, restored the status quo before the outbreak of hostilities. Further military encounters with Pakistan, at the time of the freedom struggle in Bangladesh in 1971, and then high on the snow-covered peaks of Kashmir itself in 1999, kept alive an enduring tension but reinforced the lesson that India was the dominant power in the subcontinent and that Pakistan could not secure Kashmir by force of arms.

As the Tashkent meeting came to an end, prime minister Shastri died unexpectedly of a heart attack. This precipitated a succession crisis, which coincided with a mounting economic crisis. The succession crisis was resolved by the selection of Indira Gandhi, Nehru's daughter and only child. She had acted as official hostess in the prime minister's residence for her widower father, and had been Minister of Information and Broadcasting under Shastri. By 1966, at age forty-eight, Mrs Gandhi was a widow, as her Parsi husband Feroze Gandhi (no relation to the Mahatma) had died some years before, and the mother of two sons.

Mrs Gandhi had at once to confront a critical economic situation. Monsoon failure in 1965, and a continuing drought into 1966, brought about an unprecedented decline of some 19 per cent in food grain production in one year. Faced with the spectre of famine, a desperate India turned to the United States for assistance. Grain imports averted disaster, but development had come to a dead halt. At this moment of crisis, Mrs Gandhi abandoned her father's focus on public-sector industrial investment, and set out to increase agricultural production by whatever means possible. To secure further US aid, she devalued the rupee; and, with the goal of bringing about food self-sufficiency, she turned to a new agricultural strategy pioneered by the American Ford Foundation. At its heart lay new high-yielding varieties of seeds developed in Mexico and the Philippines. Under the agricultural package programme, dissemination of these new seed varieties was to be combined with the use of chemical fertilizers and enhanced irrigation. The objective was to bring all of these inputs together in one place at one time, and so avoid the dissipation of benefits – seeds here, fertilizer there – common under the earlier plans which endeavoured to give something to everyone.

The result was the so-called 'green revolution'. In the single year 1967/8 Indian agricultural production leapt ahead by 26 per cent, and national income rose 9 per cent. Even industrial production began to pick up. Despite a huge population growth of over 2 per cent a year, India was at last making progress towards feeding her people. The green revolution, however, was not without its shortcomings. It was, first of all, simply not possible to sustain the extraordinary rates of growth of the late sixties. Then too, India was still dependent on the vagaries of the monsoon rains. Although food grain production reached a total of 100 million tonnes in 1970, it did not rise above that figure in any of the subsequent five years. Part of the problem lay in the fact that the benefits of the green revolution were unevenly distributed. The new varieties of wheat, when joined to assured irrigation on large farms, proved far more responsive to a 'take-off' in output than did rice, where the new seeds were less well suited to Indian conditions and plots were often tiny and scattered. By 1980, 75 per cent of all wheat was grown in irrigated fields, compared to only 42 per cent of rice. The wheat-growing heartland of India, above all the Punjab and Haryana, fast becoming a land of tractors and tube-wells, was, under the 'green revolution', more than ever the 'granary' of India. Rice-growing Bengal, by contrast, along with the hilly dry-farming areas of central India, where large-scale irrigation was not feasible, slipped ever further behind.

The 'green revolution' also left social disparities in its wake. Not only did the new inputs work best on large holdings, but success depended upon entrepreneurial skills, and access to credit, which the well-to-do, with their political connections, most effectively commanded. Hence, in the absence of a government commitment to anything other than maximizing output – for the new agricultural wealth was not even taxed, let alone redistributed – the poor villagers, even if marginally better off, found themselves comparatively farther behind. On the basis of this sense of deprivation among the underprivileged Mrs Gandhi was to build her political career in the 1970s. But such a challenge from below would not go uncontested. Ominously, in 1969, a group of landlords in Tamilnadu's Tanjore district confined forty-two former 'untouchables' in their huts, and burned them to the ground. Overall, although the crises of the 1960s brought about no fundamental change in the working of the Indian polity, this decade, by contrast with the optimistic expectations of the Nehru years, was a darker and more pessimistic era.

INDIRA RAJ

Installed in office as a compromise candidate by the Congress 'syndicate', Indira Gandhi was meant to be a pliable figure, whose popularity as Nehru's daughter these party bosses could turn to advantage in the elections of 1967. Her leftist sympathies, too, they calculated, could divert attention from their own conservatism. From the outset, however, Mrs Gandhi was determined to be her own master. She viewed herself as the custodian of her father's secular and socialist values, which, after an initial period of indecision, she determined to implement.

The 1967 elections, far from revitalizing the Congress, marked the beginning of the end for the powerful organization that Gandhi had set up, and Nehru had nurtured, over so many years. In the Lok Sabha the Congress majority was reduced from over a hundred to a bare majority of some twenty seats, while the opposition parties of both right, including the free enterprise Swatantra and the Hindu Jan Sangh, and the left communists and socialists, gained seats. In the states the losses were even more devastating. Communist parties came to power in West Bengal and Kerala; the Dravidian DMK, capitalizing on the language agitation, took power in Madras; while rightist coalitions claimed power in several northern states. From this time onwards, though poorly favoured with resources, Kerala embarked on a development scheme of its own which made it by the end of the century the one Indian state with near universal literacy and effective gender equality of men and women.

The 1967 electoral debacle, from which, in Bengal and Madras – Tamilnadu, the Congress never recovered, discredited the party bosses, and encouraged Mrs Gandhi, after two further years yoked uneasily with them, to break decisively with her old patrons in 1969. Expelled from the party for defying its nominee for India's president, Mrs Gandhi formed her own Congress (I) Party, and then moved swiftly to consolidate her position. She first asserted her leftist credentials by nationalizing, to popular acclaim, the country's largest banks. She then formed alliances with the Tamilian DMK and the Communists (CPI) that enabled her to stay in office. A near fifteen-year period of 'Indira Raj' had begun. The DMK alliance had one unintended effect. To secure its support, Mrs Gandhi was obliged to pour development funds into the party's home state of Tamilnadu. This in turn encouraged southerners to reconsider the value of their ties with India, and so put an end to any thought of secession.

Meanwhile, as economic growth stagnated into the early 1970s, social unrest mounted throughout India, as the discontented of all sorts – from municipal and industrial workers to the poor and the landless – took to the streets. Most ominous was the Naxalite movement, centred in West Bengal, which advocated armed struggle to bring about a Maoist-style revolution, and drew support from students and tribals as well as the dispossessed in the countryside. Mrs Gandhi moved to place herself at the head of this popular upsurge. Abandoning efforts to work through the Congress Party machinery, she appealed to the people over the heads of the country's established politicians. The success of this strategy was confirmed in the 1971 elections. Running under the banner of 'garibi hatao' (end poverty), Mrs Gandhi's fledgling Congress Party, reversing the losses of the old party in 1967, captured a surprising 352 seats in Parliament, not far short of the number her father had won for the Congress in the elections of the 1950s.

Buoyed by this electoral triumph, Mrs Gandhi continued her leftward march. Pushing through a constitutional amendment restricting the 'fundamental right' to hold property, she abolished the privy purses that had been awarded to India's princes in 1947 to sweeten the pill of states' integration. Nationalization of insurance companies and coalmines followed. In 1971 Mrs Gandhi also concluded an alliance with the Soviet Union; in so doing she brought to an end the close ties with the United States, already frayed by continued US aid to Pakistan, forged at the time of the China war. Her greatest triumph, however, was the December 1971 war with Pakistan. Since the late 1960s Pakistan had been struggling to contain the divergent interests of its two wings, in the east and west, separated by 1,000 miles of Indian territory. By 1971 Bengali anger at Punjabi dominance of the state had erupted into open rebellion. As Pakistan's ruler, General Yahya Khan, endeavoured to put down this resistance by force of arms, India moved to support the Bengalis, first by covert aid to the rebels, and then, in December, by outright invasion. The outcome was a stunning collapse of Pakistani authority in the east, and the surrender of its army, which delivered into India's hands 100,000 prisoners of war. With the emergence of the new nation of Bangladesh, Pakistan, now confined to the west, was reduced to half its former size, and India's pre-eminence on the subcontinent decisively confirmed.

Beyond these policy initiatives, the 1971 election victory opened the way to a new political order. One can identify some three elements that defined a distinctive 'Indira Raj'. One was the mobilization of the peasantry directly, rather than through the old vote brokers. This inevitably meant jumping over the dominant well-to-do rural castes in favour of seeking support from the so-called 'backward classes', as well from untouchables and Muslims, who had always seen in the Congress their only bulwark against oppression. This new political style in turn inaugurated a populist authoritarianism, or what might be called a plebiscitary democracy, in which the figure of Indira Gandhi alone mattered. The slogan 'Indira is India, and India is Indira' effectively captured this focus on the person of the leader. Inevitably, this further devalued the Congress Party organization at all levels. Indeed, to check criticism, Mrs Gandhi abandoned the practice of selecting party leaders on the basis of the support they commanded in their home regions, and instituted instead a policy of nominating 'loyalists' dependent on her favour. Over time, as its base in the countryside withered away, the Congress Party across India became little more than a coterie of sycophants clinging to its imperious leader.

Lastly, the new populism, with its use of such catchy slogans as 'garibi hatao' (eliminate poverty), risked raising expectations, especially among India's poor, that could not easily be satisfied. Despite two decades of planned development, deep poverty remained embedded in India. One 1971 survey estimated that 38 per cent of the rural population, and nearly half the urban, crowded into collections of flimsy shacks called *basti*, and lacking regular employment, lived below the level of destitution based on caloric intake. To raise the living standard of this vast number of people would be, at the best of times, a Herculean task. Mrs Gandhi's socialist measures, however, where they were not purely symbolic in nature, such as the abolition of princely purses, only nibbled at the edges of the problem. Despite the introduction of some income-generating schemes in the countryside, she dared not antagonize the well-to-do rural classes, upon whom the country depended for increased food grain production. At the same time, growing administrative corruption, together with widespread tax evasion among the wealthy, made an all-out attack on poverty nearly impossible. Even the erstwhile 'steel frame' of the Indian Administrative Service, battered by the clamorous demands of various interest groups, and the politicians who represented them, was unable to resist the corrosive demoralization that swirled about it. Trapped between the conflicting goals of economic growth and social justice, and lacking reliable administrative agency in the countryside, the government was reduced to a near ineffectuality.

Growing food shortages and increasing unemployment, made worse by the 1974 worldwide energy crisis, which precipitated an inflationary spiral, offered an opportunity to opposition politicians. Prominent among them was the old socialist and Gandhian Jayaprakash Narayan. J.P. (as he was called), who like Gandhi had renounced political office in order to serve the poor, possessed a moral authority not far short of Indira herself. Leagued with the veteran Congressman, and Indira's long-time rival, Morarji Desai, whose home state of Gujarat was the site of massive middle-class protests, he posed a formidable challenge. Mobilizing supporters in his desperately impoverished home state of Bihar, J.P. called for a mass extraparliamentary campaign of 'total revolution'. A growing crescendo of strikes and marches, fasts and sit-ins, ensued across India. Matters were finally brought to a head by a high court decision, on 12 June 1975, finding Mrs Gandhi's own 1971 election tainted by corrupt practices, and therefore invalid. Rather than resign, in a pre-emptive strike against her opponents, Mrs Gandhi two weeks later, on 26 June, proclaimed an extraordinary state of emergency.

Under the emergency regulations all civil liberties, including *habeas corpus*, were suspended; rigorous press censorship was brought into force; opposition political parties were banned; tens of thousands of Mrs Gandhi's opponents were unceremoniously thrown into jail; and the parliamentary elections set for March 1976 were postponed. In July, Parliament was convened to enact a constitutional amendment exonerating Mrs Gandhi retrospectively from any charges of electoral malpractice. From the outset, the emergency, which many middle-class Indians supported as the only alternative to a feared anarchy, was tainted by this close association with Mrs Gandhi's own political survival. While proclaiming once again a 'direct assault on poverty', the emergency created no new institutions that could carry out such a campaign. Instead, in a way reminiscent of Italian fascism, the government sought to drive India forwards by instilling a commitment to discipline and hard work among its people. Office workers showed up on time; incidents of smuggling and tax evasion fell off dramatically; an enforced labour peace helped secure renewed industrial growth. Even the weather cooperated. A good monsoon in 1975 made possible a record harvest of 121 million tonnes of food grains, accompanied by a declining rate of inflation. These apparent gains in 'efficiency' were not achieved without cost. The summary procedures by which the emergency regulations were enforced were often accompanied by a high-handed arrogance and contempt for the poor on the part of government officials. Two measures, in particular, stirred up intense popular resentment. Both were closely associated with the unchecked authority Mrs Gandhi reposed in her younger son, Sanjay Gandhi (1947–80). One was slum clearance. The old Mughal Delhi, a maze of alleyways and narrow lanes tightly confined within its walls, had for years become increasingly congested. It still remained home to a large Muslim population, as well as to numerous workshops and traders. Determined to make Delhi a modern and beautiful city, Sanjay embarked upon a massive demolition of shacks, shops, and residential quarters that cut a swath across the city right up to the gates of the Jama Masjid, and dislocated perhaps half a million people.

Control of India's burgeoning population had long been a government priority. Other than family planning slogans plastered on billboards, however, few practical measures had been taken to bring it about, with the result that not only had the absolute number of Indians continued to grow, to some 660 million by 1971, but so too, more ominously, had the rate of increase. By the 1960s it stood at over 2 per cent per annum. Sanjay took up the cause of population control with enthusiasm. Sterilization was decreed for men who had had more than two children. To meet the high targets set, the poor and the vulnerable were often dragged off by the police and forcibly sterilized. This draconian campaign terrified those who feared the loss of potency and progeny, and set back the cause of voluntary birth control in India for years to come.

The pervasive sense of disillusionment with the state that marked these years is perhaps best captured in the wildy popular film *Sholay* (1975). In it a bandit, once free, kills the family and cuts off the arms of the police officer, a local landlord or *thakur*, who had initially captured him. The thakur turns for help to two petty criminals he had once known, Jai and Veeru, and by their bravery they

together capture the villain Gabbar. In place of the state's ineffectual institutions, *Sholay* celebrates the underclass in the figure of the
hero Jai – played by the megastar Amitabh Bacchan – who gives
up his life for the thakur. In a reversal of the usual hostile imagery,
the 'feudal' landlord too is shown as fundamentally good, able to
act where the state cannot. A few years later the real-life low-caste
woman Phulan Devi in similar fashion captured the public imagination, when she escaped from a brutal marriage and gang rape by
members of the dominant village caste to lead a robber band and
seek revenge from a hideout in the maze of ravines in southern UP.
By the 1980s, in the popular imagery, the politicians often turn out
to be the 'real' criminals.

THE JANATA INTERLUDE AND INDIRA'S RETURN

Together, Sanjay's slum clearance and sterilization campaigns antagonized the two groups who had previously been Mrs Gandhi's
strongest supporters – Muslims and the poor. Hence, when Mrs
Gandhi, unaware of the resentment bubbling up underneath her,
unexpectedly called elections for March 1977 in the hope of legiti-
mating her emergency regime, she was instead swept from office.
United under the Janata Party banner, Mrs Gandhi's opponents
gained 295 seats in the Lok Sabha to Congress's 154, and so brought
to an end thirty years of uninterrupted Congress rule. Morarji Desai
took office as India's first non-Congress prime minister. India's voters clearly valued their democracy, and had no intention of surren-
dering it. As one journalist wrote of the election campaign, village
audiences in the remote countryside responded favourably 'to sophisticated arguments about civil liberties, fundamental rights, and
the independence of the judiciary'.

An ascetic Brahman, renowned for his practice of drinking his
own urine as part of his daily yoga therapy, Morarji at age eighty
presided over a fractious coalition, dominated by the rightist Jan
Sangh, but composed of an array of Congress opponents ranged
across the political spectrum from the socialists to regional parties
such as Charan Singh's agrarian Bharatiya Lok Dal. From the outset,
although united in restoring India's civil liberties, and with it a vi-
able federal system, the Janata government was hobbled by disputes

among its various constituents, and had difficulty containing the ambitions of its leaders, several of whom wished to displace Morarji Desai as prime minister in favour of themselves.

The precarious balance of interests represented in Janata required careful nurturing if the party was to succeed. This it did not get. Janata's policies, with their focus on investment in agriculture instead of industry, and a Gandhian emphasis on small-scale technology, were moderately successful. Food grain production reached records of 126 million tonnes in 1977/8 and 131 million in 1978/9. But the bickering among the party's leaders could not be brought to an end. In 1979 Morarji Desai was forced to resign in favour of Charan Singh, who as a Jat became India's first non-Brahman prime minister. Charan Singh, however, unable to muster a majority in Parliament, lasted less than a month in office. With his failure, the Janata coalition collapsed. Elections held in January 1980 brought the Congress back into office, with the presumably discredited Indira Gandhi at its head. As the country was to discover again with the swirling coalitions of the 1990s, it was no easy task to put together an opposition party that could effectively challenge Congress's long dominance of India's political system.

Resilient and indomitable as ever, Mrs Gandhi secured for the Congress in the 1980 election a commanding two-thirds majority in the Lok Sabha. Signalling a shift from the party's traditional north Indian base to the south, Mrs Gandhi herself stood for election from Andhra Pradesh. She quickly, however, resumed her personalistic style of governance. Grooming Sanjay as heir apparent, she even let him award 'tickets' for election as Congress candidates to large numbers of his own favourites and loyalists. But within six months of the election Sanjay was dead, killed in a stunt airplane crash in June 1980. A grieving Indira then turned to his elder brother Rajiv (1944–91), employed as a pilot for Indian Airlines, and charged him to take up the mantle of the family's political fortunes.

Once restored to power, Mrs Gandhi began courting voters on the basis of ethnic and religious affiliation, and cynically manipulating communalist groups for political advantage. For the most part this playing of the ethnic 'card' took place quietly, without open acknowledgement. Nevertheless, this abrogation of the Congress's traditional secularism was to be Mrs Gandhi's undoing, and it embedded in India for the first time since the 1940s a divisive communal politics. The Sikhs were the first to be caught up in this vicious new politics. Despite their position at the heart of the 'green revolution', some Sikhs, not content with formation of a Punjabi-speaking state, demanded the award to them of Chandigarh, then shared with Haryana, as the capital of Punjab alone. Others, encouraged by the enthusiasm of diaspora Sikhs in the United States, Canada, and elsewhere began to press for an autonomous, even independent, Sikh state, or Khalistan. Meanwhile, internal dissension over issues of Sikh religious practice, together with opposition to the moderate leadership of the established Akali Dal, led in the late 1970s to the rise of a young fundamentalist preacher, Sant Jarnail Singh Bhindranwale, who took up the cause of Khalistan. As the Akali Dal had supported the Janata regime, and itself controlled the Punjab government, Mrs Gandhi determined to oust it, and so gave her patronage to Bhindranwale. Such support only encouraged his extremist claims. By 1984 Bhindranwale and his armed followers had blockaded themselves in the holiest Sikh shrine, the Golden Temple in Amritsar, and vowed not leave until a Sikh state was created.

Having mounted this tiger, Mrs Gandhi now found herself unable to get off. To accept a Khalistan was impossible, for the Punjab, as a sensitive border state, was critical to India's security. Hence she decided to crush Bhindranwale's movement. This she did by sending the army to assault the Temple. Although Bhindranwale was killed, so too were thousands of other Sikhs congregated within the temple grounds; 100 soldiers fell as well. But the major casualty of this 'Operation Bluestar' – a second Amritsar massacre, after that of Jallianwalla Bagh in 1919 – was the loyalty of angry and embittered Sikhs throughout India. Among their number were Mrs Gandhi's own security guards. On 31 October 1984, as she set out to walk from her house to the office in the garden of her walled compound, two of her Sikh guards turned their weapons upon her. She died instantly.

At once public rage at the assassination of this woman, for so many years India's trusted leader, boiled up throughout the country. It quickly took as its focus Delhi's large Sikh population. Visible because of their beards and turbans, Sikh men formed an especially easy target for the mobs that roamed the city's streets seeking vengeance. For three days, gangs of arsonists and killers, in criminal collusion with the police and Congress politicians, who pointed out the houses of Sikhs, were allowed to rampage freely. Over 1,000 innocent Sikhs were murdered in Delhi alone, and thousands more rendered homeless. No one was ever brought to trial.

THE END OF A DYNASTY – RAJIV GANDHI, 1984–1989

Rajiv Gandhi in 1984 was young, handsome, and personable; as 'Mr Clean', he stood in sharp contrast with his 'godfather'-like brother. Hence after his mother's death the country turned to him at once as its next prime minister. Moving quickly to capitalize on the sympathy he had won as the only remaining son of a martyred mother, Rajiv called parliamentary elections for December 1984. With an image comparable to that of a Bombay film idol, Rajiv rode to power on the crest of the largest electoral victory ever won by the Congress Party. Its 415 seats gave the party an 80 per cent majority in the Lok Sabha, while, at over 48 per cent of the popular vote, the Congress came closer than ever before to securing the support of an absolute majority of the electorate.

In office Rajiv backed away from some of his mother's policies. He sought, albeit rather ineffectually, to revitalize the Congress Party organization. Undoing Mrs Gandhi's tight centralization of power in Delhi, he worked hard to accommodate non-Congress and regional political parties. In the Punjab he reached an accord with the Akali Dal, which enabled that party to take office in 1985. Unfortunately this agreement, which would have transferred Chandigarh exclusively to Punjab, was never fully implemented, and it did not succeed in putting an end to individual acts of terrorism, primarily by Khalistan enthusiasts. As a result the Punjab was placed under president's rule in 1987, and under a state of emergency the following year. The violence of the Sikhs was now matched by that of the paramilitary police, who swarmed over the state, harassing and detaining Sikh youths without fear of legal challenge. Only in the 1990s was civil order finally restored in Punjab.

Rajiv's most significant break with Congress Party tradition was the opening of India to the world capitalist system, and with it preaching the virtues of private enterprise. By the 1980s India had been walled off from the world economically for the better part of fifty years. Many powerful elements within Indian society found this a comfortable arrangement. Corrupt permit-issuing bureaucrats and inefficient manufacturers jointly benefited from captive markets and a cozy under-the-table circulation of 'black money'. Politicians, of the Hindu right and the socialist left alike, delighted to keep India free from the 'taint' of American culture and goods. Others, their ideas formed in colonial days, simply looked with suspicion on all capitalists as selfish and exploitative. Alert to the new world of computers and mobile capital, Rajiv sought to ally himself with the young modern managers, who, like himself, found the old 'permit Raj' constraining. Rajiv was able to take only a few beginning steps towards liberalization. Regulations governing the size of firms were lifted; taxes on wealth and inheritance reduced; and the tangle of licences restricting the import of consumer durables and high-technology products such as computers was simplified. Even after these reforms were in place, however, India remained a long way from the free market vision of Rajiv's contemporaries, Ronald Reagan and Margaret Thatcher.

Despite his innovations in economic policy, Rajiv was unable to emancipate himself wholly from his mother's habit of playing with the fire of communal politics. The Muslims this time bore the brunt of a heavy-handed intervention. The occasion was the 1985 Shah Bano decision of the Indian Supreme Court. The vexed problem of the separate Hindu and Muslim law codes, brought into existence 200 years before in the days of Warren Hastings, had never been resolved by independent India. A constitutional directive committed the new state to a uniform civil code, covering the whole of India's diverse peoples, but no such code had ever been enacted. The Nehru government had reformed and codified Hindu law, but, fearful of antagonizing Muslim opinion, had left Muslim law alone. In its Shah Bano decision, in the case of a divorced Muslim woman's claim for maintenance from her former husband, the supreme court set aside the Muslim code, which awarded such maintenance for only a few months, and instead, on the basis of the criminal law, ordered maintenance as necessary to prevent the woman from becoming destitute. This open challenge to the authority of Muslim personal law affronted much Muslim opinion, for in the charged atmosphere of communal distrust of the time, it appeared to threaten the shared values of India's vast Muslim population. In India, where Muslims were an often fearful minority, the old personal law was charged with a meaning that it did not possess in Pakistan, where the family law was substantially reformed in the 1960s.

Rajiv Gandhi cared little about the Shah Bano case himself, and no doubt would have preferred a common civil code; nevertheless he saw in the opposition to this supreme court decision a heaven-sent opportunity to draw conservative Muslim voters to the Congress cause. Hence he pushed through Parliament a bill, overturning the Shah Bano decision, that required disputes among Muslims to be settled under Muslim personal law. In justification he said that it was for the 'Muslims themselves to look at their laws', and to change them if they wished. Still, a dangerous precedent of state intervention had been set. Further, the outcome of the Shah Bano case handed a weapon to the opponents of the Congress, who began to allege that the government 'pampered' Muslims with special legislation at the expense of the Hindu majority. The obsessive focus on Muslim 'mistreatment' of women also distracted public opinion from abuses to which women throughout India were subjected, from neglect of infant girls to the brutal killing of young brides by setting them on fire so that the husband could collect a second dowry from a new wife.

Rajiv's intervention into the ethnic politics of Sri Lanka, formerly Ceylon, was to prove even more disastrous. An island divided between a Buddhist Sinhalese-speaking majority, and a large Hindu Tamil minority with ties to India's Tamils across the Palk Strait, Sri Lanka since its independence had enjoyed a precarious communal amity. In 1983, Sinhala enthusiasts determined to cleanse the southern or Sinhalese portion of the island of its Tamil residents. The violence of this purge provoked in response a Tamil resistance movement of guerilla warfare, that of the Tamil Tigers, who sought independence for the northern areas around the Jaffna peninsula.

As India's Tamils sympathized with their Sri Lankan co-religionists, Rajiv at first gave covert assistance to the rebels, by, for instance, air-dropping supplies to them in beleagured Jaffna. The conflict at a standstill, the Sri Lankan president then encouraged India to send a 'peace-keeping' force to the island. This force was charged with disarming the Tamil terrorists so that elections might take place. The Tigers, however, refused to give up their arms, instead turning them against the Indian soldiers. A bloody combat ensued, in which the Indian Army soon lost the confidence of both sides. Ultimately, in 1990, the Indian Government extricated itself from this futile struggle by simply withdrawing its troops. Nevertheless Tamil anger and bitterness at India remained. A year later, in May 1991, while Rajiv Gandhi was campaigning through Tamilnadu, a woman presumed to be a member of a Tamil Tiger terrorist group worked her way to his side in an election rally, and then detonated a bomb hidden on her person. The resulting explosion killed Rajiv Gandhi, the assassin, and a dozen bystanders.

By the time of his death, however, Rajiv was out of office, his reputation as 'Mr Clean' tarnished by a series of scandals. Of these the most serious was the Bofors affair, in which Rajiv was accused of taking 'kickbacks' from a Swedish munitions firm in return for the award of defence contracts. Rajiv responded by ousting his finance minister V. P. Singh, who in turn went into opposition. Following mid-term election losses, Rajiv went to the voters in the autumn of 1989. An electoral pact on the part of the major opposition parties not to contest seats against each other dramatically enhanced their ability to defeat Congress candidates. As a result Congress won fewer than 40 per cent of the seats in the Lok Sabha. V. P. Singh took office at the head of a minority government, built upon a precarious coalition of his own supporters together with those of the Communist parties and the newly ascendant rightist Hindu Bharatiya Janata Party (BJP). A new era in Indian politics was about to begin.

Rajiv's defeat and death effectively brought to an end some forty years of rule over India by the family of Jawaharlal Nehru. To be sure, Rajiv's widow Sonia, an Italian whom he had met as a student in England, and who remained in seclusion for years after Rajiv's death, was pulled on to the political stage in 1998; and his children may yet ultimately take up careers in politics. Still, as the years go by, especially as no member of the family was in office throughout the decade of the 1990s, the immediacy of the Nehru family name becomes ever more remote. The Nehrus, father, daughter and grandsons, will in the end be remembered above all for their role in securing India's transition to independence, and the country's subsequent consolidation as a powerful democratic nation.

It is suggestive to compare the attraction this family commands in India with that of the Kennedys in the United States. Like the Nehru family, the Kennedys enjoyed, if not always the love and affection of the nation, then a respectful admiration over many decades. The Kennedys and the Nehru family share, too, a history of tragic deaths, which has deepened the imaginative sympathy each commands from their respective nations. The parallels are almost uncanny: two towering figures, John F. Kennedy (1963) and Indira Gandhi (1984), struck down by assassin's bullets while in office at the head of the nation. Two sons, John F. Kennedy, Jr. (1999) and Sanjay Gandhi (1980), headstrong, even reckless, killed in the crash of small planes they were piloting. Two brothers, to be sure of different generations, Robert Kennedy (1968) and Rajiv Gandhi (1991), their political potential as yet barely realized, slain while on the campaign trail. Although the Kennedys did not have the extended years in power of the Nehru family, still both families embodied their respective nations, through their triumphs and tragedies, in a vibrant and personal fashion for much of the last half of the twentieth century.

9

Democratic India in the nineties: coalitions, class, community, consumers, and conflict

> We are a free and sovereign people today and we have rid ourselves of the burden of the past. We look at the world with clear and friendly eyes and at the future with faith and confidence.
>
> Prime Minister Jawaharlal Nehru, broadcast from
> New Delhi, 15 August 1947

The hopeful words of any nation's founding fathers are likely to be read with some degree of irony a half-century later. In India, half-centennial reflections on the past were occasioned not only by the country's anniversary but also by the end of the millennium, a focus for stocktaking everywhere. If the words of the founding fathers at times rang hollow, they also, in fact, predicted many successes, not least India's proud claim to the world's largest democracy (plate 9.1). A baker's dozen of general elections, by century's end, and hundreds of state elections had produced a high degree of politicization extending to those long outside the political system. In the year of the golden anniversary, K. R. Narayanan, dalit by birth, was sworn in as India's president, a powerful symbol of the progress and aspirations of 'untouchables'. The role of president, one might note, had been assumed on two earlier occasions in the half-century by a Muslim and, most poignantly, at the time of Indira Gandhi's assassination, by a Sikh. Observers also praised the Supreme Court's activism, for example in indictments of top government and political leaders for bribery and corruption as well as in favouring public-interest litigation to strengthen the effective exercise of civil liberties. India's press continued renowned for its independence and

Plate 9.1 'Election Time', as villagers consult newspaper with information about candidates.

vitality. Economic liberalization had stimulated the growth of a middle class; a major role in the global software industry; and a culture increasingly open to the larger world. And India, as a site of tourism and a producer of the arts, wisdom, and handicrafts, delighted ever-increasing numbers of consumers worldwide.

But commentators reviewing these achievements also acknowledged that the glass was in every arena also 'half empty'. The decade was marked by substantial violence directed against Muslims, and, at the end of the decade, against Christians as well. In 1992, the destruction of the 'Babri Masjid' mosque by Hindu militants was followed by an anti-Muslim pogrom that left thousands dead. The increasing influence of the Hindu nationalist party, the Bharatiya Janata (Indian People's) Party (BJP), fuelled further fears for India's secular tradition and the vitality of a religiously plural culture. The situation in Kashmir, which seemed like unfinished business from partition, became one of virtual civil war, and, like the stunning decision to test nuclear devices in 1998, meant that tensions with Pakistan continued. Class or caste tension was also evident right from the start of the decade with protests against implementation

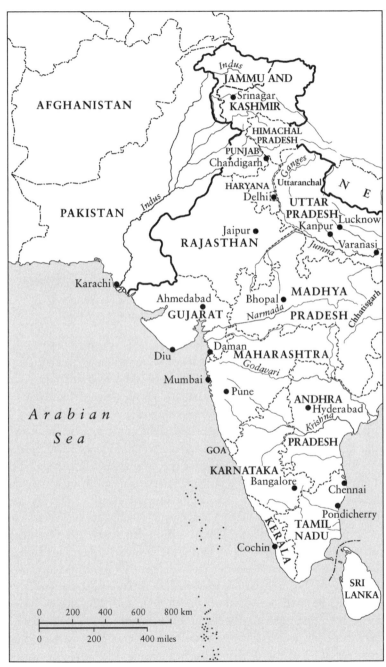

Map 4   India in 2000.

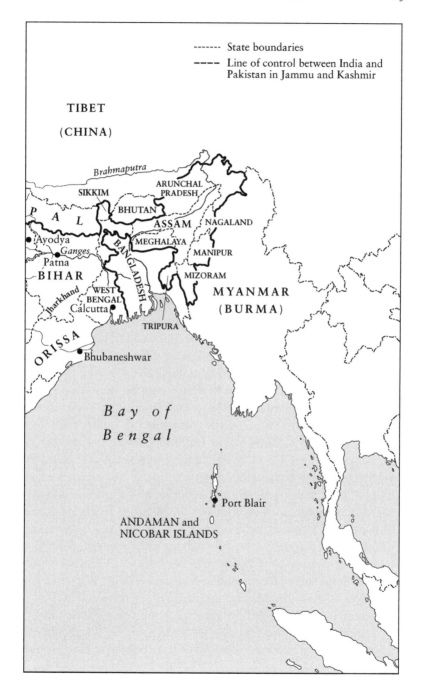

State boundaries

Line of control between India and Pakistan in Jammu and Kashmir

TIBET

(CHINA)

Brahmaputra

SIKKIM

ARUNCHAL PRADESH

BHUTAN

NEPAL

ASSAM

NAGALAND

Ayodya

Ganges

MEGHALAYA

MANIPUR

Patna

BANGLADESH

BIHAR

MIZORAM

Jharkhand

WEST BENGAL

MYANMAR

(BURMA)

Calcutta

ORISSA

TRIPURA

Bhubaneshwar

Bay of Bengal

Port Blair

ANDAMAN and NICOBAR ISLANDS

of the Mandal Commission's report in favour of additional affirmative action; and it continued with periodic episodes of violence against the lowest classes. Serious disabilities faced women, with 'dowry deaths' the most flagrant sign of their lack of power; but the unfavourable sex ratio in India and the subcontinent as a whole was a more important clue to the differential health care and nutrition for girls and women that was characteristic in a context of extreme scarcity. Lack of basic public health and education facilities, and an often- corrupt bureaucracy, constrained the freedom and life chances of much of the population. Many would point precisely to 'the burden of the past' as at least part of the explanation for these serious issues of equality, freedom, and poverty.

In the 1990s the most serious conflicts were religious conflicts, including regional conflicts that found expression through religion, and caste conflicts that were displaced on to religion. One of the most influential voices in explaining worldwide religious conflict and 'fundamentalism' in the 1990s was that of political scientist Samuel Huntington, who posited a 'clash of civilizations' as key to the conflicts both within and between nations at the end of the century. He argued that there were deep and enduring differences characteristic of civilizations like Islam, the Indic civilizations, and the West, and that, with the end of the Cold War, it would be these that would profoundly shape international relations in particular. Huntington's arguments, however superficially plausible, failed to take into account the great variety within traditions; their long history of interactions, which left none unchanged; and the great variations in patterns of interaction among civilizations. Others, more persuasively, argued that the significant influence of the past on India in regard to ethnoreligious conflict was the lingering legacy of British colonialism. There was, by this argument, no need to look to essential differences among cultures given the colonial strategy of defining corporate groups as the building blocks of society. Former areas of British colonial influence, including Northern Ireland, Palestine, and Malaysia, as well as India, all experienced severe ethnoreligious conflict after independence. In terms of the economy as well, the legacies of the colonial economy had also left India seriously disadvantaged in both social and economic development, a 'burden of the past' not easily shed.

In reviewing the events of the 1990s, however, it is necessary to go beyond extrapolation from historical patterns as explanation. In the first place, it is clear that independent India itself crafted policies that reflected profound ambivalence about whether it was to be a society of individuals or one of corporate groups. The Indian constitution, above all in the elimination of separate electorates, did indeed seek to obliterate colonial categories like 'Muslim' in favour of the liberal vision of free individuals interacting with the state. Yet the very category of 'minority', central to everyday 'common sense' and used in such bodies as the post-independence federal Minorities Commission (to address what could have been defined as 'human rights' or 'civil rights' more generally) belied the liberal goal. The old colonial policy of separate civil codes defined by religion, moreover, had been maintained, with separate personal law for each religious group. This legal pluralism was also intended to be temporary, with the goal of a Uniform Civil Code identified as one of the 'directive principles' of the new state. In fact no progress was made in this regard, and the 'Hindu' codes alone, generally speaking, proved subject to legislation and reform, emerging as the *de facto* normative law of the new state. Caste categories were also to be of no official importance and their enumeration was dropped from the census. The erstwhile 'untouchables' and the similarly disadvantaged 'tribes', however, would for a time be recognized as eligible to receive compensatory discrimination in education and employment. The contradictions inherent in social arrangements that treated individuals as members of corporate groups bedeviled social and political life in the 1990s.

It is important, however, to see that these tensions, whether in relation to religious 'minorities' or lower castes, were not continuously salient since independence but took on new virulence at the end of the century. Here a range of political and economic factors come into play, above all those associated with the dramatic changes in economic liberalization, begun to a very limited degree in the 1980s and advancing steadily in the 1990s, that marked a break with the pattern set at independence. By implementing a 'socialist pattern of society' and pulling itself up by its bootstraps, the new state had intended to end the grinding poverty and technological backwardness that was a legacy of colonial rule and that often reinforced the categories of hierarchic status. In fact, weighed down by an inefficient state sector, severe restrictions on imports, and a regime of licences and bureaucracy, more aspects of the colonial economy persisted than were changed. When change did come at the end of the century, however successful the policies proved for some classes and some sectors, it also made for increasing economic disparities that left untold hundreds of millions in grinding poverty as well as millions of others aspiring to share in economic change.

With economic liberalization, India was increasingly opened to global culture through cable and satellite television, films, consumer advertising, the Internet, and diaspora networks. With an increasingly consumer-oriented television on the one hand, and the lifestyle of those profiting in the new economy ever more visible on the other, the tensions generated by class and regional deprivation could only grow. As in the case of the green revolution, when the wealthier farmers were often clear winners, liberalization and concomitant withdrawal of protection to agriculture and the pubic sector, even more dramatically made for winners and losers. The decade saw violence directed against presumed rivals for economic preference, assertion of state and caste interests, and national assertion, militarily, culturally, and economically, against presumed threats to India's integrity.

Coca-Cola had been excluded from the Indian market in the late 1970s. It returned in 1995 with the Hindi slogan, 'jo chaahoo, so jahee' 'Whatever you desire, let it happen'. As in the United States, where 'things go better with Coke', consumption of modern goods held out hope of a better life on all fronts. To the majority of Indians, focused on gaining the bare necessities of everyday existence, consumer goods, even of an inconsequential item like Coke, were utterly beside the point. Yet many of the decade's challenges were inextricably linked to both the allure and the revulsion posed by new social relations and new values. The need of regimes to keep electoral support militated against the kind of dramatic 'structural adjustment' of some developing countries so that tensions, however dramatic, continued to be played out within the existing political structures. But change was sufficient that conflicts over class, regional interests, and those summed up by 'Hindutva', 'Hindu-ness', took on increased power to include and exclude and to shape governing policies.

By 1989, the Congress Party was no longer able to form a majority government, and no other party arose to command the kind of widespread support Congress had once enjoyed. Every government in the 1990s was a regime of coalitions. Amrita Basu and Atul Kohli have identified what they call a 'deinstitutionalization' of the Indian state evident by the 1990s with the decline not only of the Congress Party, but also of the bureaucracy, as well as of the normative institutions in place since independence – 'secularism, socialism and democracy of the Nehruvian type'. The resultant vacuum, coupled with increased democratic competition in terms both of numbers and of decline of the old hierarchies, provided the opening for the political conflicts of the decade. The most important competing parties included not only the Hindu nationalist party, but also parties representing the lower castes and various regions – the political side of what V. S. Naipaul aptly called in 1990 'a million mutinies now'. The 'burden of the past' shaped these conflicts, whether they were conflicts in the street or at the ballot box, but it is only in the new political context, shaped by the hopes and fears of the far-reaching changes engendered by liberalization and globalization, that these conflicts emerged with the salience and power that they did. India, in Atul Kohli's phrase, became 'a noisy democracy'. No thoughtful person welcomed the violence that seemed endemic in political life in the 1990s, but political life in general in this period did bring increased popular participation and increased attention to the demands of previously marginalized groups. The proliferation of group demands appears to be characteristic of democracies in developing countries and should not be dismissed as evidence of 'failure' or, necessarily, as permanent.

There were three noteworthy regimes in the nineties. In each of these, particular aspects of the transformations of the period came to the fore. The initial period of Janata Dal rule (1989–90) set the stage for the interconnected class, religious, and gender-based tensions, persistent throughout the decade, focused on what came to be seen, above all, as inappropriate concessions to Muslims and to the lower castes. The period of the Narasimha Rao, Congress (I), coalition (1991–6) marked the real beginning of economic liberalization, the cultural and economic opening to world markets, and the dismantling of debilitating state control. Finally, after an interim of

United Front coalitions (1996–8), the BJP regime (from 1998) represented new strategies of managing coalitions based on regional and other interests within, as well as a newly assertive presence, economic, cultural, and military, in the world outside.

MUSLIMS, THE 'OBCS', AND WOMEN

The year 1989 was one of momentous change worldwide and marked a significant transition in India as well. The Congress Party, even if fragmented by the 1960s, had been a remarkable institution in the first four decades of independence, providing a framework for integration, rooted in its long colonial history, that no other new nation could claim. With the general election of 1989, however, it was clear that a now attenuated Congress, tainted by charges of corruption and facing multiple rivals, no longer could win majority support. Instead, a coalition came to power that was to usher in a decade of governments built on alliances, in this initial case led by V. P. Singh and his Janata Dal party with its base among the lower-caste cultivating peasantry. For the first time, the Hindu nationalist party, the urban, upper caste BJP, was part of a ruling coalition, having come in with some 88 (of 545) Lok Sabha seats along with – strange bedfellows all – the communist parties, CPI and CPI (M). This coalition would be out in eleven months, leading more than one commentator, watching the slow collapse of the Soviet Union, to wonder if 'a somewhat similar unraveling [was] being played out . . . in democratically governed, but now virtually leaderless, India' and even to predict military rule. Such a prognosis was misplaced, but ominous events unfolding as the decade began signalled what would be endemic problems in the 1990s.

There continued to be fear of regional separatism. In 1990, the military was deployed in three states: Kashmir, Punjab, and Assam. Attention was almost immediately riveted on Kashmir, with a kidnapping that resulted in the controversial decision to release leaders of the Jammu and Kashmir Liberation Front, a party demanding a secular and autonomous Kashmir. This incident revealed the extent of disaffection in Kashmir towards Indian rule; it also signalled the end of Faruq Abdullah's ability to sustain his father's legacy as spokesman for Kashmiris. Although Hindu nationalists portrayed

Hindus in all three regional crises as victims, they especially emphasized this theme in Kashmir. Meanwhile, Punjab's Sikh separatist movement continued to simmer and in 1990 alone there were some 4,000 deaths. That year proved, however, to be the peak of militancy and of repression. A combination of a crackdown on militants and accommodation from the centre soon began the process of resuming normal political life in Punjab, and regular state-level elections were held beginning in 1992.

Similarly a movement for independence, or 'self-determination' in Assam, fuelled in part, as had been the Bangladesh crisis in Pakistan, by resentment of a kind of 'internal colonialism' in which non-Assamese in business and government positions presided over extraction of primary products from the region, also peaked in about 1990–1. There too a combination of major armed operations and incorporation into political institutions made it possible for Assam to operate within the constitutional framework. Only in Kashmir, where the larger issues related to Muslims confounded all negotiations, did a solution to a movement for regional separatism prove intractable. By the end of the decade, the Indian military presence had escalated to approximately 1 soldier to every 5 Kashmiris and some 30,000 people had died in the conflict.

Issues related to lower-caste/class aspirations and, inescapably linked to them, those related to the Muslim 'community' were also signalled at the beginning of the decade and continued to reverberate throughout. The crisis which brought the Janata coalition down was the decision to implement the long-moribund 1980 report of the Mandal Commission that had recommended reservations of federal government and public sector positions, as well as slots in institutions of higher education, for the 'Other Backward Castes' (OBCs). The OBCs were estimated to be as numerous as the Scheduled Castes and Tribes combined, and they thus together represented roughly half of the society as a whole. The Mandal recommendations brought total reservations up to the 49.5 per cent allowed by the constitution, a percentage exceeded in several of the southern states (for state positions) where the social position of the upper castes had long been challenged. The report did not hesitate to blame the higher castes, who had 'subjected the rest to all manner of injustice'. By September 1990, Delhi was at a standstill as high- and low-caste groups across north India fought and demonstrated. There were even cases of upper- and middle-class students, shown in photographs flashed across the country, setting themselves ablaze in protest. The BJP withdrew its support from the government. They and other opponents argued, as do opponents of affirmative action in the United States, that such programmes fostered social divisions, failed to reward merit, and benefited only the better-off in the disadvantaged groups. In 1992 the Supreme Court upheld the legality of the commission report and the government moved to its implementation.

The Mandal crisis coincided with a dramatic escalation on the part of the BJP, with its allied Vishva Hindu Parishad, the World Hindu Council, of their simmering demand to build a Ram temple at the precise site of a 1528 Mughal mosque in the north Indian town of Ayodhya. The support of diaspora Hindus, highly organized through the VHP, fuelled the movement throughout. The VHP had intensified pressure on this issue in the mid-1980s, gaining significantly in 1986 when a judicial decision allowed the site to be opened. In an earlier, equally problematic, government action, the mosque had been closed to worshippers when activists, claiming a miracle, inserted a Ram icon in the mosque in 1949.

The activists all along argued that the mosque builders had themselves destroyed an ancient temple, built on the very site of the birthplace of Lord Ram. Personal devotion to Ram, as well as the annual re-enactments of his story during the autumnal festival of Diwali, had long been part of religious life, particularly in the north. The Ram tradition, however, had taken on new salience through the weekly Sunday morning television broadcast of some seventy-eight episodes of the Ram epic, the Ramayana, beginning in 1987. The series was produced by the Bombay filmmaker, Ramanand Sagar, and shown on state-controlled television, Durdarshan. This was the most popular programme ever shown on Indian television, and, critics have noted, it encouraged a homogenized image of a shared story that had always had multiple regional and local forms. The story was, moreover, through its television presentation made more concrete and more historical. The gods were 'humanized' in this medium. Ram and his brother Bharat, for example, were not made up with blue skin as representations of Ram and Krishna conventionally were (as above, plate 2.5). The site of Ayodhya became more concretely a specific place on a map. The influence of the media in itself became a media event, widely commented on in news reporting and subjected to intense analysis, above all for the ritual that families and neighbourhoods practised in conjunction with viewing. The epic was a blockbuster commercial event, not only the initial production, but the associated sale of cassettes, the franchising of spin-offs, and the piggy-backing of publications and other products that tapped into the new 'Ramayana fever'. State television followed up with serialization during the following year of the second great Hindu epic, the 'Mahabharata'.

In October 1990, L. K. Advani, president of the BJP, undertook a pilgrimage across India in a Toyota transformed into a chariot. Dressing himself as Ram, he moved across the country in a brilliantly effective political strategy of collecting bricks that would build the new temple. Advani himself may have been circumspect, but the processionists favoured rhymes like 'The only place for Muslims is the graveyard (*qabarstan*) or Pakistan'. Fearing bloodshed as Advani approached the town itself, the government had him arrested, and the state government forcibly controlled an assault on the mosque in Ayodha. The image of Advani as Ram, however, persisted in the ever more influential print and television media. He was, for example, shown in a joyous but martial pose on the cover of India's equivalent of '*Newsweek*' or '*Time*' (plate 9.2). The VHP website in 2000 included a page dedicated to two 'martyrs of Ayodhya . . . felled by the bullets of Mullah Mulayam Singh Yadav's goonda raj' – the state prime minister (heading a party defined by lower-caste support) mocked as a Muslim ('mullah') and a low-caste thug ('goonda').

Many of the country's most respected professional historians, like those at Jawaharlal Nehru University who signed a widely published statement, argued that there was no evidence of destruction of a temple to build the mosque; others pointed out that Ayodhya had emerged as a Hindu pilgrimage town only under the patronage of the eighteenth-century Muslim rulers of Awadh. Still others refused to even enter a debate whose premise of putative historicity was seen as a flawed standard for public policy. But the BJP, and its ancillary organizations, had found a symbol unmatched for public mobilization. The importance of Ram's

Plate 9.2   L. K. Advani as charioteer in the guise of Lord Ram.

birthplace was, they argued, not a matter of fact but of faith. Claiming that birthplace was, they insisted, a key to 'national honour'.

These demands took place in an atmosphere of considerable communal tension. Hindu–Muslim riots had not been a continuous element in independent India. Incidents increased in the 1980s, often in the form of anti-Muslim violence, in which all too often police and other officials were complicit. One of the most horrific episodes had taken place in the poverty-stricken town of Bhagalpur and surrounding areas in Bihar in 1989. Probably 1,000 people were killed, almost all Muslim; some 40,000 were forced to leave their homes; the local administration was clearly involved in encouraging the attacks and suppressing evidence. The historian Gyanendra Pandey, who was part of an independent fact-finding mission to Bhagalpur, has argued that 'the violent slogans and demands of organizations like the VHP' now speak to a 'whole new common sense about Muslims'. This 'common sense' had become so internalized that anti-Muslim violence, he argued, should not merely be seen as an aberration, or linked, as in the Bhagalpur case, only to local economic interests:

What appears to many of us as rabid and senseless Hindu propaganda is widely believed. In one of its more restrained forms, this leads to the view that all Muslims in India are 'Pakistanis'. Following from this is the argument that local Muslims are out to create another Pakistan . . . Muslims are represented as being inherently turbulent, fanatical, violent . . . What follows from all this is of course a dread of 'the Muslim' and the demand to disarm him – by disenfranchisement and deculturisation: adopt 'our' names, 'our' language, 'our' dress . . . The emphasis in this militant Hindu propaganda is not so much on the non-violent, peaceful, tolerant character of 'the Hindus' – though astoundingly, even that proposition remains. It is rather more on how 'the Hindus' have been tolerant for too long; they are still 'too timid'; the need of the hour is 'not tolerance but courage'. (1991)

Fear of Muslims, often linked to economic anxieties, was intensified by key events in the 1990s. The decade began with the return of migrant workers with disposable income as the Gulf War escalated in the Middle East. Their presence stimulated exaggerated notions of flows of money from rich Saudis. There was an influx of poor Bangladeshi 'infiltrators' seeking land and a livelihood in the north-east. There was anger at the 'pampering' of Muslims by the continuation of the colonial policy of a separate Muslim civil code, erroneously assumed to be key, through polygamy, to Muslim population growth. As the situation in Kashmir worsened during the 1990s, there was fear of losing part of the nation.

In relation to women, although no issues as dramatic as the Roop Kunwar sati or the Shah Bano court case took place, women's problems were also visible from the beginning of the decade. Reports of violence against women were frequent, above all in the form of 'dowry burnings' of women whose husbands and their families had decided they had failed to bring adequate resources to the family. Some 11,000–15,000 of these deaths were estimated to take place each year. Energized in part by the Government of India report on the status of women in 1975, the decade of the eighties had seen a range of protective legislative acts passed. Yet critics insisted that the laws, targeting dowry abuses, rape, and other violence against women, and even fetal gender determination to select for male off-spring, had been poorly conceived and rarely led to convictions. To many, one strategy for addressing women's needs was to treat them, on the model of Scheduled Castes and Tribes, as a disadvantaged group.

A significant development of the 1990s was the constitutional amendment passed in 1992 giving enhanced power to elected municipalities and village panchayats. In these local bodies, women were accorded one-third of the seats along with one-third of the *sarpanch*, or village chief, positions (which would rotate among villages). Karnataka had pioneered the use of reservations for women in the 1980s, and Rajiv Gandhi had proposed the same reservation at a national level as part of a move to institutionalize democratically elected village councils. A full one-half of those women elected, beginning in the mid-nineties, were dalit or other lower-caste members, a development possible in part because lower-class women were more accustomed to working in public than were more privileged women. In addition to addressing issues related to health, education, and development, women in particular energized protests against liquor stores, which women rightly saw as undermining their men folk, often on the part not only of the shop owners but of upper castes and employers who encouraged alcohol consumption. The women panchayat members also intervened in domestic crises. In one 1999 newspaper interview, an angry former male village head, a Brahman, commented on one lower-caste sarpanch, 'The Government has turned power upside down. The Government is making these people sit on top of us. We are the rulers, but now she is ruling.' There were many obstacles for women, but many opportunities as well. The BJP government in 2000 continued to seek similar reservation for women in Parliament and the state legislatures. Several women emerged in unexpected public roles during the decade. Dr Kiran Bedi proved brilliantly successful as director general of New Delhi's prisons. Phulan Devi, the low-caste woman gang-raped by upper-caste men, whose revenge as part of a robber band riveted the public in the

1980s, emerged from prison to enter politics and be celebrated in a controversial Hindi film as the 'Bandit Queen'. And anti-Muslim Hindu women activists, above all Uma Bharati and Sadhvi Rithambara, were in the forefront of militant popular oratory over Ayodhya.

Gendered imagery was central in the majoritarian discourse about Muslims and lower castes in the 1990s. For the Hindu nationalists, Muslim men were foreign marauders who had 'violated' the motherland and the women of India. Muslim men, in echoes of the colonial discourse about Indian men in general, oppressed their women. Muslim women, however, could be redeemed by submission to Hindu men. Lower-class women had long been the prey of the upper class. Women's submission was taken to define 'masculinity' and 'honour'. These themes were present not only in explicitly ideological statements but also in film and other imaginative literature.

By the end of the decade it was clear that the most oppressed members of Indian society – the low castes, the poor, and the illiterate – had been joining political parties and voting in ever-growing numbers, as had women. Many were supporting caste- and regionally based parties seen as sympathetic to their interests. These parties were, literally, able to speak their language. In a remarkable life story (recorded from her conversations), an 'untouchable' Pariah woman in Tamilnadu, Viramma, described how the party workers came through the village every evening, urging poor, rural people to seek education, fight oppression, and defy the divisions of caste. Dubious of the possibilities of change herself, Viramma added nonetheless, speaking of the movie star M. G. Ramachandran who founded the Anna DMK and led the Tamilnadu state government for a decade until 1987, 'Look at M. G. R., he'd give his life for us.'

Recent surveys have shown that it has been the poor in India who believe more profoundly than the privileged in democracy and the importance of their vote. Uttar Pradesh, historic home of the Congress Party, for example, saw two non-Brahman, non-upper-caste parties play ever larger roles in state politics; Mayawati, a Dalit woman leader of the Bahujan Samaj Party, whose core support was Dalit, served two brief terms as Chief Minister in the late 1990s. The Samajwadi Party whose core was Muslim and Yadav (traditionally

the cow herders' caste, which was categorized as OBC) also saw
their leader, Mulayam Singh Yadav, head the state government of
Bihar in the nineties.

It is striking that no party emerged in post-independence India to
represent Muslims as an interest group. Muslims long looked to the
Congress Party, with its tradition of secularism, as their protector,
but that link had frayed by the 1990s. Contrary perhaps to most
people's assumptions, outside the Jama'at-i Islami in Kashmir, there
was no Muslim 'fundamentalist' party based on Islamic principles.
There have been commentators who assume that the Hindu nationalist party must have been a 'reaction' to Muslim fundamentalism,
but such axiomatic logic has no basis in fact. Indeed there was no
organized Muslim political movement in India at all in the whole
half-century after partition. The largest organization of Muslims in
India, as in Pakistan and Bangladesh, was the transnational Tablighi
Jama'at, whose historic centre was near the Sufi shrine of Hazrat
Nizamu'd Din in New Delhi. The movement emphasized an internal mission to other Muslims to cultivate impeccable standards in
worship and the morality of everyday behaviour coupled with a
'counter-culture' eschewal of entertainment and consumer goods. A
movement offering individuals a space of dignity and community, it
also fostered withdrawal from the public arena.

RSS, BJP, VHP, AND THE SANGH PARIVAR

The cluster of Hindu nationalist organizations that emerged into
public view around the Ram temple issue was known as the Sangh
Parivar, the Sangh 'Family' of organizations. At the core was
the Rashtriya Swayamsevak Sangh, the Association of National
Volunteers (RSS), the cadre-based paramilitary organization founded in 1925, whose branches (*shakhas*) trained youth in physical
strength and self-discipline and fostered a resurgent Hindu ideology.
The RSS had emerged into dramatic visibility when one of its members assassinated Gandhi, and the organization had subsequently
been banned. The most prominent members of the BJP, including
Atal Bihari Vajpayee and L. K. Advani, were both long associated
with the RSS. They had been among the founding members of the
post-independence Jan Sangh political party, which, in the aftermath

of Jan Sangh participation in the Janata Party coalition (1977–9), was reborn as the BJP. Other RSS-linked organizations targeted respectively university students, workers, and peasants; still others focused on education and social uplift among tribals (where there was fear of Christian influence) and on rural areas.

The centrally important VHP was established in 1964, organizing Hindu sectarian leaders to confront Christian missionary activity and to disseminate Hindu teachings worldwide. It was intended to be a cultural and social service organization, with fears and programmes that echoed reform movements back to the Arya Samaj. Its website in 2000 identified a range of activities that included educational and vocational training for widowed and abandoned women; programmes to train 'low-caste' priests, particularly in 'tribal' and slum areas; a social reform programme focused on caste and dowry; and programmes to repair and utilize abandoned temples. The Bajrang Dal, the army named after Ram's faithful monkey companion, Hanuman, operated under the wing of the VHP; its members were widely regarded as toughs always ready to fight Muslims. The Shiv Sena, initially a Maharashtrian party virulently opposed to labour immigration from other states, was now loosely linked to the Parivar as well. All these organizations provided not only ideology, but also community, mutual support, and upward mobility to men and women across the generations. With their mapping of militant religion on to the modern nation-state, the Parivar organizations were far from 'traditional' and shared many characteristics with similar twentieth-century movements worldwide.

One critical element in the power of the Hindu nationalist movement in the nineties was the close connection between religious community and class. As Mandal and other measures seemed to challenge the interests of the middle class, the BJP, whose core supporters were small businessmen, traders, and white-collar workers, escalated a rhetoric that denied the relevance of class in favour of the unity of religion. In this sense Muslims could be seen as playing a role as scapegoat for problems not of their making and as a foil for creating majoritarian identity. More than one commentator saw a desire to distract attention from 'Mandal' – which entailed economic competition among Hindus – in the campaign for 'mandir' (temple) – which could unite Hindus against an 'outsider'.

The Muslim population in India, whose relative disadvantage could be measured by low representation in government employment and share of higher education, was, moreover, economically and politically linked to the threatening lower classes both materially and politically. Of the regional crises, at the end of the nineties, only Kashmir, which served as 'confirmation' of the threat Muslims posed to Hindus, continued to be intractable.

'KFC' AND ECONOMIC LIBERALIZATION

In the aftermath of the V. P. Singh government, a short-lived successor coalition came in under the socialist Chandra Shekhar (Janata-S). His government faced a now desperate balance of payments crisis, exacerbated in the short run by soaring oil prices associated with the Gulf War. It was clear by the time of the general elections that the most pressing issue facing any new government would be the implementation of long-resisted measures of macro-economic adjustment. In the general election of May 1991, Congress, Janata, and the BJP dominated the campaign. It was in this campaign that Rajiv Gandhi, who in fact had already shown his support in principle for economic reforms, met his death at the hands of a Tamil Tiger suicide bomber.

Almost immediately, Congress Party leaders turned to Rajiv's devastated widow, Sonia, to offer her, the last adult member of the family, the Congress Presidency. She turned down the offer, craving privacy for herself and her two children. At the end of the decade, although Italian by birth and wholly inexperienced in public life, she would fitfully take on Congress leadership as bearer of the family legacy. But in 1991 it was the elderly P. V. Narasimha Rao (b. 1921), who had served earlier as foreign minister under both Indira and Rajiv, who emerged as the compromise leader of the party in Rajiv's stead. With support from Tamilnadu's AIADMK (a regionally based power which had split from the Dravida Munnetra Kazhagam), the Muslim League, and the communist CPI (M), Rao formed a fragile Congress (I) ministry. The BJP, its percentage in the Lok Sabha increased from 11.4 per cent in 1989 to 23.2 per cent with 119 seats, now led the opposition. Rao's tenure would last a full, if shaky, five-year term (1991–6), marked not only by further anti-Muslim mobilization but also by dramatic changes in economic policy.

On 6 December 1992, Hindu nationalist 'karsevaks', from across north India and even the south, converged on the old mosque in Ayodhya and tore it down, brick by brick. The police and UP authorities at best simply stood by as sadhus, militant activists, urban youth, and outright toughs surged over the tomb. Thirteen Muslims were murdered with pickaxes and knives; journalists were beaten and their cameras seized. VHP activists were central in this, as they had been in the earlier assault on the mosque in 1990. In the aftermath of the 1992 attack, massive anti-Muslim riots spread throughout India, killing thousands of people, almost all of them Muslim, of whom a large proportion was in Bombay. There the Shiv Sena Party and its leader, Bal Thakeray, with connivance of police and civic officials, spearheaded the assault. BJP and VHP leaders moved to dissociate themselves from the violence. The Narasimha Rao government, itself widely faulted for not having acted sooner, dismissed the four BJP-led state governments and arrested top BJP leaders.

The anti-Muslim mobilization took place against a worsening economic crisis in India. Problems evident during the preceding decade had made clear that the cherished 'socialist pattern of development', with its state controls, subsidies, and public-sector enterprises, had faltered badly. The government's fiscal deficit almost doubled during the 1980s; India's rank as an industrial nation fell; its exports of manufactured goods, already infinitesimal, declined at a time when the share of developing countries in exported manufactured goods was increasing. The governments of the 1980s had all tried piecemeal economic liberalization, exempting more industries from licensing, replacing quotas on imported goods with tariffs, and allowing somewhat more expansion of larger companies. Rajiv, despite his strong majority government, could not win support within his own party for a more comprehensive liberalization policy that was seen to depart from the dual themes of self-reliance and aid for the poor. These issues, motivated in large part by the fear of losing support among voters, meant that liberalization throughout the nineties would be hedged by compromise.

The Narasimha Rao government faced staggering annual debt payments, depleted foreign exchange reserves, and a credit rating so

Plate 9.3 The Cyber Towers of Andra Pradesh's planned 'Hitech City', Hyderabad.

low that it was forced to put up gold reserves to secure foreign loans. At this point, there seemed no option but to turn to the International Monetary Fund and the policies of 'structural adjustment' that they required. The collapse of the Soviet Union, moreover, had both discredited centralized planning and terminated agreements that had committed the USSR to importing more manufactured goods from India during the 1990s. The government's first budget, orchestrated by the Finance Minister, Dr Manmohan Singh, committed it to a range of reforms in return for which it received a $1.4 billion IMF loan. The rupee was devalued 20 per cent and made partially convertible, export subsidies were abolished, tariffs were lowered, the number of public-sector industries was reduced, and licences for most industries ended. A stock exchange was launched. Attempts were made to simplify and rationalize taxes. India thus took part in a worldwide transition in which national economies were increasingly integrated into a global economic system. In the first three years of the reforms, the annual rate of growth reached 7 per cent.

One particularly successful arena of the new economy was software development. Bangalore in Karnataka emerged as the Indian 'Silicon Valley', while Andhra Pradesh, under a visionary chief minister, undertook to create a new 'Hitech City' promising not only a technological infrastructure but an urban and governing environment conducive to global business undertakings (plate 9.3). Among those especially encouraged to invest were so-called 'NRIs', or 'non-resident Indians'. Many of these were entrepreneurs who had migrated to the United States, where they founded such major firms as Sun Microsystems and Hotmail. By the late 1990s, a quarter of the high-tech companies in California's 'Silicon Valley' were run by Indian immigrants, and the South Asian community as a whole on a per capita basis was the wealthiest in the nation.

The BJP and the left parties came together to deplore the Rao–Singh economic policies, decrying them as the end of economic self-sufficiency. They argued that reforms were the route to unemployment and inflation, and nothing more than an opportunity for a small elite to be corrupted by foreign luxury culture and goods. Particularly after the Ayodhya crisis at the end of 1992, BJP opposition to government economic policies increased, giving the impression of an attempt to win short-term political goals at a difficult time for the party. An agreement reached by an earlier Congress ministry in Maharashtra and the Enron Corporation to construct India's largest power project was stopped in its tracks in 1995 by opposition from the Shiv Sena and the BJP, who argued that the interests of Indian consumers had been sacrificed. Time, money, and credibility were jeopardized, and the availability of badly needed power delayed. Yet the project, in the end, was in fact resumed and completed with only minor changes. Protests forcing the temporary closing of Kentucky Fried Chicken (KFC) outlets, a symbol of Western taste and extravagance, similarly attracted a great deal of attention. However abortive the protests, or strategic the political opposition, the fear of Western imperialism and even of deindustrialization ran deep.

The anxiety surrounding economic opening involved not only fear of competition but also apprehension that liberalization would bring with it a threat to India's indigenous culture and its moral or 'family values' (a phrase used in 1998 in the BJP election manifesto). A problematic symbol of Indian pride in the 1990s was success for Indian women in Miss World and Miss Universe contests. On this occasion the 'left', dismayed at female commodification, and the 'right', appalled at seeing women's 'charms' displayed on the public stage, united in opposition. A photo of Miss Universe 2000 (of dozens on the worldwide web in 2000) summed up much of the new global lifestyle with an image both cosmopolitan and 'ethnically chic' (plate 9.4). The daughter of an Air Force officer, from the cosmopolitan city of Bangalore and a student at Bombay University, Lara Dutta's hobbies were those of the young global elite – rock-climbing, para-gliding, bungee-jumping – as was her career goal to become a documentary film director. Beauty pageant success evoked anxiety along with pride.

In addition to the economic–moral arguments based on swadeshi, two quite different critiques were also made in relation to the economic reforms, under both the Rao ministry and the governments that followed. One was simply that the reforms did not go far enough. At every point, political leaders worried about losing their constituents and about possible social unrest were they to curtail inefficient government industries that would, for example, require massive lay-offs. They were unwilling to end subsidies that kept low the prices of basic food commodities, or to

Plate 9.4   Lara Dutta, Miss Universe 2000.

impose taxation on agriculture. There were multiple constituencies fearful of reforms, including the middle classes, who benefited from subsidies on fertilizer, power, and communications; workers employed in inefficient public-sector enterprises; bureaucrats who profited from patronage; and lower-caste cultivators who wanted more allocations. All this meant that the nineties saw mounting government deficits. A further and related problem was the inability of governments to address an aged and inadequate infrastructure, evident in all aspects of power, transportation, and communication.

The second major critique, the failure on the part of successive governments to invest adequately in human capital, was articulated most eloquently by Amartya Sen, who won the Nobel prize for economics in 1998:

After fifty years of independence, half the adults in India are illiterate (indeed more than two-thirds of the adult women cannot read or write.) In this respect, India today stands well behind where Japan stood at the time of the Meiji restoration in the mid-nineteenth century, and far distant from what South Korea, Taiwan, China, Thailand and other countries in east and south-east Asia achieved well before their market-oriented economic expansion began... Indian reformist leaders... have failed to acknowledge the role of widespread literacy and numeracy and other forms of social achievement (completed land reform, good health care, etc.) which permit a shared and participatory process of economic expansion. India has not had difficulty in raising its overall rate of economic growth by removing constraints and restrictions and by making use of opportunities of trade... But a large part of Indian society remains excluded from the range of economic opportunities.

There has been debate over the proportion of the population benefiting from recent economic change. Although commentators have rightly emphasized the growth of a middle class, it is now clear that earlier estimates of their numbers were exaggerated and that the gap between the middle class and the rest of society grew as a result of the reforms. One rough clue to consumption at the end of the nineties was the figure for television ownership, about 62 million. The 'middle class', able to purchase cars and other consumer goods, was estimated at no more than 150 million, while those living in extreme poverty, earning the equivalent of one dollar a day, were more than twice that many. In 1999 India's population joined China's in reaching the one-billion mark. Controlling population growth seemed a critical step in reducing poverty, but economists like Amartya Sen argued that reducing population growth required not solely contraception but provision of education, employment, and health services that would make it rational for families to have fewer children. Regional variation in these measures of social and economic well-being in India was extreme. Kerala on the south-west coast, for example, enjoyed a gender ratio, literacy level, and population growth rate, if not per capita income, nearly equal to that of first world countries.

With substantial political opposition to more far-reaching economic reform, and the limitations imposed by the deficits in infrastructure and social capital, the pace of change slowed by mid-decade. In the three years beginning 1996/7, the rate of growth in the domestic product fell to 5 per cent. The country was somewhat insulated when the south-east Asian economic crisis hit, in part because of its incomplete integration into the global marketplace. It was not, however, primarily the economic situation that precipitated a decisive defeat for the Congress Party in the national election of 1996. Equally important was the revelation of a major financial scam in 1992 involving collusion of officials of the State Bank of India and foreign-owned private banks. In 1994 the government was hit again by a series of corruption scandals that even lead to indictments against cabinet ministers. As a result the May 1996 election gave the BJP, now with some 194 seats, a plurality in Parliament. A. B. Vajpayee (b. 1926) was sworn in as prime minister, but, unable to form a government as Congresss and the multiparty United Front cooperated in support of secularism, he lasted only twelve days. Two fragile United Front coalitions, comprised of socialist, lower-caste, regional, and leftist parties followed, the first headed by Karnataka's chief minister, H. D. Deve Gowda, the second by a long-time Congress statesman, Inder Kumar Gujral (b. 1919). It was Gujral who presided over India's fifty-year celebration of independence.

In the February 1998 election, the Congress (I) decline was checked by the brave campaign of Sonia Gandhi, who became both Congress (I) president and leader of the Congress (I) in Parliament. In the lead up to both the 1998 and the 1999 election, increasing violence erupted against the Christian minority, typically poor 'tribals' in places like Gujarat and Orissa. The climate created by the VHP and other members of the Parivar against Christians in general, as 'foreigners' who were slandered as less than 'real' Indians, and against Sonia in particular, as a Roman Catholic and putative agent of Rome, was clearly a tool to influence the vote. The BJP won 179 of 545 Lok Sabha seats, with roughly the same share, approximately 25 per cent, of votes polled, as Congress (I) secured. The BJP took office as head of a coalition, of which the southern regional parties were a critical component, which lasted little more than a year.

The BJP-led coalition was always at risk as its members, typically demanding patronage as the price of loyalty, threatened to withdraw. The largest block in the coalition was the Tamilnadu-based AIADMK led by the film actress and former chief minister, Jayalitha Jayaram, who faced multiple charges of corruption in Tamilnadu. Her withdrawal of support over demands expected to help her case ultimately brought about the government's collapse. In the subsequent thirteenth general election held in October 1999, however, the BJP was again returned to power, proudly claiming to be the first incumbent party returned to office since 1984. With only 183 seats of their own, showing little change from the previous election, they depended on the loyalty of their electoral alliance. It appeared during their first year in office that the BJP, with a platform ironed out in advance with its partners, had now achieved a more stable base of power. With 114 seats, the Congress became the opposition, and three-dozen other parties claimed anywhere from 1 to 33 seats. India's political parties by decade's end routinely maintained home pages, the BJP's providing both current and archival information (plate 9.5).

BJP: PRAGMATISM AND THE NUCLEAR OPTION

On 15 August, Independence Day, 2000 prime minister Vajpayee summarized his goals for the nation and the achievements of his party's tenure:

In the middle of the last century, Mother India won her freedom after a long and exemplary struggle against colonial rule. We have many proud achievements to our credit in nation building in the first five decades of Freedom. However, we also have many dreams that are yet unrealized. Learning proper lessons from the past, we must re-dedicate ourselves to the task of building a strong, prosperous, and egalitarian India; an India that is free of every trace of underdevelopment; a caring and compassionate India; and an India that regains her rightful role in shaping the destiny of the world in the new century and the new millennium... The most important achievements [since the BJP came to power in 1998] – and this is an achievement not so much of the Government, but of the entire country – has been that India is a stronger, more secure, and much more self-confident nation today than in the past. When we approached the people of India for a mandate... we had promised that national security would be one of our

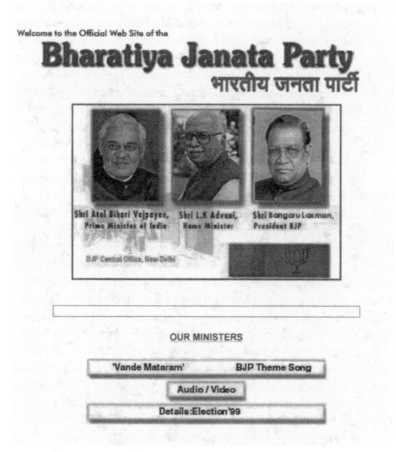

Plate 9.5   Introductory pages of the official Bharatiya Janata
Party website.

first and foremost priorities. We fulfilled this promise with our historical
action of exercising the nuclear option at Pokharan in May 1998...the
very countries that imposed sanctions against us...[now] view India with
greater respect than in the past.

The statesmanlike tone of Vajpayee's address marked a fundamental
shift in the thrust of the BJP programme. Once in power the party
pragmatically sought to distance itself from many aspects of its earlier policies and promises. To maintain support from its coalition
partners it could do no other. In the economic sphere, the BJP, for

all its tradition of swadeshi, found the move to liberalization ir-
reversible. As for Hindutva, there were no steps towards building
the Ayodhya temple, still under judicial scrutiny; there was no effort to move towards a Uniform Civil Code (that would replace
the personal law of the minority communities); there was no action on abrogating Article 370 of the Constitution that prohibited
outsiders from owning land in Kashmir. The BJP claimed to be offering 'genuine secularism', in contrast to what the Parivar liked to
call Nehruvian 'pseudo-secularism', which meant, they insisted, that
minorities were coddled and favoured.

Arguably, anti-Muslim sentiment was deflected on to the international scene where a range of issues identified Muslims as a threat
surrounding India, whether in Kashmir, Bangladesh (with 'infiltrators' across the border), or the Middle East, where India dramatically reversed its tradition of Palestinian sympathy to recognize and
support Israel. The decision to test nuclear weapons in May 1998
was justified as a response to China, but was understood by Pakistan,
who immediately responded with their own tests, as a challenge to
them. Nuclear capability was clearly intended as further assertion of
India's hegemony in its region. Pakistan's inept intrusions in Kargil
across the Line of Control in the spring of 1999 were widely condemned not only in India but beyond, and provoked a major crisis
and loss of lives on both sides. In all these actions, Vajpayee had
support far beyond his own party. Tough in relation to Muslims outside India, the party could distance itself from much in the Hindutva
ideology of the non-political Parivar groups, above all the VHP and
the RSS.

In the economic arena, the BJP attempted the same balancing
act of depending on Parivar mobilization of popular support while
charting a somewhat independent course of action. The BJP had
been a severe critic of both Congress and United Front liberalization. Nonetheless, once in power, the regime put economic reforms
at the centre of their coalition's programme, promising a growth rate
of 7–8 per cent and control of the fiscal deficit. Like their predecessors, they were unable to move quickly towards the integrated policies necessary to secure these goals, in their case in part because of
internal divisions. Swadeshi opposition, especially to foreign investment in consumer goods, ran deep in the BJP and the Sangh Parivar
generally. The very term *swadeshi* was redolent of the traditions

of the nationalist movement from the beginning of the twentieth century and one that conjured up fears of foreign control, now in the guise of the IMF (International Monetary Fund), World Bank, GATT (General Agreement on Trade and Tariffs), and WTO (World Trade Organization). Nonetheless, the BJP struggled to achieve what Christophe Jaffrelot called 'a division of labor', with Vajpayee, who had taken leadership of the party from Advani precisely because he was perceived as more moderate, on one side, and the RSS and other elements of the Parivar continuing to pursue a Hindu nationalist agenda, on the other. Advani, in the centrally important position of home minister, was a powerful voice for the positions of the RSS. The first year of BJP power continued the disappointing economic performance of the previous two years.

By the end of 1998, however, Vajpayee had enacted policies that would encourage critically needed foreign investment. Investment was no longer limited to manufacturing and infrastructure but permitted even in consumer goods. There was no longer a requirement of Indian majority control of joint ventures. The BJP took other measures it had also earlier opposed, including amendment to the Patents Act to conform to WTO rules and allowing foreign investment in insurance. By the end of the decade it was clear that, however great their differences might be on the principles of secularism, the reformers in the BJP and those in Congress (I) shared more than they differed when it came to economic policy. On the one hand, concerns for the interests of developing countries in the context of globalization, issues given wide international attention at the 1999 WTO conference in Seattle and subsequently, were being treated seriously beyond mere invocation of swadeshi. On the other hand, reformers in both parties agreed that the critical issues were privatization, excess subsidies, and foreign investment – even if all were wary of doing too much. However incomplete, there was, after forty years of socialism, a national consensus by the end of the 1990s in favour of economic liberalization. In Vajpyaee's words, 'Swadeshi, in today's context, is anything that promotes . . . [strengthening] India's economic base.' By 1999 the economic slow-down of the previous three years seemed to have been turned around.

As with the Hindutva agenda, the government's nuclear tests advanced the regime's new economic policy. By defying the West, long

Plate 9.6   Introducing computerized voting in rural India.

committed to non-proliferation at the cost of late-comers, on the
issue of nuclear testing, the government deflected domestic criticism
of its economic liberalization as a 'sell-out' to the old imperial powers. In 2000, however, the most popular show on television was
not a Hindu epic, but the Indian version of *Who Wants to be a
Millionaire* with the film idol, Amitabh Bacchan, once celebrated
for his roles as an anti-establishment hero, handing out the prizes
to the lucky 'crorepati'. Winners included not only engineers and
executives but, in a deliberate move to expand viewer identification
with participants, milkmen and housewives as well. A show like this
depends on the dreams of a consumer society.

   A particular focus of hope in the economy was in the potential
of technology to leap over existing impediments of old policies and
inadequate infrastructure. Vajpayee won considerable credit for his
move to reduce government monopolies and licensing in telecom-
munication. There were dramatic examples of rural populations,
armed with cellular phones and solar-powered computers, gaining
new access to weather and marketing information, to 'e-commerce'
facilities, and to government bureaucracy. The Election Commission
pioneered the use of computers for rural voting (plate 9.6). New
communications also offered India unusual opportunities in a new

Plate 9.7 'Indianexus' web page providing information for doing business in Bangalore.

kind of 'service' sector, namely the export of services that included computer software programming; clerical services, for example for medical transcription; and engineering services. Other service areas that began to emerge as potential exports included higher education in English; research, including clinical trials in such areas as pharmaceuticals; entertainment, both film and music; even transport repair and maintenance; and telemarketing. In these arenas, the Internet played a critical role (plate 9.7), and the Indian diaspora population – no longer thought of as a 'brain drain' – proved an invaluable resource.

What of Advani's own claim that by 15 August 2000 the most important achievement of his regime had been the decision to develop a nuclear capacity? That decision, despite its clear implications for foreign policy, was rooted in domestic considerations and played well, for the most part, to an internal audience convinced that the BJP had shown itself tough towards the Muslim powers on its borders and tough towards the West. This decision was not without critics, many of whom were appalled at what made South Asia, in US President Clinton's words, the most dangerous place in the world. Others, especially within India, opposed such a diversion of resources when India's strength in the long run, to say nothing of the immediate needs of its weakest citizens, required the provision of desperately needed support for public health and education. In Advani's words, however, echoing the claims of the VHP activists after the destruction of the Babri Masjid, India had gained 'respect'.

HISTORY MATTERS

Ideologies and policies of modern nation-states are all rooted in a linear narrative history that defines what is often called 'full citizenship', a citizenship that goes beyond mere legal definition to describe those understood as entitled to play a role in the state. Often these narratives create an 'Other', or more than one, which serves to enhance the cohesion of the 'full citizens' of the nation. In Parivar narratives, Muslims, and to a lesser extent Christians and the West, played that role. The distorted image of Muslims in history was widely taken as fact.

The distinguished Indo-Trinidadian writer V. S. Naipaul later abjured many of his early judgments about India, published in a book whose telling title was *An Area of Darkness* (1964). But he clung, nonetheless, to an old understanding of India's past that demonized Muslims:

What I hadn't understood in 1962 [he wrote in 1990], or had taken too much for granted, was the extent to which the country had been remade; and even the extent to which India had been restored to itself, after its own equivalent of the Dark Ages – after the Muslim invasions, and the detailed, repeated vandalizing of the North, the shifting empires, the wars, the eighteenth-century anarchy. The twentieth-century restoration of India to itself had taken time.

This distorted view of the historical role of India's Muslims, constructed by colonial writers to justify and explain their own rule, became central to Hindu nationalist ideology.

In a world of nuclear weapons, of community-based violence, and of the desperate poverty most evident in the growing urban subproletariat of India's cities, the story India tells about its own past may seem a small matter to emphasize among issues of concern in India at century's end. The BJP and its Parivar allies, however, did not think so. They worked steadily throughout the 1990s to disseminate a version of India's past consonant with their Hindutva agenda. A history biased towards Hindutva contributes to the continuing marginalization of non-Hindus. The Parivar attempt to deliberately control a dimension of public intellectual life as central as national history puts at risk, moreover, the openness and vitality that foster the high-quality intellectual and artistic work India has long produced.

Almost immediately upon taking office in 1998, the minister of education, Murli Manohar Joshi, began appointing scholars sympathetic to the Hindu nationalist interpretation of history to national academic bodies, including the Indian Council of Historical Research, the Indian Council of Social Science Research, and the Indian Institute of Advanced Studies. A government plan presented in late 1998 to 'Hinduize' the school system with teaching of Hindu texts and 'values' was shouted down by a dozen state ministers of education and others who argued that the BJP was attempting to destroy the secular fabric of the country with the introduction of specious depictions of Muslims as foreign collaborators and oppressors.

In 2000, the BJP-appointed president of the ICHR recalled two volumes of the Towards Freedom series, in press with Oxford University Press, edited by two distinguished historians, Sumit Sarkar and K. N. Panikkar. The volumes covered the period of the 1940s and were likely to shed unfavourable light on the role of RSS members in such events as the Gandhi assassination. This act was widely condemned as one of several official actions on the part of both the central government and BJP-ruled states that threatened academic freedom. The issue of biased 'communalism' in the writing of Indian history was one that professional historians had criticized in India for decades, often with great success, but in the 1990s the problem accelerated, many believed, to the point that it appeared to challenge fundamental premises of intellectual standards and national identity.

Nehru's heartfelt wish for his country in 1947 was to shed 'the burden of the past'. The attempt by the BJP to construct a 'hindu-ized' version of the past gave Nehru's phrase a new meaning in which the 'burden' became not the past itself but a vision constructed of that past. In the same year in which Nehru spoke, the year of independence, 1947, the distinguished historian of medieval India, Mohammad Habib, delivered the presidential address to the Indian History Congress. His comments were the more poignant for being spoken by a person of Muslim descent. Habib rejoiced in the freedom of his beloved country, 'the sacred land where the black gazelles graze and the *munja* grass grows and the *pan*-leaf is eaten, and where the material and the spiritual are organically interwoven.' He faced the tragedy of partition violence with clear eyes as many others in the years to follow did not: 'Mussalmans, Sikhs and Hindus have proved themselves almost equally guilty; and this mark of disgrace on the forehead of our generation will be remembered for years to come.' With the insight of a social historian, he pinpointed the importance of the enduring divisions of class in contrast to the limited and shifting relevance of what he called not 'religious' but 'culture groups' – sects, philosophical schools, religious orders, sangha – for most aspects of historical experience. These communities in the present day, he argued, though linked with the earlier groups in name, in the context of colonial rule had become self-seeking or 'communalist'.

Habib turned to his fellow professional historians at this critical time, exhorting them to hold to professional standards. 'History', he said 'is quickly exported from the academy to the *bazaar*' and, quoting a medieval historian, '"shopkeepers who cannot distinguish white from black and black from white, confidently venture to pass judgments on historical matters"' – a description historians of the 1990s might well have found uncannily apt. Habib added, in conclusion:

The historian must speak the truth. . . . A state-dominated interpretation of history is one of the most effective means of sabotaging democracy. A free India implies a free history of India in which every point of view has a right to be heard. Free and untrammeled discussion will lead us to the truth; and there is no other way of reaching it.

India's achievements since independence in sustaining freedom and democracy have been singular among the world's new nations, though no one would claim the work, especially in regard to the poverty that constrains freedom for so many, is done. In that continuing struggle, 'a free history of India', as Habib put it, a history viewed, to use the phrase Nehru used for a general outlook on the world, 'with clear and friendly eyes', does indeed matter, as do the historical stories and myths that sustain all our individual and collective lives.

BIOGRAPHICAL NOTES

AHMAD KHAN, Sayyid (1817–1898). Scion of a family who served first the Mughals and then the British, Sayyid Ahmad was employed by the East India Company in its judicial administration. During the revolt of 1857 he saved the lives of his British colleagues at Bijnor, and subsequently wrote an essay on the causes of the revolt calling the British to account for their failure to respect the opinion of their Indian subjects. Encouraging Muslims to participate in Western learning, in 1877 he founded the Mohammedan Anglo-Oriental College at Aligarh. In his religious writings he advocated an interpretation of the Qur' an based on the conviction that its teachings accorded with 'the laws of nature'. In 1886 he founded the Mohammedan Educational Conference. Arguing that Western liberal constitutionalism was unsuited to India he refused to participate in the Indian National Congress.

BENTINCK, Lord William Cavendish (1774–1839). Governor of Madras 1803–07; recalled as a result of the army mutiny at Vellore. Served as British governor of Sicily during the Napoleonic wars. Returned to India as governor-general (1828–35). Introduced controversial reductions in government expenditure as well as liberal reforms, most notably the abolition of sati (1829) and the introduction of English education (1835).

CLIVE, Robert (1725–74). Appointed writer in the East India Company service in 1743, Clive was posted to Madras. In 1747 during the War of the Austrian Succession he obtained a commission as an ensign, and participated in campaigns against the French and their chosen rulers in the Carnatic. Gaining renown for his successful defence of Arcot in 1751, Clive returned to England in 1753, only to return again to India in 1756 with the rank of lieutenant-colonel. On the outbreak of the Seven Years' War, he moved to secure the position of the British in Bengal, first by defeating the Nawab Suraj-ud-daula (February 1757), and then by overthrowing him at the famous battle of Plassey (June 1757). As governor of Bengal (1758–60), Clive secured an immense fortune. He served a second term as governor of Bengal from 1765 to 1767, following the British takeover of the revenue administration of the province.

CURZON, George Nathaniel (1859–1925). Educated at Eton and Oxford, as a Conservative member of Parliament he served as under-secretary for India (1891–92) and for foreign affairs (1895–98). During the 1890s he travelled widely throughout central and eastern Asia. As governor-general and viceroy of India (1899–1905), he worked energetically to re-organize its administration. He presided over the Delhi durbar of 1903, and created the North-West Frontier Province, but secured the enmity of educated Indians by his 1905 division of Bengal along communal lines. After his return from India he was elevated to the House of Lords. During the First World War he served in the coalition governments of Asquith and Lloyd-George. From 1919 to 1924 he was British Foreign Secretary.

GANDHI, Indira (1917–1984). The only child of Jawaharlal Nehru and widowed mother of two sons (Rajiv (1944–91) and Sanjay (1947–80)), she served as a minister in the government of Lal Bahadur Shastri (1964–66). On his death in 1966 she took office as prime minister of India despite her limited administrative experience but with a background as her father's official hostess, leadership in the Youth Congress, and association with leftist causes. Narrowly re-elected in 1967, she decisively split with the old Congress leadership two years later to form a separate Congress party. Running on a populist slogan, her Congress (I) swept the polls in 1971. In June 1975, after she was found guilty of election malpractice in her 1971 race, she suspended the constitution and declared a state of national emergency. Her defeat in the subsequent election of March 1977 ended thirty years of Congress rule. She was returned to power in 1980. On 31 October 1984 she was assassinated by two of her Sikh guards, resentful of her armed attack on the Golden Temple in Amritsar the previous June.

GANDHI, Mohandas Karamchand (1869–1948). Member of a bania caste family that served in the princely states in Gujarat, Gandhi studied law in London (1888–91). Unable to find work in Bombay, he practised law in South Africa from 1893 to 1914. There he set up his first ashram, and, while working to secure the rights of South Africa's Indian residents, devised the ideas of 'satyagraha'. On his return to India Gandhi made Ahmedabad his base, and from there launched peasant and labour protests in Bihar and Gujarat in 1917–18. In 1919 he led the India-wide protest against the Rowlatt Acts. In September 1920 he secured support of the Indian National Congress for his strategy of non-violent non-cooperation with the British. In 1930 he led the famed 'salt march' to the sea; the subsequent year, following the signing of the Gandhi–Irwin Pact, Gandhi represented the Congress at the second round table conference in London. Though remaining symbolic head of the Indian nationalist movement, Gandhi retired from active engagement in politics after the mid-1930s. He was assassinated by a Hindu enthusiast on 30 January 1948.

GOKHALE, Gopal Krishna (1866–1915). Born of a Chitpavan Brahman family, Gokhale was educated in Bombay, and then settled in Poona, where he became a teacher in Fergusson College. He was a member of the Deccan Education Society, and secretary of the Poona Sarvajanik Sabha (1890). He was elected a member of the Bombay Provincial Legislative Council in 1899, and of the Imperial Legislative Council in 1902, where he advocated a programme of so-called 'Moderate' political activism on behalf of Indian constitutional reform. In 1905 he founded the Servants of India Society to work for social reform.

HASTINGS, Warren (1732–1818). Hastings joined the East India Company's service in 1750. He served as resident at the court of Murshidabad (Bengal) from 1757 to 1760, and as governor-general (1772–85). As governor-general Hastings had to deal with the concerted opposition of a majority of his council, but he succeeded in placing the Company's finances on a sound footing, in part by mulcting his Indian allies, and secured the Company's position in Bengal by containing Maratha advances. A patron of Indian culture, Hastings founded the Asiatic Society of Bengal (1784). On his return to England, he was impeached in the House of Commons for his arbitrary methods of governance. After an extended trial, he was acquitted in 1795.

IQBAL, Muhammad (1873–1938). Iqbal studied at Government College, Lahore, Cambridge, and Germany, completing a doctorate in philosophy and qualifying as a barrister. He is widely recognized as an important religious thinker and as the most influential poet of Urdu in the twentieth century. His themes include 'selfhood' and the injunction to constant striving, opposition to capitalism and imperialism, and the celebration of a utopian vision associated with 'the East', Asia, and above all, Islam. In his presidential address to the All-India Muslim League in 1930, he espoused the idea of territorial consolidation of Muslims within India. His writings include *The Reconstruction of Religious Thought in Islam*, based on lectures delivered in 1928. In 1931 and 1932 he participated in the round table conferences in England.

JINNAH, Muhammad Ali (1875–1948). Born into a business family, Jinnah studied law in London, returning to India in 1896. A leading figure in the Bombay Bar, he was active in Congress politics, as a close associate of G. K. Gokhale, and in the Muslim League, which he joined in 1913. Throughout his career he worked to secure separate electorates, reservation of seats, and weightage for Muslims in electoral politics. He disliked Gandhi's techniques of non-cooperation and civil disobedience; he did not support the Khilafat Movement; and he failed to find agreement with Congress over constitutional guarantees for Muslims. In 1931 he withdrew to a law practice in London, but in 1935 returned to India to campaign on behalf of the Muslim League and, after 1940, to press for a separate Muslim polity. He was the first governor-general of Pakistan (1947–48).

MACAULAY, Thomas Babington (1800–59). A reformist Whig, Macaulay was secretary of the Board of Control for India (1832–34). He then went to India as member of the governor-general's council (1834–38). While in Calcutta, he was appointed president of the commission for composing a criminal code for India, and he authored the famous 'Minute on Education' (1835) which put forward the case for government support of English language instruction. On his return to England he served as secretary of war (1839–41), and wrote a classic history of England, as well as other essays.

NEHRU, Jawaharlal (1889–1964). A Kashmiri Brahman, whose father Motilal was a wealthy lawyer and Congress politician, Nehru studied at Trinity College, Cambridge (1907–10) and became a barrister in 1912. A follower of Gandhi, but also a Fabian socialist, Nehru participated in the various non-cooperation movements and served as president of the Indian National Congress (1930). In the early 1940s Gandhi chose Nehru as his successor. Hence Nehru became vice-president of the viceroy's council in the transition government of 1946–47, and prime minister of independent India in August 1947. His years as prime minister were marked by the institutionalization of democracy, the beginnings of state-directed economic development, and a foreign policy devoted to non-alignment in the Cold War.

ROY, Rammohun (*c.* 1774–1833). Bengali Brahman educated in Persian, Arabic, and Sanskrit and self-educated in English through business connections to British civil servants and employment in the East India Company. An outspoken advocate of ethical monotheism, social reform, and political liberalism, he was among the founders of an association called the Brahmo Samaj in 1828. His writings include translations of the Upanishds, *The Precepts of Jesus* (1820), textbooks, newspapers, tracts, and petitions. He died in England, where he had travelled to lobby Parliament for improvements in the government of India.

TAGORE, Rabindranath (1861–1941). A Bengali Brahman, grandson of the industrialist Dwarakanath Tagore and son of the reformer Debendranath Tagore, Tagore was a renowned poet and writer. In 1901 he founded a rural school at Santiniketan, Bengal; later (1918) this school became the Visva-Bharati University. He composed the hymn 'Jana, Gana, Mana', adopted after independence as India's National Anthem. He was awarded the Nobel prize for literature in 1913 for *Gitanjali*, a set of Bengali poems. His novel *The Home and the World* is an evocative account of the 1905 Bengal partition. Never a committed follower of Gandhi, he nevertheless renounced his British knighthood to protest the Amritsar massacre (1919).

TILAK, Bal Gangadhar (1856–1920). A Chitpavan Brahman, resident of Poona, Tilak helped found the Deccan Education Society (1885) and Fergusson College. Breaking with the 'Moderates' in 1890, he established two newspapers, the Marathi language weekly *Kesari* and its English counterpart *The Mahratta*. In the pages of these papers he criticized the British-sponsored Act of Consent Bill (1891) and the plague control measures adopted five years later. During these years he organized two festivals – one devoted to the Maharashtrian hero Shivaji, and one dedicated to the Hindu god Ganesh. In 1897 his willingness to condone the assassination of a British official led to Tilak's jailing for sedition. As a leader of the nationalist 'Extremists', he was subsequently (1908–14) incarcarated in Mandalay, Burma for six years. On his return from Burma Tilak helped found (1916) the Home Rule League.

BIBLIOGRAPHIC ESSAY

This section makes no attempt to provide a comprehensive listing of works on modern India. For recent authoritative studies of major topics in Indian history, containing excellent bibliographies, the reader is encouraged to consult the volumes in the New Cambridge History of India series (Cambridge University Press). Individual volumes in this series are cited below as appropriate. Other scholarly studies of various topics are included for each chapter to extend the necessarily brief discussion in this book.

All authors mentioned in the text are identified by citation of the works from which the quotations, or other references, were taken. So far as possible, the indented extracts from original sources were drawn from readily accessible works, which readers may wish to consult to obtain a further insight into India's past. Such source volumes are listed together, and separately from the scholarly works, for each chapter.

PREFACE

The 'subaltern studies' collective over the last twenty years has made an immense contribution to rethinking the history of India. Readers are advised to consult the ten volumes of the Subaltern Studies series published by Oxford University Press, Delhi (1982–99). A selection of essays from the earlier volumes was published as *Selected Subaltern Studies*, ed. Ranajit Guha and Gayatri Chakravorty Spivak (Oxford and New York: Oxford University Press, 1988). For an appraisal of the 'subaltern studies' enterprise see the essays collected in Vinayak Chaturvedi, ed., *Mapping Subaltern Studies and the Postcolonial* (London: Verso, 2000).

Benedict Anderson, *Imagined Communities* (London: Verso, 1983; revised edn 1991) has been immensely influential in shaping studies of nationalism over the last decade. For India, Partha Chatterjee, *The Nation and its Fragments* (Princeton: Princeton University Press, 1994) has stimulated much debate about the nature of nationalist thought. For an alternative narrative of Indian 'modernity' see Dipesh Chakrabarty, *Provincializing Europe* (Princeton: Princeton University Press, 2000).

1: SULTANS, MUGHALS, AND PRE-COLONIAL INDIAN SOCIETY

For discussion of India's place in the larger world order see John F. Richards, 'Early Modern India and World History', *Journal of World History* 8: 2 (1997), pp. 197–209; and Janet Lippman Abu-Lughod, 'The World System in the Thirteenth Century: Dead-End or Precursor?', in Michael Adas, ed., *Islamic and European Expansion: the Forging of a Global Order* (Philadelphia: Temple University Press, 1993), pp. 75–102. For the Orientalist 'triptych' see David Arnold's volume in the New Cambridge History of India series, *Science, Technology and Medicine in India* (2000), ch. 1.

For a general account of the Sultanate period see Romila Thapar, *A History of India*, vol. i, chs. 12–14 (Harmondsworth: Penguin, 1966). Important recent regional studies include Richard Eaton, *The Rise of Islam and the Bengal Frontier, 1204–1760* (Berkeley: University of California Press, 1993); Cynthia Talbot, *Precolonial India in Practice: Society, Region, and Identity in Medieval Andhra* (Oxford and New York: Oxford University Press, 2000); and Philip B. Wagoner, *Tidings of the King: a Translation and Ethnohistorical Analysis of the Rayavacakamu* (Honolulu: University of Hawaii Press, 1993). On bhakti movements see John Stratton Hawley and Mark Juergensmeyer, *Songs of the Saints of India* (Oxford and New York: Oxford University Press, 1988); and the selections in Wm. Theodore de Bary, Stephen Hay, and I. H. Qureshi, eds., *Sources of Indian Tradition*, vol. i (New York: Columbia University Press, revised edn 1988).

The best general account of the Mughal Empire is John F. Richards, *The Mughal Empire* (1993) in the New Cambridge History of India series. For a useful collection of essays see Muzaffar Alam and Sanjay Subramaniam, eds., *The Mughal State 1526–1750* (Oxford and Delhi: Oxford University Press, 1998). 'Classic' works include Irfan Habib, *The Agrarian System of Mughal India* (Bombay: Asia Publishing House, 1963); and M. Athar Ali, *The Mughal Nobility Under Aurangzeb* (1966; revised edn Oxford and Delhi: Oxford University Press, 1997). For a stimulating comparative account of the 'gunpowder' empires see Marshall G. S. Hodgson, *The Venture of Islam*, vol. ii (Chicago: University of Chicago Press, 1974). For Babar see Stephen F. Dale, 'Steppe Humanism: the Autobiographical Writings of Zahir al-Din Muhammad Babur, 1483–1530', *International Journal of Middle Eastern Studies* 22 (1990), pp. 37–58.

Important studies of the period include Stephen Blake, *Shahjahanabad: the Sovereign City in Mughal India* (Cambridge: Cambridge University Press, 1991); Catherine B. Asher, *Architecture of Mughal India* (1992) in the New Cambridge History of India; Sanjay Subramaniam, *The*

Political Economy of Commerce: Southern India, 1500–1650 (Cambridge: Cambridge University Press, 1990); and, for a stimulating account of the nature of 'caste', Susan Bayly, *Caste, Society and Politics in India from the Eighteenth Century to the Modern Age* (1999) in the New Cambridge History of India series, ch. 1.

Extracted quotations are taken from Ross E. Dunn, *The Adventures of Ibn Battuta: a Muslim Traveller of the Fourteenth Century* (Berkeley: University of California Press, 1986); for Babar, from Gulbadan Begam, *The History of Humayan*, trans. Annette S. Beveridge (1902; reprint Delhi: Low Price Publications, 1994); and, for Abu'l Fazl, from *Sources of Indian Tradition*, ed. de Bary, Hay and Qureshi.

2: MUGHAL TWILIGHT: THE EMERGENCE OF REGIONAL STATES AND THE EAST INDIA COMPANY

Eighteenth-century India has been the subject of extensive recent revisionist historiography. The best study of Mughal decline is Muzaffar Alam, *The Crisis of Empire in Mughal North India, 1707–1748* (Oxford and Delhi: Oxford University Press, 1986). Among the studies of particular regions the most useful are J. S. Grewal, *The Sikhs in the Punjab* (1990) in the New Cambridge History of India; Richard B. Barnett, *North India Between Empires: Awadh, the Mughals, and the British, 1720–1801* (Berkeley: University of California Press, 1980); Bernard S. Cohn, 'Political Systems in Eighteenth-Century India: the Benares Region', in Bernard S. Cohn, *An Anthropologist Among the Historians* (Oxford and Delhi: Oxford University Press, 1987), pp. 683–99; Stewart Gordon, *Marathas, Marauders, and State Formation in Eigthteenth-Century India* (Oxford and Delhi: Oxford University Press, 1994), and his *The Marathas 1600–1818* (1993) in the New Cambridge History of India; and Andre Wink, *Land and Sovereignty in India: Agrarian Society and Politics under the Eighteenth-Century Maratha Swarajya* (Cambridge: Cambridge University Press, 1986).

For religion and society see Susan Bayly, *Saints, Goddesses, and Kings: Muslims and Christians in South Indian Society, 1700–1900* (Cambridge: Cambridge University Press, 1989). Ralph Russell and Khurshidul Islam, *Three Mughal Poets: Mir, Sauda, Mir Hasan* (Cambridge, Mass.: Harvard University Press, 1968) is an excellent introduction to late Mughal culture. There are numerous studies of the operations of the European trading companies in Mughal and eighteenth-century India. For general accounts see Om Prakash, *European Commercial Enterprise in Precolonial India* (1998) in the New Cambridge History of India; and the works of K. N. Chaudhuri, especially his *The Trading World of Asia and the English East India Company, 1660–1760* (Cambridge: Cambridge University Press, 1978).

The transition to colonialism can be studied in Sudipta Sen, *Empire of Free Trade* (Philadelphia: University of Pennsylvania Press, 1998); C. A. Bayly, *Rulers, Townsmen, and Bazaars: North Indian Society in the*

Age of British Expansion, 1770–1870 (Cambridge: Cambridge University Press, 1983); and P. J. Marshall, 'The British in Asia: Trade to Dominion, 1700–1760', summarizing much of his own scholarship, in P. J. Marshall, ed., *The Oxford History of the British Empire*, vol. II, *The Eighteenth Century* (Oxford: Oxford University Press, 1998), pp. 487–507. Two volumes in the New Cambridge History of India ought also to be consulted: P. J. Marshall, *Bengal: the British Bridgehead – Eastern India, 1740–1828* (1988); and C. A. Bayly, *Indian Society and the Making of British India* (1988). For a stimulating revisionist account see D. A. Washbrook, 'Progress and Problems: South Asian Economic and Social History, *c.* 1720–1860', *Modern Asian Studies* 22 (1988), pp. 57–96.

Extracted quotations are taken from, for Bhimsen, J. F. Richards, 'Norms of Comportment Among Imperial Mughal Officers', in Barbara D. Metcalf, ed., *Moral Conduct and Authority* (Berkeley: University of California Press, 1984); H. T. Sorley, *Shah Abdul Latif of Bhit: his Poetry, Life and Times* (Oxford and Lahore: Oxford University Press, 1966 edn [1940]); for Ananda Ranga Pillai, Stephen Hay, ed., *Sources of Indian Tradition*, vol. II (New York: Columbia University Press, 1988); and Michael H. Fisher, ed., *The Travels of Dean Mahomet* (Berkeley: University of California Press, 1997).

3: THE EAST INDIA COMPANY RAJ, 1772–1850

For the structure and functioning of the Company state see Bernard Cohn, 'The Language of Command and the Command of Language', in Nicholas Dirks, ed., *Colonialism and its Forms of Knowledge* (Princeton: Princeton University Press, 1996); Rosane Rocher, 'British Orientalism in the Eighteenth Century', and David Ludden, 'Orientalist Empiricism', in Carol Breckenridge and Peter van der Veer, eds., *Orientalism and the Postcolonial Predicament* (Philadelphia: University of Pennsylvania Press, 1993); C. A. Bayly, *Empire and Information: Political Intelligence and Social Communication in North India* (Cambridge: Cambridge University Press, 1996); and Radhika Singha, *A Despotism of Law* (Oxford and Delhi: Oxford University Press, 1998).

The ideas that sustained British rule are explored in several classic works. Among them are Ranajit Guha, *A Rule of Property for Bengal* (1963; revised edn Durham: Duke University Press, 1996); David Kopf, *British Orientalism and the Bengal Renaissance* (Berkeley: University of California Press, 1969); and Eric Stokes's influential *The English Utilitarians and India* (Oxford: Clarendon Press, 1959). An important article is David Washbrook, 'Law, State, and Society in Colonial India', *Modern Asian Studies* 15 (1981).

Recent studies worth consulting on particular topics include Matthew Edney, *Mapping an Empire* (Chicago: University of Chicago Press, 1997);

Ajay Skaria, *Hybrid Histories: Forests, Frontiers, and Wilderness in Western India* (Oxford and Delhi: Oxford University Press, 1999); Seema Alavi, *The Sepoys and the Company* (Oxford and Delhi: Oxford University Press, 1995); Thomas Trautmann, *Aryans and British India* (Berkeley: University of California Press, 1997); and Michael Fisher, *Indirect Rule in India* (Oxford and Delhi: Oxford University Press, 1993). For issues of gender in the colonial period see the various essays, including especially that by Lata Mani on sati, in Kumkum Sangari and Sudesh Vaid, eds., *Recasting Women: Essays on Colonial History* (New Delhi: Kali for Women, 1989). The quotation discussing sati by an English resident of Calcutta is from Eliza Fay, *Original Letters from India (1779–1815)*, ed. E. M. Forster (London: Hogarth Press, 1986). For the bhadralok, and Calcutta social life more generally, see Pradip Sinha, *Calcutta in Urban History* (Calcutta, 1978); and S. N. Mukherjee, 'Class, Caste and Politics in Calcutta, 1815–38', in E. Leach and S. N. Mukheree, eds., *Elites in South Asia* (Cambridge: Cambridge University Press, 1970). On resistance movements, Ranajit Guha's influential *Elementary Aspects of Peasant Insurgency in Colonial India* (Oxford and Delhi: Oxford University Press, 1984) should be consulted.

Extended quotations are taken from Sita Ram, *From Sepoy to Subedar* (London: Routledge, 1970); for Halhed, from Rosane Rocher, 'British Orientalism' (citied above); for Valentia, from Curzon of Kedleston, *British Government in India* (London: Cassell & Co., 1925); for Trevelyan, from G. O. Trevelyan, *The Life and Letters of Lord Macaulay* (London: Longmans, Green, 1876).

4: REVOLT, THE MODERN STATE, AND COLONIZED SUBJECTS, 1848–1885

Much has been written about the 1857 revolt. Especially useful are Eric Stokes, *The Peasant Armed* (Oxford: Clarendon Press, 1986), and Rudrangshu Mukherjee, *Awadh in Revolt* (Oxford and Delhi: Oxford University Press, 1984). The latter adopts a populist view of the uprising which contrasts with Stokes's delineation of caste and clan antagonisms. Eric Stokes, *The Peasant and the Raj* (Cambridge: Cambridge University Press, 1978) sets the uprising in the larger setting of British agrarian policy. For the consequences of the revolt, especially as these affected British policy, see Thomas R. Metcalf, *The Aftermath of Revolt: India, 1857–1870* (Princeton: Princeton University Press, 1964). The attitudes and assumptions that shaped Indian governance under the Crown are assessed in Thomas R. Metcalf, *Ideologies of the Raj* (1994) in the New Cambridge History of India series. An earlier, though still stimulating, account is Francis Hutchins, *The Illusion of Permanence* (Princeton: Princeton University Press, 1967).

The institutions of the Raj are examined in, among other works, David Omissi, *The Sepoy and the Raj* (Basingstoke: Macmillan, 1994); David

Arnold, *Colonizing the Body* (Berkeley: University of California Press, 1993); Nicholas Dirks, 'Castes of Mind', *Representations* 37 (1992); Dane Kennedy, *Magic Mountains* (Berkeley: University of California Press, 1996); Bernard Cohn, 'Representing Authority in Victorian India', in Eric Hobsbawm and Terrence Ranger, eds., *The Invention of Tradition* (Cambridge: Cambridge University Press, 1983); Gauri Vishwanathan, *Masks of Conquest: Literary Study and British Rule in India* (New York: Columbia University Press, 1989). For the layout of the colonial city see J. B. Harrison, 'Allahabad: a Sanitary History', in K. Ballhatchet and J. Harrison, eds., *The City in South Asia* (London: Curzon Press, 1980); for the organization of the municipality see Narayani Gupta, *Delhi Between Two Empires, 1803–1931* (Oxford and Delhi: Oxford University Press, 1981), and Douglas Haynes, *Rhetoric and Ritual in Colonial India: the Shaping of a Public Culture in Surat City* (Berkeley: University of California Press, 1991).

Extracted source quotations are taken from John Beames, *Memoirs of a Bengal Civilian* (London: Chatto and Windus, 1961; reprint New Delhi: Manohar, 1984); Syed Ahmed Khan, *The Causes of the Indian Revolt* (1858, 1873; reprint Oxford and Karachi: Oxford University Press, 2000); Keshab Chandra Sen, 'Lectures in India', in Hay, ed., *Sources of Indian Tradition*, vol. II; Harischandra is quoted in Vasudha Dalmia, ' "The Only Real Religion of the Hindus": Vaishnava Self-Representation in the Late Nineteenth-Century India', in V. Dalmia and H. von Stietencron, eds., *Representing Hinduism: the Construction of Religious Identity and National Identity* (New Delhi: Sage, 1995); and Nazer Ahmad, *The Taubatu'n-Nasuh* (in Urdu), ed. M. Kempson (London: W. H. Allen and Co., 1886).

5: CIVIL SOCIETY, COLONIAL CONSTRAINTS, 1885–1919

For the Indian economy in the later nineteenth century the two classic nationalist accounts are Romesh Chunder Dutt, *The Economic History of India*, vol. II (1904; reprinted Delhi: Publications Division, Government of India, 1960), and Dadabhai Naoroji, *Poverty and Un-British Rule in India* (1901; reprint Delhi: Publications Division, Government of India, 1962). A useful general account of the entire period of Crown rule and beyond is B. R. Tomlinson, *The Economy of Modern India, 1860–1970*, (1993), in the New Cambridge History of India series. For the growth of Indian industry most authoritative are the works of Rajnarayan Chandavarkar, especially his *The Origins of Industrial Capitalism in India* (Cambridge: Cambridge University Press, 1994). A stimulating study of labour culture, challenging standard Marxist interpretations, is Dipesh Chakrabarty, *Rethinking Working Class History: Bengal, 1890–1940* (Princeton: Princeton University Press, 1989). For environmental history see David Arnold and Ramchandra Guha, eds., *Nature, Culture, Imperialism: Essays on the Environmental History of South Asia* (Oxford and Delhi: Oxford University Press, 1995).

On early Indian nationalism older but still valuable works include Anil Seal, *The Emergence of Indian Nationalism* (Cambridge: Cambridge University Press, 1968); Stanley Wolpert, *Tilak and Gokhale* (Berkeley: University of California Pres, 1962); and John Gallagher, Gordon Johnson, and Anil Seal, eds., *Locality, Province, and Nation* (Cambridge: Cambridge University Press, 1973). On social change and the growth of community identities, see Sandria Freitag, *Collective Action and Community: Public Arenas and the Emergence of Communalism in North India* (Berkeley: University of California Press, 1989); Gyanendra Pandey, *The Construction of Communalism in Colonial North India* (Oxford and Delhi: Oxford University Press, 1990); and the essays in part 2 of Sumit Sarkar, *Writing Social History* (Oxford and Delhi: Oxford University Press, 1998).

Important studies exist for several of the major late nineteenth-century reform movements. On non-Brahman activism see Rosalind O'Hanlon, *Caste, Conflict, and Ideology: Mahatma Jotirao Phule and Low Caste Protest in Nineteenth-Century Western India* (Cambridge: Cambridge University Press, 1985); on the Arya Samaj, Kenneth Jones, *Arya Dharm: Hindu Consciousness in Nineteenth-Century Punjab* (Berkeley: University of California Press, 1976); on Harischandra, Vasudha Dalmia, *The Nationalization of Hindu Traditions* (Oxford and Delhi: Oxford University Press, 1997). For contemporaneous Muslim movements see Barbara Daly Metcalf, *Islamic Revival in British India: Deoband, 1860–1900* (Princeton: Princeton University Press, 1982); and David Lelyveld, *Aligarh's First Generation* (Princeton: Princeton University Press, 1977). For the Sikhs see Richard Fox, *Lions of the Punjab* (Berkeley: University of California Press, 1985). For the debates between and within communities see Kenneth W. Jones, ed., *Religious Controversy in British India* (Albany: State University Press of New York, 1992). For the politics of 'swadeshi' the classic study is Sumit Sarkar, *The Swadeshi Movement in Bengal, 1903–1908* (New Delhi: People's Publishing House, 1973).

For issues of gender relations see Mrinalini Sinha, *Colonial Masculinity: the 'Manly Englishman' and the 'Effeminate Bengali' in the Late Nineteenth Century* (Manchester: Manchester University Press, 1995); Barbara Daly Metcalf, *Perfecting Women: Maulana Ashraf Ali Thanawi's 'Bhishti Zewar'* (Berkeley: University of California Press, 1990); Rokeya Sahkhawat Hossain, *Sultana's Dreams and Selections from the Secluded Ones*, ed. and trans. Roushan Jahan (New York: Feminist Press, 1988); and the excerpts included in Susie Tharu and K. Lalita, *Women Writing in India*, 2 vols. (New York: Feminist Press, 1992, 1993). For art and architecture in late nineteenth-century India see Tapati Guha-Thakurta, *The Making of a New 'Indian' Art: Artists, Aesthetics and Nationalism in Bengal* (Cambridge: Cambridge University Press, 1992); Partha Mitter, *Art and Nationalism in Colonial India, 1850–1922* (Cambridge: Cambridge University Press, 1994); and Thomas R. Metcalf, *An Imperial Vision: Indian Architecture and Britain's Raj* (Berkeley: University of California Press, 1989).

Extended source quotations are taken for Naoroji, from Hay, ed., *Sources of Indian Tradition*, vol. II; from Rudyard Kipling, *Kim* (1901; reprint edn New York and Oxford: Oxford University Press, 1987); for Akbar, from Ralph Russell, *Hidden in the Lute: an Anthology of Two Centuries of Urdu Literature* (Harmondsworth and Delhi: Viking Penguin, 1995); for 'Bande Mataram', from Hay, ed., *Sources of Indian Tradition*, vol. II; and for Iqbal from *Iqbal: a Selection of Urdu Verse*, ed. and trans. D. J. Matthews (London: University of London, School of Oriental and African Studies, 1993).

6: THE CRISIS OF THE COLONIAL ORDER: REFORM, DISILLUSIONMENT, DIVISION, 1919–1939

The literature on Gandhi is vast. It is best to start with his autobiography, *My Experiments with Truth* (Boston: Beacon Press, 1957), and Rudrangshu Mukherjee, ed., *The Penguin Gandhi Reader* (Harmondsworth and Delhi: Penguin, 1993). Gandhi's political role in India is authoritatively assessed in Judith Brown, *Gandhi's Rise to Power: Indian Politics, 1915–1922* (Cambridge: Cambridge University Press, 1972), and her *Gandhi and Civil Disobedience, 1928–1934* (Cambridge: Cambridge University Press, 1977). For the 1919 Rowlatt satyagraha, see Ravinder Kumar, ed., *Essays on Gandhian Politics* (Oxford: Clarendon Press, 1971); for Chauri Chaura see the postmodernist analysis of Shahid Amin, *Event, Metaphor, Memory: Chauri Chaura, 1922–1992* (Oxford and Delhi: Oxford University Press, 1995). For stimulating general accounts of the nationalist encounter with colonialism, including useful discussions of Gandhi, see Ashis Nandy, *The Intimate Enemy: Loss and Recovery of Self Under Colonialism* (Oxford and Delhi: Oxford University Press, 1983); and Partha Chatterjee, *Nationalist Thought and the Colonial World: a Derivative Discourse?* (Oxford and Delhi: Oxford University Press, 1986).

There exist good accounts of nationalist politics in most of India's provinces. See especially David Hardiman, *Peasant Nationalists of Gujarat: Kheda District* (Oxford and Delhi: Oxford University Press, 1981); Majid Siddiqi, *Agrarian Unrest in North India: the United Provinces, 1919–1922* (Delhi: Vikas, 1978); and, for the Dravidian movement in South India, Sumathi Ramaswamy, *Passions of the Tongue: Language Devotion in Tamil India, 1891–1970* (Berkeley: University of California Press, 1997). For the Khilafat see Gail Minault, *The Khilafat Movement: Religious Symbolism and Political Mobilization in India* (New York: Columbia University Press, 1982).

The course of the negotiations between the Congress and the Raj is examined in a number of works, most notably D. A. Low, ed., *Congress and the Raj, 1917–47* (Columbia, Mo.: South Asia Books, 1977), and his *Britain and Indian Nationalism, 1929–1942* (Cambridge: Cambridge

University Press, 1997). On the economic history of the late colonial period see Amyia Kumar Bagchi, *Private Investment in India, 1900–1939* (Cambridge: Cambridge University Press, 1972); Claude Markovits, *Indian Business and Nationalist Politics, 1931–1939* (Cambridge: Cambridge University Press, 1985); and B. R. Tomlinson, *The Political Economy of the Raj, 1914–1947* (London: Macmillan, 1979).

Extended source quotations are taken, for Gandhi from Mukherjee, *The Penguin Gandhi*, and from Shahid Amin, 'Gandhi as Mahatma', *Subaltern Studies 3* (1984); for Nehru from Hay, ed., *Sources of Indian Tradition*, vol. II; and for Azad, from Hay, ed., *Sources of Indian Tradition*, vol. II.

7: THE 1940S: TRIUMPH AND TRAGEDY

Numerous memoirs and extensive collections of documents illustrate the events leading up to independence and partition. From the British side the most exhaustive is the set of twelve volumes entitled *India, the Transfer of Power, 1942–1947*, edited by N. Mansergh, E. W. R. Lumby and Penderel Moon (London: Her Majesty's Stationery Office, 1970–83). A comparable compilation from the Indian side is now in the process of publication. A useful volume of essays is Mushirul Hasan, ed., *India's Partition: Process, Strategy, Mobilization* (Oxford and Delhi: Oxford University Press, 1993). General narrative accounts include R. J. Moore, *Endgames of Empire* (Oxford and Delhi: Oxford University Press, 1988), his *Churchill, Cripps, and India* (Oxford: Oxford University Press, 1979), and, for the princes, Ian Copland, *The Princes of India in the Endgame of Empire, 1917–1947* (Cambridge: Cambridge University Press, 1997). Ayesha Jalal's *The Sole Spokesman: Jinnah, the Muslim League and the Demand for Pakistan* (Cambridge: Cambridge University Press, 1985), though controversial, remains essential for understanding the origins of Pakistan.

The politics of the Punjab are explored in David Gilmartin, *Empire and Islam: Punjab and the Making of Pakistan* (Berkeley: University of California Press, 1988); while those of Bengal are assessed in Joya Chatterjee, *Bengal Divided: Hindu Communalism and Partition* (Cambridge: Cambridge University Press, 1995). For the Bengal famine see Paul Greenough, *Prosperity and Misery in Modern Bengal: the Famine of 1943–44* (Oxford and New York: Oxford University Press, 1982).

The social history of the partition, with its massacres and abductions, is only now being assessed, and much remains unpublished or in article form. Readers should consult Ritu Menon and Kamla Bhasin, *Borders and Boundaries: Women in India's Partition* (New Delhi: Kali for Women, 1998); Urvashi Butalia, *The Other Side of Silence: Voices from the Partition of India* (Harmondsworth and New Delhi: Penguin, 1998); and the special issue of the Australian journal *South Asia* published as D. A. Low and Howard Brasted, eds., *Freedom, Trauma, Continuities: Northern India and Independence* (New Delhi: Sage, 1998).

Extended source quotations are taken, for Jinnah and Savarkar, from
Hay, ed., *Sources of Indian Tradition*, vol. II; and for Nehru from Jawaharlal
Nehru's *Speeches*, vol. I (Delhi: Publications Division, 1958).

8: CONGRESS RAJ: DEMOCRACY AND DEVELOPMENT, 1950–1989

For the political development of independent India the most useful general survey is Paul Brass, *The Politics of India since Independence* (1990)
in the New Cambridge History of India series. The most recent general
history of the period is Bipan Chandra, Aditya Mukherjee and Mridula
Mukherjee, *India After Independence* (Harmondsworth and New Delhi:
Viking Penguin, 1999). The best studies of India's political economy during
the years of Congress dominance are Francine Frankel, *India's Political
Economy, 1947–1977* (Princeton: Princeton University Press, 1978), and
Lloyd and Susanne Hoeber Rudolph, *In Pursuit of Lakshmi: the Political
Economy of the Indian State* (Chicago: University of Chicago Press, 1987).
There are many studies by development economists. Those interested may
wish to consult the numerous works of the Nobel prize winner Amartya
Sen, and Pranab Bardhan, *The Political Economy of Development in India*
(Oxford and Delhi: Oxford University Press, 1985). Sunil Khilnani, *The
Idea of India* (London: Hamish Hamilton, 1997; New York: Farrar Straus
Giroux, 1998) provides an accessible introduction to Indian nationhood
since independence.

9: DEMOCRATIC INDIA IN THE NINETIES: COALITIONS, CLASS, COMMUNITY, CONSUMERS, AND CONFLICT

The best general study of the growth of religious nationalism in India
is Peter van der Veer, *Religious Nationalism* (Berkeley: University of
California Press, 1994). On the Ayodya mosque controversy, though not
including the 1992 destruction of the mosque, see Sarvepalli Gopal, ed.,
Anatomy of a Confrontation: the Babri Masjid – Ramjanmabhumi Issue
(New Delhi: Viking, 1991). For the politics of the BJP see Christophe
Jaffrelot, *The Hindu Nationalist Movement in Indian Politics* (New York:
Columbia University Press, 1996); and Thomas Blom Hansen, *The Saffron
Wave* (Princeton: Princeton University Press, 1999). Paola Bacchetta's
forthcoming book on the RSS (New Delhi: Kali for Women, 2001) should
be consulted for the role of a gendered ideology in shaping the activities of
the Hindu right. For a stimulating discussion of recent politics, especially
those of the regions, see the articles collected by Atul Kohli and Amrita
Basu as 'Community Conflicts and the State in India', in the *Journal of
Asian Studies* 56 (1997).

For the growing links between cinema, television, and politics see
Purnima Mankekar, *Screening Culture, Viewing Politics: an Ethnography
of Television, Womanhood, and Nation* (Durham: Duke University Press,

1999); and Philip Lutgendorf, *The Life of a Text* (Berkeley: University of California Press, 1991). For the Dalit life story see Viramma, Josiane Racine, and Jean-Luc Racine, *Viramma – Life of an Untouchable* (London: Verso, 1997). Numerous websites give valuable information regarding India's political parties, as well the country's engagement with global business. Drawn on here, for the VHP, RSS, and BJP respectively, are *www.vhp.org*, *www.rss.org*, and *www.bjp.org*.

Extended quotations are taken, for Nehru, from his *Collected Speeches*, vol. 1; for Gyan Pandey, from his edited *Hindus and Others: Questions of Identity in India Today* (New Delhi: Viking, 1993); for Amartya Sen, from his *Development as Freedom* (New York: Vintage Anchor, 2000); for Vajpayee's Independence Day speech, from the official BJP website; for V. S. Naipaul, from his *A Million Mutinies Now* (New York: Viking Penguin, 1991); and for Mohammed Habib from the website *www.geocities.com/ a_habib/Dada/ihc.html*.

INDEX

Index